The Law of Command Responsibility

The Law of Command Responsibility

M.P.W. Brouwers (ed.)

The Law of Command Responsibility
M.P.W. Brouwers (ed.)

ISBN: 978-90-5887-050-6

Published by:

Wolf Legal Publishers (WLP)
P.O. Box 31051
6503 CB Nijmegen
The Netherlands
Tel: +31 24 355 19 04
Fax: +31 84 837 67 00
E-Mail: info@wolfpublishers.nl
www.wolfpublishers.com

Table of Contents

Introduction

International criminal tribunals have been entrusted with the judicial powers to hold natural persons individually criminally responsible, for the most serious international crimes, like genocide, crimes against humanity and other war crimes.[1] Yet these international tribunals are limited in their investigative powers, and thus not capable of trying every single individual who took part in these international crimes. As a result, the international tribunals will have a strong focus on the 'superiors' of organized groups of individuals, like the military. This is where 'the law of command responsibility' will play a crucial role, as a legal tool for the international tribunals, to impose criminal liability on superiors, for the crimes of their subordinates.[2]

Under international humanitarian law superiors will have a duty to ensure that their subordinates will comply with the rules of international humanitarian law in armed conflicts.[3] Superiors will have this duty because of their position of command over, and their influence on, their subordinates.

This book will elaborate on issues related to the application and development of the law of *command responsibility* or *superior responsibility*. The next two chapters will clarify the evolution and the nature of the law of command responsibility. This will be followed by the elements of command responsibility, such as the 'superior-subordinate relationship', the mental elements: 'knew or had to know' and the 'failure to prevent and punish'. Finally a brief comment will be made on the practical application of the law of command responsibility,

---

1 See the statutes of the International Criminal Court, the International Criminal Tribunal for the former Yugoslavia, the International Criminal Tribunal for Rwanda, the Special Court of Sierra Leone, the 'Khmer Rouge tribunal', the Special Tribunal for Lebanon, and the law on the establishment of the Extraordinary Chambers in the Courts of Cambodia for the Prosecution of Crimes Committed During the period of Democratic Kampuchea. (See the attached documents for the relevant articles of these statutes)

2 It is not mandatory that a subordinate is identified by name, the fact that the perpetrators are identified as a part of a group controlled by the superior will be enough. See the *Blaškić* Judgment, paragraph 217 and the *Brima et al.* Judgment, paragraph 790.

3 International Humanitarian law: international rules to limit the effects of armed conflict for humanitarian reasons. The Geneva Conventions and the Hague Conventions are the main examples.

such as the phases of 'investigation and prosecution', 'trial' and the 'conviction and sentence'.
This book will primarily be based on the case-law of the International Criminal Tribunal for the former Yugoslavia (ICTY), the International Criminal Tribunal for Rwanda (ICTR) and the Special Court for Sierra Leone (SCSL), which have taken the lead in the legal development of the law of command responsibility (see for example the ICTY's Hadzihasanovic Appeal Judgment summary, the Akayesu ICTR's Trial Judgment and the SCSL's Brima et al. Trial Judgment in the attached documents). There will also be elaborated on the role of the International Criminal Court (ICC), which has a different legal view on some aspects with regard to the law of command responsibility (see the attached documents for the Bemba ICC pre-trail decision).

Evolution of the law of command responsibility

The principle of responsible command is a fundamental principle of humanitarian law, in which the doctrine of command responsibility has its roots.[4] The Fourth Hague Convention on the Laws and Customs of War on Land did not provide for individual responsibility, but placed a responsibility upon the belligerent party.

This has been confirmed in Article 3:

> 'A belligerent party which violates the provisions of the said Regulations shall, if the case demands, be liable to pay compensation. It shall be responsible for all acts committed by persons forming part of its armed forces.'

The Yamashita trial – 1945: The first conviction based on command responsibility (see the attached documents)

The birth of the doctrine of command responsibility is generally linked to the trial of General Tomoyuki Yamashita (However, it is also very interesting to notice the post First-World War case of Emil Müller, see the attached documents).[5] Tomoyuki Yamashita was the commanding general of an Army Group of Japanese Army in the Philippines from 9 October 1944 until Japan's surrender on 3 September. General

---

[4] See Meloni 2010, p. 35 and Mettraux 2009, p. 53.
[5] See for example Meloni 2010, p. 42; Slye and Van Schaack 2009, p. 274, and Mettraux 2009, p. 5.

Yamashita was therefore the last commander of the Japanese Army before the Allied landed on the Philippines.

During the months that Yamashita was in command, his subordinates in the Japanese Army killed thousands of civilians. On 19 January 1946 the International Military Tribunal for the Far East (IMTFE), which had its seat in Tokyo, was established to charge the most important Japanese war criminals. However, as for Yamashita, the United States decided not to wait for the International Tribunal: they set up a United States Military Commission. The case against him was that he as: 'a commander of armed forces of Japan at war with the United States of America and its allies, unlawfully disregarded and failed to discharge his duty as commander to control the operations of the members of his command, permitting them to commit brutal atrocities and other high crimes against the people of the United States and of its allies and dependencies, particularly the Philippines; and he [...] thereby violated the laws of war.'[6] However, in the charges there was no direct link between these crimes and the fact that the defendant actually committed these crimes. Yamashita was to be held responsible for every crime that had been committed by a soldier of the Japanese forces under his command.

On 7 December 1945 the Military Commission sentenced General Yamashita to death, although many were not convinced that the prosecution had been able to prove that the defendant had ordered the crimes committed by his army, or that he had effective knowledge of them.[7] Yamashita maintained that he as the defendant, did not know about the horror committed by his men, and that his subordinates had not followed his orders. Yamashita stated that if he had known of the atrocities, he would have done anything to prevent them from happening. As the defendant explained during the trial, American bombers had disconnected him from his soldiers, by bombing the communication facilities. Yamashita declared that because of this, he only learned afterwards about the shocking acts of his men. The military judges rejected this theory of Yamashita, considering that in a case like this, in which the crimes are brutal and extensive, and there is no effective attempt by the commander to discover and control them, such a commander may be held responsible, even criminally liable, for the lawless acts of his troops.[8]

---

6 See the Judgment of the United States Military Commission, Manila, 8 October 1945- 7 December 1945. As referred to in Mettraux 2009, p. 6.

7 Meloni 2010, p. 44.

8 Meloni 2010, p. 45.

Commanders thus were deemed to have a clear responsibility to ensure that their subordinates respect international humanitarian law. This can also be concluded from other post-Second World War case law, like the Eichmann case and the Abbaye Ardenne case (see the attached documents).

The first codification of the doctrine of command responsibility: Articles 86 and 87 of the Additional Protocol I of 1977 to the Geneva Conventions

It took many years before the doctrine of command responsibility was finally codified. This because of the fact that neither the first Draft Codes of the Offences against the Peace and Security of Mankind nor the Draft Statute for an International Criminal Law (1950-1954), contained any article on command responsibility. Some would say that 'the absence is indicative of the fact that at the time no agreement had been reached at the international level on the notion and formulation of the doctrine'.[9]

The first codification of the doctrine of command responsibility can be found in the Articles 86 and 87 of the Additional Protocol I of 1977 to the Geneva Conventions. It is important to notice that these articles do not directly address individuals: it establishes obligations on States. Article 86(2) confirms the responsibility of the superior who violates his duties to act, and reads as follows:

> '2. The fact that a breach of the Conventions or of this Protocol was committed by a subordinate does not absolve his superiors from penal or disciplinary responsibility, as the case may be, if they knew, or had information which should have enabled them to conclude in the circumstances at the time, that he was committing or was going to commit such a breach and if they did not take all feasible measures within their power to prevent or repress the breach.'

Article 87 Add. Prot. I (duty of commanders) reads as follows:

> '1. The High Contracting Parties and the Parties to the conflict shall require military commanders, with respect to members of the armed forces under their command and other persons under their control, to prevent and, where necessary, to suppress and to report to competent authorities breaches of the Conventions and of this Protocol.

[9] Meloni 2010, p. 65.

> 2. In order to prevent and suppress breaches, High Contracting Parties and Parties to the conflict shall require that, commensurate with their level of responsibility, commanders ensure that members of the armed forces under their command are aware of their obligations under the Conventions and this Protocol.
> 3. The High Contracting Parties and Parties to the conflict shall require any commander who is aware that subordinates or other persons under his control are going to commit or have committed a breach of the Conventions or of this Protocol, to initiate such steps as are necessary to prevent such violations of the Conventions or this Protocol, and, where appropriate, to initiate disciplinary or penal action against violators thereof.'

In the light of the above, the first Additional Protocol to the Geneva Conventions marks a fundamental step towards the definitive recognition of the doctrine of command responsibility in international law. Although it is debated whether as a whole the Protocol has achieved customary law status, this seems certain with regard to Article 86(2) which, as the jurisprudence of the ICTY also confirmed, may be recognized as a rule of customary law.[10] Given its status of customary rule, its applicability is not limited to States that have ratified the Protocol and it is not contingent upon its implementation in domestic law.

In these modern times, the concept of command responsibility has been further developed by the various international tribunals, for instance: the International Criminal Tribunal for the former Yugoslavia (ICTY), the International Criminal Tribunal for Rwanda (ICTR) and the Special Court for Sierra Leone (SCSL). These international tribunals contribute to this development with their statutes and their jurisprudence.[11]

---

10 *Čelebići* Judgment, paragraph 333.

11 Statute of the International Criminal Tribunal for the former Yugoslavia, UN Doc. S/RES/827 (1993), Art. 7(3); Statute of the International Criminal Tribunal for Rwanda, UN Doc. S/RES/955 (1994), Art. 6(3); Statute of the Special Court for Sierra Leone, *Agreement Between the United Nations and the Government of Sierra Leone on the Establishment of a Special Court for Sierra Leone*, 16 January 2002, Art. 6(3); Statute of the "Khmer Rouge Tribunal," Law on the Establishment of Extraordinary Chambers in the Courts of Cambodia for the Prosecution of Crimes Committed During the Period of Democratic Kampuchea, Art. 29; Rome Statute of the International Criminal Court, circulated as document A/CONF.183/9 of 17 July 1998 and

Nature of the law of command responsibility

When studying the concept of command responsibility, it is important to understand its nature. Therefore, the fundamental question to be asked is: is the concept of command responsibility based on the fact that superiors are indirectly being held responsible for criminal acts of their subordinates (liability for an omission), or, does the concept of command responsibility entail a form of liability for superior's own, personal misconduct (liability for an commission)?
The answer to the question above must be: both. The ICTY has clarified, in the *Halilović* Judgment (see the attached documents), that the concept of command responsibility is a form of liability for an omission, as the ICTY confirmed that 'a commander is not responsible as though he had committed the crime himself.' Instead, the superior incurs criminal liability for his or her failure to comply with the duty that international law imposes on superiors to prevent or punish crimes committed by their subordinates.[12] However, on the other hand, the wording of the statutes of the ICC and of the Special Tribunal for Lebanon confirm that superiors may be held *'responsible for* crimes [...] committed by subordinates', which indicates that the concept of command responsibility is a form of liability for a commission.[13]

Elements of command responsibility

To hold a person individually criminally responsible under the concept of command responsibility for an international crime, three legal elements must be met:

1. A relationship of *subordination* between the direct perpetrators of the unlawful acts and the superior;

2. The superior *knew or had reason to know* that his or her subordinates were committing, had committed, or were about to commit abuses (the *mens rea* element); and

---

corrected by process-verbaux of 10 November 1998, 12 July 1999, 30 November 1999, 8 May 2000, 17 January 2001 and 16 January 2002, Art. 28; Statute of the Special Tribunal for Lebanon, UN Doc. S/RES/1757 (2007), Art. 3(2).

12 *Halilović* Judgment, paragraph 54. The SCSL has confirmed this approach in the *Brima et al.* Judgment, paragraph 783.

13 ICC Statute, Article 28 and the Special Tribunal for Lebanon Statute, Article 3(2).

3. The superior failed to take adequate steps to prevent or punish abuses (the *actus reus* element).

Relationship of subordination[14]

The doctrine of command responsibility does not only apply to military commanders, but also to others who poses a form of authority: for example political leaders and civilian superiors.[15] It ultimately depends on the actual power of control that the superior has on the acts of his subordinates.[16] The ICTY, the ICTR and the SCSL all apply the *effective control test*, for determining whether there is a situation of actual power of control.[17] This brings us to the question in what situation the "effective control" test is met. The answer to this question must be, that this has to be determined on the basis of the evidence of each particular case.[18] However, the following factors may be generally indicative of an superior's position of authority: the official position, the capacity to issue orders, the position in the military or political structure, and the actual tasks that he or she performed.[19]

---

14 Recommended reading: Meloni 2010, chapters 3.3 and 4.3, Mettraux 2009, chapter 9; Slye and Van Schaack 2009, chapter 10; Nybondas 2010, chapter 2.4.2.1.

15 *Čelebići* Appeal Judgment, paragraph 226; *Aleksovski* Appeal Judgment, paragraph 76; *Baglishema* Appeal Judgment paragraph 51; *Kajelijeli* Appeal Judgment, paragraph 85; *Brima et al.* Judgment, paragraph 782.

16 *Halilović* Judgment, paragraph 57. This actual power of control, does not necessarily have to be a formal one: *de jure power*. The command responsibility of a superior can also be based on the *de facto power* of control: *Čelebići* Appeal Judgment, paragraph 195; *Kajelijeli* Appeal Judgment, paragraph 85; *Brima et al.* Judgment, paragraph 784. It is also important to notice that it is not required that the subordinate is directly subordinated to its superior, since the ICTY clarified that the doctrine of command responsibility also applies to a subordinate which is several steps down in the chain of command: *Čelebići* Appeal Judgment, paragraph 303; *Halilović* Judgment, paragraphs 60-63

17 In other words, does the superior 'has the material ability to prevent and punish criminal conduct?': *Čelebići* Appeal Judgment, paragraph 256; *Kajelijeli* Appeal Judgment, paragraph 86; *Brima et al.* Judgment, paragraph 784.

18 Mettraux 2009, pp. 156-159.

19 The ICTY has held that it is permissible to *presume* that possession of a formal *de jure* power results in 'effective control' unless proof to the contrary is provided: *Čelebići* Appeal Judgment, paragraph 197. In regard to irregular armed groups, the ICTR has confirmed that the superior's *de facto*

As the ICTY confirms in the *Čelebići* case (see the attached documents): 'The power or authority to prevent or to punish does not solely arise from de jure authority conferred through official appointment. In many contemporary conflicts, there may be only de facto, self proclaimed governments and therefore de facto armies and paramilitary groups subordinate thereto. Command structure, organized hastily, may well be in disorder and primitive. To enforce the law in these circumstances requires a determination of accountability not only of individual offenders but of their commanders or other superiors who were, based on evidence, in control of them without, however, a formal commission or appointment. A tribunal could find itself powerless to enforce humanitarian law against de facto superiors if it only accepted as proof of command authority a formal letter of authority, despite the fact that the superiors acted at the relevant time with all the powers that would attach to an officially appointed superior or commander.'[20]

Mental element: 'knew or had reason to know'[21]

In order for a superior to acquire command responsibility, it must also be proven that the superior either had *actual knowledge*, or *had reason to know*, that his or her subordinates were committing, or were about to commit crimes.[22] A superior's *actual knowledge* can be established through circumstantial evidence, such as: the scope of the illegal acts, and the period of time and geographical location in which they occurred.[23] Whether it can be established that a superior *had reason to know*, depends on the central question whether information was available to the superior which would have put him on notice of crimes committed by his subordinates.[24] This available information can be interpreted broadly. For example, the awareness of a military

authority will play a crucial role in determining if he or she meets the effective control test. This *de facto* authority can for example be concluded by the fact that the superior had first entitlement to the profits of war and that the superior was protected by personal security guards, loyal to him or her, akin to a modern praetorian guard: *Brima et al.* Judgment, paragraph 788.

20 *Čelebići* Appeal Judgment, paragraph 195.

21 Recommended reading: Meloni 2010, chapters 3.5 and 4.6, Mettraux 2009, chapter 10; Slye and Van Schaack 2009, chapter 10; Nybondas 2010, chapter 2.4.2.2.

22 Mettraux 2009, p. 194.

23 *Halilović* Judgment, paragraph 66 and *Brima et al.* Judgment, paragraph 792.

24 *Čelebići* Appeal Judgment, paragraph 241; *Brima et al.* Judgment, paragraph 794; *Blaškić* Appeal Judgment, paragraph 62.

commander of the fact that one of his subordinates has a violent character, or has a drinking problem, may be enough to establish the knowledge requirement.[25] This has also been confirmed in the ICTR's *Bagilishema* case: 'The reason to know standard does not require that actual knowledge, either explicit or circumstantial, be established. Nor does it require that the Chamber satisfied that the accused actually knew that crimes had been committed or were about to be committed. It merely requires that the Chamber be satisfied that the accused had some 'general information' in his possession, which would put him on notice of possible unlawful acts by his subordinates.'[26]

It is important to notice that the ICC Statute differs somewhat from the other international criminal tribunals, when it comes to the mental element of command responsibility.[27] Article 28 confirms two separate standards: one for military commanders and one for non-military commanders ('other superiors'). For the military commander the knowledge test will remain the same: the accused knew or had reason to know that subordinates were committing illegal acts. This is in contrast with the ICC's standard for non-military commanders (other superiors), because for this type of commander to incur liability, the prosecutor must show that the accused either knew, or *consciously disregarded information that clearly indicated* that subordinates were committing or were about to commit illegal acts.[28] This approach was followed in the ICTR's *Kayishema and Ruzindana* case, which confirmed that: 'In light of the objective of Article 6(3) which is to ascertain the individual criminal responsibility for crimes as serious as genocide, crimes against humanity and violations of Common Article 3 to the Geneva Conventions and Additional Protocol II thereto, the Chamber finds that the Prosecution must prove that the accused in this case either knew, or *consciously disregarded information* which clearly indicated or put him on notice that his subordinates had committed, or were about to commit acts in breach of Articles 2 to 4 of this Tribunal's Statute.'[29]

So it can be concluded that, not only must the prosecutor show that the accused non-military commander had some kind of information regarding illegal acts committed by his subordinates, but also that the non-military commander chose not to consider or to act upon it. This

[25] *Halilović* Judgment, paragraph 68; *Čelebići* Appeal Judgment, paragraph 238.
[26] *Bagilishema* Appeal Judgment, reasons and paragraph 28.
[27] Mettraux 2009, pp. 195-197.
[28] Nybondas 2010, pp. 35 and 36.
[29] *Kayishema and Ruzindana* Judgement, paragraph 228.

might make it more difficult to effectively prosecute non-military commanders through command responsibility.[30]

'Failed to take adequate steps to prevent or punish abuses'[31]

The doctrine of command responsibility includes two legal duties for superiors: the duty to prevent future illegal acts by their subordinates, and the duty to punish past illegal acts by their subordinates.[32]

As to the superior's duty to prevent, a superior must intervene as soon as he becomes aware of the planning or preparation of crimes to be committed by his subordinates.[33] It is not certain whether or not the concept of command responsibility, in relation to the duty to prevent, requires an element of causation. Where the statutes of the ICTY, ICTR and the SCSL do not require an element of causation, the ICC Statute does in Article 28: 'as a result of'.[34]

The superior's duty to punish arises once one of his or her subordinates has committed an illegal act.[35] It is important to notice that a superiors failure of his or her duty to prevent, cannot be cured by punishing the subordinates afterwards.[36] This is also confirmed in the ICTY's *Blaškić* case (see the attached documents): 'The failure to punish and the failure to prevent involve different crimes committed at different times: the failure to punish concerns past crimes committed by subordinates, whereas the failure to prevent concerns future crimes of subordinates.'[37]

The ICTR trial chamber's reasoning in the *Musema* case, shows the suggestions by the judges, of measures to prevent and to punish, the defendant could have taken in that particular case: 'The Chamber finds that it has been established beyond reasonable doubt that Musema

30 Nybondas 2010, pp. 123 and 124.

31 Recommended reading: Meloni 2010, chapters 3.6, 4.5 and 4.8; Mettraux 2009, chapter 4.1.5; Slye and Van Schaack 2009, chapter 10; Nybondas 2010, chapter 2.

32 Meloni 2010, p. 114.

33 *Brima et al.* Judgment, paragraph 798.

34 *Blaškić* Appeal Judgment, paragraph 77. Meloni 2010, p. 173.

35 If the superior does not have the power to punish, he or she is obligated to report the illegal act(s) to the competent authorities: *Halilović* Judgment, paragraph 97.

36 *Halilović* Judgment, paragraph 72.

37 *Blaškić* Appeal Judgment, paragraph 83.

exercised de jure authority over employees of the Gisovu Tea Factory while they were on Tea Factory premises and while they were engaged in their professional duties as employees of the Tea Factory, even if those duties were performed outside factory premises. The Chamber notes that Musema exercised legal and financial control over these employees, particularly through his power to appoint and remove these employees from their positions at the Tea Factory. The Chamber notes that Musema was in a position, by virtue of these powers, to take reasonable measures, such as removing, or threatening to remove, an individual from his or her position at the Tea Factory if he or she was identified as a perpetrator of crimes punishable under the Statute. The Chamber also finds that, by virtue of these powers, Musema was in a position to take reasonable measures to attempt to prevent or to punish the use of Tea Factory vehicles, uniforms or other Tea Factory property in the commission of such crimes. The Chamber finds that Musema exercised de jure power and de facto control over Tea Factory employees and the resources of the Tea Factory.'[38]

The statutes of all international criminal tribunals confirm that the superior must take the 'necessary and reasonable measures' to fulfill the duty to prevent and the duty to punish.[39] The superior must have taken such necessary and reasonable measures that could have been taken given the superior's degree of effective control over his or her subordinates.[40] What constitutes such measures depends on the evidence.[41] However, the ICTY has defined both measures in the *Blaškić* case: 'Necessary measures' are those required to discharge the obligation to prevent or punish, in the circumstances prevailing at the time. 'Reasonable' measures are those which the commander was in a position to take in the circumstances prevailing at the time.'[42]

The ICTY's judges have been aware of the risk of expecting more than was within the capacity of a superior at the time of the violations. As the ICTY reasoned in the *Čelebići* case, it must: 'be recognized that international law cannot oblige a superior to perform the impossible. Hence, a superior may only be held criminally responsible for failing to take such measures within his powers [...] or within his material possibility.'[43]

---

[38] *Musema* Judgment, paragraph 880.

[39] See the Attached Documents.

[40] *Blaškić* Appeal Judgment, paragraph 72.

[41] What matters is whether the superior had the 'material ability' to act: *Halilović* Judgment, paragraph 73; *Brima et al.* Judgment, paragraph 798.

[42] *Blaškić* Judgment, paragraph 333.

[43] *Čelebići* Appeal Judgment, paragraph 395.

Practical application of the law of command responsibility[44]

This section will show a glance of the practical application of the law of command responsibility in cases before the ICTY.

Investigation and prosecution

The legal process at the Tribunal is set in motion by the Prosecutor. It is the Prosecutor who decides when to initiate an investigation, what to investigate, which persons to prosecute and what the charges should be. The materials collected through investigations are used for raising indictments against suspected perpetrators. Defendants may be charged with one or both of the two types of individual criminal responsibility; firstly, for personally committing, ordering, planning, instigating or aiding and abetting crimes under the Tribunal's jurisdiction and secondly, for being in a position of authority and failing to prevent or punish the commission of such crimes by subordinates: command responsibility.[45]

However, before a person can be accused and arrested, the indictment has to be confirmed by a judge who must be satisfied that there is enough evidence to support the charges. Once the indictment has been confirmed, the indictment will be served on the accused. The accused will be offered the choice to surrender to the ICTY voluntarily. If the accused will not surrender voluntarily, the competent Judge will issue a warrant for his or her arrest. After the accused has been arrested, he or she is immediately transferred to the ICTY's detention facility in The Hague, The Netherlands. In a short time after the transfer, the accused will make an initial appearance before the Tribunal. At that moment the accused will plead guilty or not guilty to charges against him or her. If the accused pleads not guilty, the pre-trial phase will start. During this phase, the prosecution team will for example prepare a document (pre-trial brief) which outlines the evidence which the prosecution plans to use during the trial to prove the commission of the crimes and the responsibility of the accused.

Trial

Trial proceedings at the ICTY are held before a Trial Chamber which consists of three judges without a jury. The Trial Chambers form the

44 Website of the ICTY: www.icty.org

45 See also the section on 'Conviction and sentence'.

first level of a two-tier court system, the Appeals Chamber being the second.

The fundamental principle of the presumption of innocence places a positive burden of proof on the prosecution and explains why a prosecution case will often feature many more witnesses and exhibits than the defense case. The question is, whether the prosecution manages to prove the guilt of the accused with so compelling evidence that the judges will have no reasonable doubt in the guilt of the accused. Witnesses can play a crucial role in proving this, three examples of categories of witnesses are:
Insider witnesses: many of the Tribunal's accused are high-level political, military or police leaders who are accused of planning crimes and ordering others to commit them. Persons who were close to the accused, called "insider witnesses," can provide the court with evidence about their actions and state of mind. The evidence gained from their testimony is often crucial for establishing the degree of responsibility of the accused.

Expert Witnesses: these witnesses are professionals who provide their expert opinion, under oath, on topics such as military doctrine, political structures, national laws in the former Yugoslavia, demographics, financial transactions, and forensic evidence. They help the judges to determine the circumstances in which crimes were committed, the accused's authority over their subordinates, the identity and number of victims found in mass graves, the number of victims killed in an area, among others.

International witnesses: diplomats or foreign military officers who were active in the conflict area at the time are sometimes called to testify for the Prosecution, especially if they held meetings with the suspects or other high-ranking civilian or military officials. They may, for instance, be able to provide proof that the suspect was informed about certain atrocities or military operations.

Conviction and sentence

In the world of international criminal justice, superiors will have, in relation to their subordinates, a greater responsibility in ensuring that the law is not violated. The superior's greater responsibility can be explained by the position of authority he or she fulfills, whether it is civilian or military. This position of authority gives rise to both duty and trust which, if broken or abused, would tend to aggravate the sentence.[46] The ICTY has concluded that it would be inconsistent to punish a simple perpetrator with a sentence equal or greater than that of its superior, this has been confirmed in the *Blaškić* case: 'when a commander fails in his duty to prevent the crime or to punish the perpetrator thereof he should receive a heavier sentence than the subordinates who committed the crime insofar as the failing conveys some tolerance or even approval on the part of the commander towards the commission of crimes by his subordinates and thus contributes to encouraging the commission of new crimes. It would not in fact be consistent to punish a simple perpetrator with a sentence equal or greater to that of the commander.'[47]

Finally, it must be noticed that where that the accused has both ordered and failed to prevent or punish crimes of its subordinates, the ICTY have expressed a preference for convicting the superior on the basis of the direct form of liability. This has also been confirmed in the *Blaškić* case: 'The Appeals Chamber considers that, in relation to a particular count, it is not appropriate to convict under both Article 7(1) (listing forms of direct and accessory responsibility) and Article 7(3) (superior responsibility) of the (ICTY) Statute. Where both forms of responsibility are alleged under the same count, and where the legal requirements pertaining to both of these heads of responsibility are met, a Trial Chamber should enter a conviction on the basis of Article 7(1) only, and consider the accused's superior position as an aggravating factor in sentencing.'[48]

Conclusion

The law of command responsibility plays a crucial role, as a legal tool for the international tribunals, to impose criminal liability on superiors, for the crimes of their subordinates

To establish command responsibility, it is necessary to show that the accused had 'effective control' over his or her subordinates. This situation of effective control can manifest itself by a formal *de jure* superior-subordinate relationship or a *de facto* superior-subordinate relationship. It must also be established that the superior 'knew' or 'had reason to know' that the subordinates had committed or were about to commit crimes. Finally, the superior must have failed to prevent the

[46] *Akayesu* Judgment, Sentence.

[47] *Blaškić* Judgment, paragraph 789.

[48] *Blaškić* Judgment, paragraph 91.

illegal acts committed its subordinates, or the superior must have failed to punish its subordinates for those actions. The superior is obliged to take the 'necessary and reasonable measures' to fulfill these two duties, to the extent that he or she had the 'material ability to act.'

Literature

Mettraux 2009
G. Mettraux, *The Law of Command Responsibility*, Oxford: Oxford University Press 2009.

Slye & Van Schaack 2009
R. C. Slye & B. Van Schaack, *International Criminal Law,* New York: Aspen Publishers 2009.

Meloni 2010
C. Meloni, *Command Responsibility in International Criminal Law,* The Hague: T. M. C. Asser Press 2010.

Nybondas 2010
M. L. Nybondas, *Command Responsibility and its Applicability to Civilian Superiors,* The Hague: T. M. C. Asser Press 2010.

Other recommended literature

Mettraux 2006
G. Mettraux, *International Crimes and the ad hoc Tribunals*, Oxford: Oxford University Press 2006.

Van Sliedregt 2011
E. van Sliedregt, *Individual Criminal Responsibility in International Law,* Oxford: Oxford University Press 2011.

Jurisprudence

DECISIONS OF NATIONAL COURTS

Emil Müller, German Supreme Court, 30 May 1921. (see the attached documents)

Yamashita, U.S. Military Commission, Manila, 7 December 1945. (see the attached documents)

Abbaye Ardenne, Canadian Military Court, Aurich, 28 December 1945. (see the attached documents)

Eichmann, Israel Supreme Court, Jerusalem, 29 May 1962. (see the attached documents)

INTERNATIONAL CRIMINAL TRIBUNAL FOR THE FORMER YUGOSLAVIA (ICTY)

Prosecutor v. Aleksovski, Case No. IT-95-14/1-A, Judgment, 24 March 2000. (see the attached documents)

Prosecutor v. Delalić et al., Case No. IT-96-21-A, Judgment, 20 February 2001 ('*Čelebići* Appeal Judgment'). (see the attached documents)

Prosecutor v. Blaškić, Case No. IT-95-14, Judgment, 3 March 2000.

Prosecutor v. Blaškić, Case No. IT-95-14-A, Appeal Judgment, 29 July 2004. (see the attached documents)

Prosecutor v. Halilović, Case No. IT-01-48-T, Judgment, 16 November 2005. (see the attached documents)

Prosecutor v. Halilović, Case No. IT-01-48-A, Appeal Judgment, 16 October 2007 . (see the attached documents)
Prosecutor v. Hadžihasanović, Case No. IT-01-47-T, Judgment, 15 March 2006. (see the attached documents)

INTERNATIONAL CRIMINAL TRIBUNAL FOR RWANDA (ICTR)

Prosecutor v. *Akayesu*, Case No. ICTR-96-4-T, Judgment, 2 September 1998. (see the attached documents)

Prosecutor v. *Kayishema and Ruzindana*, Case No. ICTR-95-1-T, Judgment, 21 May 1999.

Prosecutor v. *Musema*, Case No. ICTR-96-13-T, Judgement, 27 January 2000.

Prosecutor v. *Akayesu*, Case No. ICTR-96-4-A, Appeal Judgment, 1 June 2001.

Prosecutor v. Baglishema, Case No. ICTR-95-1A-A, Appeal Judgment (Reasons), 3 July 2002.

Prosecutor v. Ntagerura et al., Case No. ICTR-99-46-T, Judgment and Sentence, 25 Feb. 2004.

Kajelijeli v. The Prosecutor, Case No. ICTR-98-44A-A, Appeal Judgment, 23 May 2005.

SPECIAL COURT FOR SIERRA LEONE (SCSL)

Prosecutor v. Brima et al., Case No. SCSL-04-16-T-613, Judgment, 20 June 2007. (see the attached documents)

Prosecutor v. Brima et al., Case No. SCSL-04-16-A , Appeal Judgment, 22 February 2008.

INTERNATIONAL CRIMINAL COURT (ICC)

Prosecutor v. Bemba, Case No. ICC-01/05-01/08 , ICC Pre-Trial Decision on the Charges of the ICC, 15 June 2009. (see the attached documents)

ATTACHED DOCUMENTS

STATUTE OF THE INTERNATIONAL CRIMINAL TRIBUNAL FOR THE FORMER YUGOSLAVIA

Article 6
Personal jurisdiction

The International Tribunal shall have jurisdiction over natural persons pursuant to the provisions of the present Statute.

Article 7
Individual criminal responsibility

1. A person who planned, instigated, ordered, committed or otherwise aided and abetted in the planning, preparation or execution of a crime referred to in articles 2 to 5 of the present Statute, shall be individually responsible for the crime.

2. The official position of any accused person, whether as Head of State or Government or as a responsible Government official, shall not relieve such person of criminal responsibility nor mitigate punishment.

3. The fact that any of the acts referred to in articles 2 to 5 of the present Statute was committed by a subordinate does not relieve his superior of criminal responsibility if he knew or had reason to know that the subordinate was about to commit such acts or had done so and the superior failed to take the necessary and reasonable measures to prevent such acts or to punish the perpetrators thereof.

4. The fact that an accused person acted pursuant to an order of a Government or of a superior shall not relieve him of criminal responsibility, but may be considered in mitigation of punishment if the International Tribunal determines that justice so requires.

STATUTE OF THE INTERNATIONAL TRIBUNAL FOR RWANDA

Article 5: Personal jurisdiction

The International Tribunal for Rwanda shall have jurisdiction over natural persons pursuant to the provisions of the present Statute.

Article 6: Individual Criminal Responsibility

1. A person who planned, instigated, ordered, committed or otherwise aided and abetted in the planning, preparation or execution of a crime referred to in articles 2 to 4 of the present Statute, shall be individually responsible for the crime.

2. The official position of any accused person, whether as Head of State or Government or as a responsible Government official, shall not relieve such person of criminal responsibility nor mitigate punishment.

3. The fact that any of the acts referred to in articles 2 to 4 of the present Statute was committed by a subordinate does not relieve his or her superior of criminal responsibility if he or she knew or had reason to know that the subordinate was about to commit such acts or had done so and the superior failed to take the necessary and reasonable measures to prevent such acts or to punish the perpetrators thereof.

4. The fact that an accused person acted pursuant to an order of a Government or of a superior shall not relieve him or her of criminal responsibility, but may be considered in mitigation of punishment if the International Tribunal for Rwanda determines that justice so requires.

STATUTE OF THE INTERNATIONAL CRIMINAL COURT

Article 22
Nullum crimen sine lege

1. A person shall not be criminally responsible under this Statute unless the conduct in question constitutes, at the time it takes place, a crime within the jurisdiction of the Court.
2. The definition of a crime shall be strictly construed and shall not be extended by analogy. In case of ambiguity, the definition shall be interpreted in favour of the person being investigated, prosecuted or convicted.
3. This article shall not affect the characterization of any conduct as criminal under international law independently of this Statute.

Article 23
Nulla poena sine lege

A person convicted by the Court may be punished only in accordance with this Statute.

Article 24
Non-retroactivity ratione personae

1. No person shall be criminally responsible under this Statute for conduct prior to the entry into force of the Statute.
2. In the event of a change in the law applicable to a given case prior to a final judgement, the law more favourable to the person being investigated, prosecuted or convicted shall apply.

Article 258
Individual criminal responsibility

1. The Court shall have jurisdiction over natural persons pursuant to this Statute.
2. A person who commits a crime within the jurisdiction of the Court shall be individually responsible and liable for punishment in accordance with this Statute.
3. In accordance with this Statute, a person shall be criminally responsible and liable for punishment for a crime within the jurisdiction of the Court if that person:
   (a) Commits such a crime, whether as an individual, jointly with another or through another person, regardless of whether that other person is criminally responsible;

(b) Orders, solicits or induces the commission of such a crime which in fact occurs or is attempted;

(c) For the purpose of facilitating the commission of such a crime, aids, abets or otherwise assists in its commission or its attempted commission, including providing the means for its commission;

(d) In any other way contributes to the commission or attempted commission of such a crime by a group of persons acting with a common purpose. Such contribution shall be intentional and shall either:

(i) Be made with the aim of furthering the criminal activity or criminal purpose of the group, where such activity or purpose involves the commission of a crime within the jurisdiction of the Court; or

(ii) Be made in the knowledge of the intention of the group to commit the crime;

(e) In respect of the crime of genocide, directly and publicly incites others to commit genocide;

(f) Attempts to commit such a crime by taking action that commences its execution by means of a substantial step, but the crime does not occur because of circumstances independent of the person's intentions. However, a person who abandons the effort to commit the crime or otherwise prevents the completion of the crime shall not be liable for punishment under this Statute for the attempt to commit that crime if that person completely and voluntarily gave up the criminal purpose.

3 *bis.* In respect of the crime of aggression, the provisions of this article shall apply only to persons in a position effectively to exercise control over or to direct the political or military action of a State.

4. No provision in this Statute relating to individual criminal responsibility shall affect the responsibility of States under international law.

Article 26
Exclusion of jurisdiction over persons under eighteen

The Court shall have no jurisdiction over any person who was under the age of 18 at the time of the alleged commission of a crime.

Article 27
Irrelevance of official capacity

1. This Statute shall apply equally to all persons without any distinction based on official capacity. In particular, official capacity as a Head of State or Government, a member of a Government or parliament, an elected representative or a government official shall in no case exempt a person from

criminal responsibility under this Statute, nor shall it, in and of itself, constitute a ground for reduction of sentence.

2. Immunities or special procedural rules which may attach to the official capacity of a person, whether under national or international law, shall not bar the Court from exercising its jurisdiction over such a person.

Article 28
Responsibility of commanders and other superiors

In addition to other grounds of criminal responsibility under this Statute for crimes within the jurisdiction of the Court:

(a) A military commander or person effectively acting as a military commander shall be criminally responsible for crimes within the jurisdiction of the Court committed by forces under his or her effective command and control, or effective authority and control as the case may be, as a result of his or her failure to exercise control properly over such forces, where:

(i) That military commander or person either knew or, owing to the circumstances at the time, should have known that the forces were committing or about to commit such crimes; and

(ii) That military commander or person failed to take all necessary and reasonable measures within his or her power to prevent or repress their commission or to submit the matter to the competent authorities for investigation and prosecution.

(b) With respect to superior and subordinate relationships not described in paragraph (a), a superior shall be criminally responsible for crimes within the jurisdiction of the Court committed by subordinates under his or her effective authority and control, as a result of his or her failure to exercise control properly over such subordinates, where:

(i) The superior either knew, or consciously disregarded information which clearly indicated, that the subordinates were committing or about to commit such crimes;

(ii) The crimes concerned activities that were within the effective responsibility and control of the superior; and

(iii) The superior failed to take all necessary and reasonable measures within his or her power to prevent or repress their commission or to submit the matter to the competent authorities for investigation and prosecution.

Article 29
Non-applicability of statute of limitations

The crimes within the jurisdiction of the Court shall not be subject to any statute of limitations.

Article 30
Mental element

1. Unless otherwise provided, a person shall be criminally responsible and liable for punishment for a crime within the jurisdiction of the Court only if the material elements are committed with intent and knowledge.

2. For the purposes of this article, a person has intent where:

   (a) In relation to conduct, that person means to engage in the conduct;

   (b) In relation to a consequence, that person means to cause that consequence or is aware that it will occur in the ordinary course of events.

3. For the purposes of this article, "knowledge" means awareness that a circumstance exists or a consequence will occur in the ordinary course of events. "Know" and "knowingly" shall be construed accordingly.

Article 31
Grounds for excluding criminal responsibility

1. In addition to other grounds for excluding criminal responsibility provided for in this Statute, a person shall not be criminally responsible if, at the time of that person's conduct:

   (a) The person suffers from a mental disease or defect that destroys that person's capacity to appreciate the unlawfulness or nature of his or her conduct, or capacity to control his or her conduct to conform to the requirements of law;

   (b) The person is in a state of intoxication that destroys that person's capacity to appreciate the unlawfulness or nature of his or her conduct, or capacity to control his or her conduct to conform to the requirements of law, unless the person has become voluntarily intoxicated under such circumstances that the person knew, or disregarded the risk, that, as a result of the intoxication, he or she was likely to engage in conduct constituting a crime within the jurisdiction of the Court;

   (c) The person acts reasonably to defend himself or

herself or another person or, in the case of war crimes, property which is essential for the survival of the person or another person or property which is essential for accomplishing a militar y mission, against an imminent and unlawful use of force in a manner proportionate to the degree of danger to the person or the other person or property protected. The fact that the person was involved in a defensive operation conducted by forces shall not in itself constitute a ground for excluding criminal responsibility under this subparagraph;

(d) The conduct which is alleged to constitute a crime within the jurisdiction of the Court has been caused by duress resulting from a threat of imminent death or of continuing or imminent serious bodily harm against that person or another person, and the person acts necessarily and reasonably to avoid this threat, provided that the person does not intend to cause a greater harm than the one sought to be avoided. Such a threat may either be:

(i) Made by other persons; or

(ii) Constituted by other circumstances beyond that person's control.

2. The Court shall determine the applicability of the grounds for excluding criminal responsibility provided for in this Statute to the case before it.

3. At trial, the Court may consider a ground for excluding criminal responsibility other than those referred to in paragraph 1 where such a ground is derived from applicable law as set forth in article 21. The procedures relating to the consideration of such a ground shall be provided for in the Rules of Procedure and Evidence.

Article 32
Mistake of fact or mistake of law

1. A mistake of fact shall be a ground for excluding criminal responsibility only if it negates the mental element required by the crime.

2. A mistake of law as to whether a particular type of conduct is a crime within the jurisdiction of the Court shall not be a ground for excluding criminal responsibility. A mistake of law may, however, be a ground for excluding criminal responsibility if it negates the mental element required by such a crime, or as provided for in article 33.

Article 33
Superior orders and prescription of law

1. The fact that a crime within the jurisdiction of the Court has been committed by a person pursuant to an order of a Government or of a superior, whether militar y or civilian, shall not relieve that person of criminal responsibility unless:

   (a) The person was under a legal obligation to obey orders of the Government or the superior in question;

   (b) The person did not know that the order was unlawful; and

   (c) The order was not manifestly unlawful.

2. For the purposes of this article, orders to commit genocide or crimes against humanity are manifestly unlawful.

LAW ON THE ESTABLISHMENT OF EXTRAORDINARY CHAMBERS IN THE COURTS OF CAMBODIA FOR THE PROSECUTION OF CRIMES COMMITTED DURING THE PERIOD OF DEMOCRATIC KAMPUCHEA

CHAPTER VIII INDIVIDUAL RESPONSIBILITY

Article 29

Any Suspect who planned, instigated, ordered, aided and abetted, or committed the crimes referred to in article 3 new, 4, 5, 6, 7 and 8 of this law shall be individually responsible for the crime.

The position or rank of any Suspect shall not relieve such person of criminal responsibility or mitigate punishment.

The fact that any of the acts referred to in Articles 3 new, 4, 5, 6, 7 and 8 of this law were committed by a subordinate does not relieve the superior of personal criminal responsibility if the superior had effective command and control or authority and control over the subordinate, and the superior knew or had reason to know that the subordinate was about to commit such acts or had done so and the superior failed to take the necessary and reasonable measures to prevent such acts or to punish the perpetrators.

The fact that a Suspect acted pursuant to an order of the Government of Democratic Kampuchea or of a superior shall not relieve the Suspect of individual criminal responsibility.

STATUTE OF THE SPECIAL TRIBUNAL FOR LEBANON

Article 3
Individual criminal responsibility

1. A person shall be individually responsible for crimes within the jurisdiction of the Special Tribunal if that person:

(a) Committed, participated as accomplice, organized or directed others to commit the crime set forth in article 2 of this Statute; or

(b) Contributed in any other way to the commission of the crime set forth in article 2 of this Statute by a group of persons acting with a common purpose, where such contribution is intentional and is either made with the aim of furthering the general criminal activity or purpose of the group or in the knowledge of the intention of the group to commit the crime.

2. With respect to superior and subordinate relationships, a superior shall be criminally responsible for any of the crimes set forth in article 2 of this Statute committed by subordinates under his or her effective authority and control, as a result of his or her failure to exercise control properly over such subordinates, where:

(a) The superior either knew, or consciously disregarded information that clearly indicated that the subordinates were committing or about to commit such crimes;

(b) The crimes concerned activities that were within the effective responsibility and control of the superior; and

(c) The superior failed to take all necessary and reasonable measures within his or her power to prevent or repress their commission or to submit the matter to the competent authorities for investigation and prosecution.

3. The fact that the person acted pursuant to an order of a superior shall not relieve him or her of criminal responsibility, but may be considered in mitigation of punishment if the Special Tribunal determines that justice so requires.

STATUTE OF THE SPECIAL COURT FOR SIERRA LEONE

Article 6

Individual criminal responsibility

1. A person who planned, instigated, ordered, committed or otherwise aided and abetted in the planning, preparation or execution of a crime referred to in articles 2 to 4 of the present Statute shall be individually responsible for the crime.

2. The official position of any accused persons, whether as Head of State or Government or as a responsible government official, shall not relieve such person of criminal responsibility nor mitigate punishment.

3. The fact that any of the acts referred to in articles 2 to 4 of the present Statute was committed by a subordinate does not relieve his or her superior of criminal responsibility if he or she knew or had reason to know that the subordinate was about to commit such acts or had done so and the superior had failed to take the necessary and reasonable measures to prevent such acts or to punish the perpetrators thereof.

4. The fact that an accused person acted pursuant to an order of a Government or of a superior shall not relieve him or her of criminal responsibility, but may be considered in mitigation of punishment if the Special Court determines that justice so requires.

5. Individual criminal responsibility for the crimes referred to in article 5 shall be determined in accordance with the respective laws of Sierra Leone.

EMIL MÜLLER CASE

JUDGMENT IN THE CASE OF EMIL MULLER

30 MAY 1921

IN THE NAME OF THE EMPIRE

In the criminal case against Emil Muller, barrister, and Captain in the Reserve (retired), of Karlsruhe, born on 24 July, 1877, in Mannheim, for crimes and offences against sections 122, 143, 55, 59, 1, 121, 7, of the Military Penal Code and section 74 of the Imperial Penal Code, the second Criminal Senate of the Imperial Court of Justice at a sitting held in public on 30 May, 1921, at which there took part as Judges, The President of the Senate, Dr. Schmidt, and the Imperial Justices, Dr. Sabarth, Dr. Paul, Backs, Dr. Schultz, Dr. Kleine, Hagemann, as officials of the Public Prosecutor's Department, The Oberreichsanwalt, Dr. Ebermayer and Lingemann, Counsel of the Public Prosecutor's Department, as Clerk of the Court, Risch, official, after oral evidence.

The accused is sentenced to six months' imprisonment for having ill-treated subordinates in nine instances; for having tolerated such ill-treatment in one instance; for having dealt with subordinates in four instances contrary to the regulations; and for having insulted subordinates in two instances. On the remaining charges he is acquitted. The costs of the proceedings in respect of the charges, for which sentence has been passed, are imposed upon the accused, and those in respect of the charges, on which the accused has been acquitted, are imposed upon the Imperial Exchequer. The Imperial Exchequer is also to bear the whole of the expenses con- nected with the first-mentioned cases, including the necessary expenses of the accused.

By Right

REASONS OF THE DECISION

In March, 1918, the accused, who was then a captain in the Reserve, commanded the II Company of the Gelsenkirchen Landsturm Battalion. In this capacity he was, in the beginning of April, placed in command of a camp for English prisoners of war at Flavy-le-Martel, which was being put in order by the battalion. He shared these duties with the commander of No. I Company, but each company took over a separate portion of the camp, and took up its quarters with the prisoners of war assigned to it. No commandant of the camp as a whole was appointed.

The duties of the company commanders consisted solely in housing, feeding and supervising their prisoners, and in arranging, day by day, to provide the troops requisitioned for outside work. They had nothing to do with the regulation of this work it- self or settling the hours of labor. This was the business of the commander of the battalion and of his subordinates. The company commanders took over a camp which was found empty. In the camp there were barracks and other buildings. These were the only buildings in the neighborhood. The company commanders had no choice of other buildings.

The accused held this position from the beginning of April until 5th May, 1918, that is to say, for a period of about five weeks. On the 4th May he was given leave, as he needed treatment for neurosis of the heart. He left the camp on 5th May and never returned.

The camp had shortly before been taken from the English during the so- called March offensive, and had previously been used by them as a camp for the temporary reception of German prisoners of war. It was in a wretched condition. It lay in a marshy and completely devastated district immediately behind the fighting line, where everything was still in constant movement. During the time the English had been in possession of it, it was unfit for human occupation. The witness Roeder, who at that time and indeed at the end of January and beginning of February, 1918, had taken part in the war on the English side, and had often come there as interpreter, gave reliable evidence that the accommodation had been defective in the extreme. In the two residential barracks, which together afforded room for some 300 prisoners only, double that number had been quartered. These barracks had a muddy, unboarded floor. There were no beds, but only some rotten wood- wool, which was infected with vermin. Windows and roofing were leaky. There were but two small so-called trench stoves so that the German prisoners had suffered from the cold in winter. The latrines were as primitive and unwholesome as can be imagined. There was a complete absence of sanitary arrangements, and also almost a complete absence of facilities for cooking and washing as well as of rugs. As a consequence of all this, numerous prisoners had become sick with influenza and intestinal troubles, especially with dysentery. Many had died. All had complained of the plague of lice. Even the English guard had suffered heavily. An English doctor had endeavored in vain to remove these defects.

The accused found the camp in precisely this condition, and had to do his best with it. The position was rendered more difficult for him because he was obliged to quarter over 1,000 men in the barracks as fresh prisoners were constantly arriving. Further, all the wells roundabout were ruined. The food allotted was insufficient, and during the first days he had no medical assistance. Finally he was obliged to detail daily very many men for heavy outside work, and the prisoners were already in a quite exhausted condition when they came under him. They were inadequately equipped with uniforms on arrival, as also with underclothes, rugs and so on. The accused at once set energetically to work to effect an improvement. On the one hand he sent many memoranda to his superiors emphatically demanding delivery of supplies in order to draw their attention to the conditions, and he made pressing demands for what was wanting (his report of 20th April, 1918, particularly is worthy of notice), and by urgent representations, both verbal and in writing, he in fact obtained many things. For example, medical assist- ance was allotted to him as early as the third day. Furthermore, he himself took in hand the improvement of the camp as far as was possible. He formed a working party from what labor was left in the camp. He had wells sunk, stoves installed, proper latrines laid out, cooking and washing places provided, and he fought the plague of lice first by the means of powder and finally by getting a disinfecting station set up. He also succeeded in getting some improvement in the food, and occasionally he got the outside work made easier. On one occasion he procured soap as well as extra food and luxuries from Belgium. On another he managed to get hold of some clothing which was not intended for his men at all. Several times he procured some horse-flesh, and he detailed those prisoners, who were particularly weak, for duty in the kitchens and bakeries where they could get more food. He showed thereby that he had sympathy with his prisoners and that he was not insensible to their real needs.

in spite of all this the position of the prisoners became continuously worse. Food remained insufficient. (The causes of this lay in the shortage of nourishing food prevailing at that time owing to the blockade.) The strength of the prisoners had not grown equal to the strenuous outside work. This work was necessitated by the fighting and, in determining it, the accused had in general no influence. Most of the prisoners grew weaker and weaker and they often collapsed at their work or on the march to their place of work as well as at the roll-calls in camp. Furthermore, infectious diseases broke out in the shelters, which were already overrun with lice and infected with germs of disease. The prisoners did not keep themselves clean and were un- able to change either uniform or underclothing. At first there was not any sufficient quantity of disinfectant. Thus nearly all the prisoners suffered to a great extent from lice and ulcers, many also from intestinal catarrh. Finally dysentery, which already in the time of the English had been rampant there, broke out again, at first in isolated cases and then it spread rapidly. This epidemic developed after the departure of the accused in such a manner that a large proportion of the prisoners had to be transferred into the interior to Stendal, where many more died from it. In the camp itself the number of deaths from dysentery is said to have been considerable, but not until after the departure of the accused.

But no responsibility of any kind rests upon the accused for this wretched aggravation of the conditions. As has been stated above, he had perceived the danger in good time and had done everything to prevent it. That in this respect he attained but little was due to the circumstances which were beyond both him and also his immediate superiors. It was not possible at that time to take adequate care of the troops' and prisoners' camps close behind the battle zone. Nevertheless, in a short time the accused did an astonishing amount towards improving his camp and he laid the foundations, whereby in the course of the succeeding months (when a quieter period came along) this camp could be converted into a relatively well-equipped prisoners' camp. Later, not only his superiors but also the medical inspectors repeatedly acknowledged this to be so. He has the reputation of having been an able, energetic and conscientious officer, who always carried through the tasks which were imposed upon him and who always maintained good order. His immediate superior, the commander of the battalion, Major v. Bomsdorf, confirms this in particular. It cannot be disputed that as camp commandant he displayed these characteristics and that in this capacity he showed meritorious industry. In particular he cannot be reproached with not having endeavored in good time to get the camp free from epidemics. Any such an attempt at that time would have been hopeless. The cases of sickness from dysentery were then still sporadic; there was no question of a real epidemic. It has been conclusively proved that during the whole period of his command at the camp there was only one case of death among the prisoners under him and that this took place shortly before his departure and was not attributable to dysentery. The neighboring company in the camp was in a similar condition. It is true that intestinal catarrh was already very prevalent as well as lice, ulcers and a general loss of vigor. These troubles were, however, universal in the camps of that district, and it was on this account that steps could not reasonably be taken for providing fresh quarters, a step which at that time would have been scarcely possible on any large scale.

So far, therefore, as the general conditions in the prisoners' camp at Flavy-le-Martel are concerned, the accused must not only be acquitted of any blame, but it should be placed on record that the zeal with which he carried out his duties deserves high praise. On the other hand, the same cannot be said about the way in which he treated the prisoners individually or his in methods of maintaining order. It was precisely owing to his zeal and his natural tendency for an impetuous and rigorous action (combined with a serious condition of nervous overstrain) that prompted him to commit a series of excesses, which constituted a breach not only of his official duties but also of the criminal law. These excesses cannot be justified by the circumstances. His attitude towards the prisoners was hard and over-severe, sometimes even brutal, and in other cases it was at least contrary to regulations. He treated them not as subordinates, and it was as such that he ought to have regarded his prisoners, but he treated them more like convicts or inmates of penitentiaries. His methods were those of the convict prison or such like institutions, although even on this standard his conduct could not be tolerated. The court has heard of his ill-treating prisoners by hitting and kicking them. He allowed his staff to treat them in the same manner. Insults were hurled at the prisoners and there was other ill-treatment which was contrary to the regulations. He habitually struck them when he was on horseback, using a riding cane or a walking stick; several prisoners have stated that they were struck with a riding whip, but this must be a mistake as the accused did not possess one.

In detail the following instances are held proved:

I. Ill-treatment 1. According to the evidence of the witness Lovegrove the accused when on horseback struck the prisoner Millsom across the shoulders with his riding cane. Roll-call was being taken and Millsom marched past slackly and had a pipe in his mouth. Millsom himself is no longer alive.

2 and 3. In at least two cases the accused ordered prisoners to be bound to posts. In the first case, which he himself admits, this was done to a man whom he suspected of having been ringleader in an intended mutiny. The accused asserts that he made this man stand for about 10 minutes and or- dered all the others to march past him; this being intended as a warning to the others. It has not been possible to establish the details of this incident. The fact remains, however, that, as the witness Thornton has said, there never was any question of a mutiny, but only an arrangement to make a joint complaint, in the first place to the accused himself, and if opportunity arose to his superiors. The accused had found this out by questioning the prisoners concerned through an interpreter. The court cannot accept that he seriously believed from what he heard that a mutiny was intended.

The accused admits that there may have been a second case of tying a prisoner to a post, but he will not call it to mind more precisely. It remains doubtful whether this second occasion related to a man who had stolen some oats (witness Ray) or to one of the prisoners who evaded work (wit- ness non-commissioned officers, Biela, Rose, Ellis, Nelms and Sharp). It is possible that there were several such incidents as the several descriptions vary a good deal from each other. But only one case can, however, be held to be proved. Biela has given evidence that in this case, the accused ordered the prisoners to be tied up for three days, two hours each day, and that the accused himself showed Biela how it was to be done. Biela then modified the severity of the punishment, entirely on his own accord, and omitted the third day's tying up altogether.

It has not been established that in these cases the accused either ordered or allowed that these prisoners should be so tied up that they were compelled to gaze continuously in the sun. If anything of the kind actually took place, it may have been because the non-commissioned officers or soldiers who carried out the order acted on their own responsibility; there is no proof that the accused had any knowledge of it. However, even without this in- human method of carrying out the order, the tying up remains a very severe measure which cannot be justified in any way. This form of service punishment was done away with by an Imperial decree of 26th May, 1917, and certain remarks of the accused seem to show that this decree, which had been duly published and was much discussed, was not unknown to him. He probably ordered this tying up, not so much as a punishment but rather as a means of securing order generally and of putting a stop to insubordination. Of this, however, so far as the court can see, there was no reason- able fear, and the employment of this severe measure cannot be considered otherwise than as a case of ill-treatment under the conditions then obtaining.

4. On one occasion the accused struck, apparently only with his hand, the interpreter Sacof, because this man reported to him a complaint of an- other man who was asking for more bread.

5. The accused while on horseback struck a prisoner who was suffering from a bad foot. At roll-call this prisoner had raised his leg to show it to the accused, but the accused hit him across his leg with his riding cane. The man cried out, fell down and had to be carried into barracks (witness Stiles).

The witness Drewcock gave evidence as to further cases of ill-treatment. They happened in a tent-camp which was put up about the middle of April at the railway station and was intended for use by prisoners who were on their way elsewhere. The accused was not appointed commandant of this tent-camp, but the supervision of the prisoners' maintenance there had been transferred to him. He undoubtedly had duties there and during this time he had authority over the prisoners in the camp. In carrying out these duties:

6. He thrashed the prisoner Batey with his walking-stick. This man be- came ill while at work outside the camp and, although violently attacked by the sentries who did not believe in his inability to work, he refused to work any further. The sentries reported him to the accused on their return and Batey repeated that he was ill and emphatically asked for a doctor. The accused got furious over this, as he thought that Batey was a malingerer; he then belabored him in the manner already stated.

7 and 8. In two cases at least the accused struck with his stick prisoners who were asking for improved conditions, particularly for more food. The accused excuses himself for doing this by stating that the prisoners in the tent-camp had frequently obtained double rations surreptitiously. This, however, cannot justify his violence against prisoners making requests to him.

9. The accused once struck Drewcock at roll-call when he (the accused) was riding in amongst the prisoners, who did not at once give way to him. He struck him across his wounded knee with his riding cane so hard that an abscess developed and later had to be cut. The accused could not have foreseen this, for the wounds on Drewcock's knee were not visible to him. But the blow must have been a heavy one.

In general the accused has admitted that it was his practice to enforce discipline, in cases of irregular behavior by means of light blows. He will not as a rule tax his memory about the details. He explains, however, it would have been impossible to attain rigid discipline if he had tolerated any lengthy explanations, especially as he and the prisoners could not understand each other's language. There may be some truth in this and there were no doubt serious difficulties in commanding such a camp. But nevertheless the accused never had any right to get over these difficulties by means of endless acts of violence.

Three further similar cases (namely those under 1, 2 and 5 of the indictment) come under the heading of treating prisoners contrary to the regulations; see under IV, 1 to 3 later. The charge under 1, 4, of the indictment is not proved. The accused is alleged to have struck the witness Lawrence in his face with the handle of a riding whip. Lawrence alone gives evidence of this, but Lawrence has not impressed the court as a credible witness. He has shown strong animosity, he has exaggerated everything far beyond the accounts of the other witnesses and he has told of monstrous happenings. For example he asserts that he saw the accused dismount at the burial of a prisoner, get down into the open grave and snatch away from the dead man the rug in which he was shrouded. This is demonstrably untrue. While the accused was at the camp one burial only took place in the camp and this by orders of the accused was conducted in an absolutely proper manner. The corpse was placed in a coffin and the accused had ordered a wreath to decorate it.

II. Toleration of ill-treatment by Subordinates

Here only one instance has been proved with certainty. A prisoner moved in the ranks while at evening roll-call. He was harshly rebuked by Sergeant- Major Schubert. The accused saw the incident and called out something to Schubert who thereupon knocked the prisoner down with his fist. The prisoner was then carried away (witness Stiles). It is to be assumed that the accused at least tolerated and approved of this brutal treatment, even if it was not done on his orders.

On the other hand his guilt is not proved in connection with a second instance. A sentry guard was driving the prisoners out of the barracks to roll- call one morning and hit the witness Lovegrove on the hip with the butt-end of his rifle, perhaps because he did not come out sufficiently quickly. Love- grove certainly thinks that he saw the accused, who was standing close by, laugh at this. But he can easily have been mistaken, and in any case it is not clear whether this ill-treatment had not taken place before the accused either noticed it or could prevent it. Therefore no case of knowingly per- mitting this when he could have prevented it (section 143 Military Penal Code) can be established here.

III. Insults

The witnesses Peace and Sacof declare that the accused generally abused and threatened the prisoners a good deal and that he frequently spoke of them as "Englishmen" and "Schweinhunde" (pig-dogs). This however is too vague to be regarded as proof of any actual insulting of particular in- dividuals. But the witness Thornton reports two instances which are different. The accused said of a sick prisoner who was found to be in a dirty condition: "Away with the English 'Dreckschwein' (mire-pig)" (or words to that effect). These were serious personal insults and were wounding to national feeling and they are all the more serious because both the prisoners concerned were entirely blameless. For in the first instance the man had intestinal trouble and had been refused permission to leave the ranks at roll-call to go to the latrines and it was in consequence of this that he was in a filthy condition. The second instance concerned a prisoner who was seriously ill, half eaten by lice, and was to be washed by doctor's orders. He died the very next morning. There was no reason to insult men in so unhappy a condition, least of all for such insults to come from an officer and a man of education.

IV. Treatment of Subordinates contrary to Regulations

1. According to the statement of the witness Lovegrove the accused once saw two recumbent sick men lying down; they were so weak that they could not stand up before him and were groaning pitifully. But the accused is said to have got angry and impatient and to have kicked them. This is not construed as a case of ill-treatment, although it is thus alleged in the indictment. There is a possibility that the accused did not wish to hurt the men, whose sickness he apparently did not yet believe to be real, but that he only wished to secure that his order to get up was immediately obeyed. It is not clear that the kicking was particularly violent or painful. Clearly, however, in each instance this constituted a treatment of the sick contrary to regulations. These assaults are considered therefore to amount to one offence against Section 121 of the Military Penal Code.

2. While Lovegrove himself was once marching past the accused, he did not turn his head sufficiently, so the accused pulled him out of the ranks by the ear and Lovegrove was then, according to his story, pushed to and fro. This also, despite the indictment, was only a case of treatment contrary to regulations, namely, merely an irregular attempt to put a prisoner right without any intention to ill-treat him.

3. The same holds good about the accused riding on horseback into the prisoners. (I, 5, of the indictment.) The accused admits that he liked, as soon as he appeared at roll-call, to ride quickly up to the ranks. He thought this was a suitable way of ensuring proper respect for himself and of making the prisoners attentive. According to the evidence of almost all the English and also of some German witnesses, he frequently rode so far into the ranks, that the ranks were broken. The prisoners scattered on all sides and many, who could not get out of the way quickly enough, were thrown down by the horse. Such excesses when riding up to a body of men is altogether contrary to regulations and is to be condemned. This is also the opinion of the military expert, General v. Fransecki. In the present case this has not been construed as

ill-treatment, solely because no actual riding down or breaking up the ranks was intended and because as a matter of fact nobody was injured. The accused was prompted purely by excessive keenness. The several instances constitute one continuous action.

4. Finally, the accused, likewise acting continuously, often forced work on sick prisoners. When he could not muster the full complement of workers demanded or when supplementary demands arrived, he forcibly sent everyone out, even those entered as sick or who were obviously incapable of work; he tolerated no opposition. This is stated by numerous prisoners (Sacof, Goldberg, Tingle (medical orderly), Lovegrove, Peace, Abrahams, Nelms and Brett in complete agreement), and the German witness Benker confirms it. The accused cannot answer this by pleading that he considered many of these alleged sick to be malingerers or that his strict orders obliged him to send out the numbers of workers that were demanded. For the first excuse contradicts the evidence of the witnesses, who declare that there could have been no doubt about the sickness of many of the men in question. With regard to the second excuse the military advisers v. Kuhl and v. Fransecki declare that there was certainly a great and urgent need of workers and that the necessity for a scrupulous supplying of the demands for them had been enjoined upon the commandants of the camp. But they had been expressly told to avoid including weak or sick prisoners, because the maintenance of the prisoners in a healthy condition was just as much to the interest of the administration of the army as it was in that of humanity. These considerations the accused in his excessive zeal constantly ignored and that is an offence which it is not easy to estimate, especially when the wretch- ed health conditions in this camp are considered.

The case mentioned in IV, 1, 6, of the indictment must be excluded here. The witness Ray was made to chop wood for an hour, because, owing, it is said, to weakness, he did not salute. It was not certain that Ray was really too weak for this kind of penal work or that he was ordered to do it by the accused. Ray, who had received the order from Sergeant-Major Schubert, only supposes this, but the sergeant-major may have been acting independently.

Further, it is also not proved that the accused refused medical assistance to sick prisoners (IV, 3, of the indictment). His plea that he sent the men, who reported sick, to the medical authorities has remained unanswered.

The charges made in IV, 2, 4, and 5 have been satisfactorily explained. If prisoners washed their faces in dirty water, this was not because the accused directed them to do so, but because they did not trouble to change the water in the trough at the proper time and it was at all times possible to change this water. As regards the dying man who was covered with vermin, water was poured over him and he died the following day; but this treatment was given under medical orders and in a considerate way, though it is true that he was insulted by the accused while being washed. (See above under III.) The treatment itself did him no harm (witness Terlinson). The accused took some small photographs of the camp, especially of the latrine when the prisoners were using it, to commemorate his service as commandant. He did this with a feeling of pride in the improvements effected by him. He might well have done this in a less objectionable manner. But in taking the photographs he had no intention of insulting the prisoners. If several prisoners thought that in doing this the accused was mocking them, this was due to their preconceived idea that the accused was animated by feelings of spiteful malignity towards them. This preconceived idea about the accused has shown itself on other occasions (looking into the mortuary; behavior when complaints were being made, &c.). But the court has found no definite facts to prove any such feelings on the part of the accused. Accordingly on all these points (as well as those under 1, 4, and II, 1, of the indictment) the accused is acquitted. The charge in IV, 6 (the tying up of the man who stole oats) has been decided as a case of ill- usage (see above I, 2/3).

So far as the accused is guilty his offences have throughout been committed in his capacity of superior towards his subordinates and while he was carrying out his duties. He served continuously in the camp.

Thus it has been definitely established: That the accused was at the prisoners' camp at Flavy-le-Martel from the beginning of April until 5th May, 1918, and that the following separate incidents took place:

I. In nine instances he deliberately kicked or struck English prisoners of war, his subordinates, or otherwise physically ill-treated them or caused in- jury to their health.

II. In one instance, as commanding officer of a military detachment, he allowed one of his subordinates, a non-commissioned officer, deliberately to strike an English prisoner of war with his fist. The accused thereby with knowledge permitted the committing of a criminal act, which he could have prevented, and which he was officially bound to prevent.

III. In two instances he insulted English prisoners of war, his subordinates, by using words of abuse.

IV. In four instances he is guilty of treating English prisoners of war, his subordinates, contrary to the regulations and as in the cases I to IV, he did this whilst carrying out his duties.

He is thus liable to punishment for crimes and offences according to Section 122, paras. 1, 143, 121; paras. 1, 55 (2), 53, 7, of the Military Penal Code; Section 74 of the Imperial Penal Code (cf. the Imperial Law of 18th December 1919 and 24th March 1920, which deals with the prosecution of war crimes and offences).

In deciding the extent of his punishment the following factors have had to be taken into consideration:

The accused is in no wise guilty to the extent which might appear from the results of the preliminary proceedings. The trial before this court has vindicated him on many points; in others it has proved that his offences were not so serious as had been expected. As has already been stated, he has been an able officer, who faithfully tried to do his duty; who always strove to win the appreciation of his superiors, and who had hitherto secured such appreciation in full measure throughout his long years of war service. Then, however, he was suddenly confronted with an unusually difficult situation. He was obliged to take over the, to him, novel position of commandant of prisoners of war, and this in one of the most disturbed battle areas, close up against the front, in a devastated and unhealthy neighborhood and at a time of most severe scarcity of all necessaries of life. The accused had, so to speak, to create out of nothing, a camp to house the unending stream of prisoners. All these burdens were placed upon him at a time when he was already almost breaking down as a result of war strain and an old heart complaint, and was afflicted with serious nerve trouble (witness Kesseler, doctor of medicine). In spite of all this, he showed himself, generally speaking, equal to his task and carried out the administration of the camp as such as well as possible.

But in his personal treatment of the prisoners (and for this his temperament was less suited), he erred seriously. Instead of earning the prisoners' confidence, he got a reputation among them for being a tyrant and a nigger- driver. But here, too, his excesses were only due to that military enthusiasm which worked him up to an exaggerated conception of military necessity and discipline. He made insufficient allowance for the special conditions in which prisoners in war-time find themselves. He showed himself severe and lacking in consideration but not deliberately cruel. His acts originated, not in any pleasure in persecution, or even in any want of feeling for the sufferings of the prisoners; but in a conscious disregard of the general laws of humanity. Had this not been so, he would not have generally troubled so much about the well-being of the prisoners, and his acts of ill treatment would have caused more serious injury to those concerned than has been proved to have occurred. Not a single case has had really serious consequences.

It must be emphasized that the accused has not acted dishonorably, that is to say, his honor both as a citizen and as an officer remains untarnished. None the less the choice given by law (Sections 121, 122, 55 of the Military Penal Code) between imprisonment and detention in a fortress, cannot be decided in favor of the latter. There has been an accumulation of offences, which show an almost habitually harsh and contemptuous and even a frankly brutal treatment of prisoners entrusted to his care. His conduct has sometimes been unworthy of a human being: these factors the court considers decisive. When he mixed with the prisoners there was seldom anything but angry words, attempts to ride them down, blows and efforts to push them out of his way: he never listened patiently to their grievances and complaints: he had no eyes for their obvious sufferings: he cared little for the individual, if only he could secure order among the prisoners collectively. It is impossible to consider his conduct as a number of separate instances of rash actions which he regretted: it appears rather as a deliberate practice of domineering disregard for other men's feelings. It is no justification that his methods were intended to secure discipline. It is also no excuse that the conditions had been brutalized by war. The only possible excuse for him was that he was overexcited: that he feared disorder, and that he did not know how to handle men. But even so, it must be recalled that he had under him prisoners who were peculiarly unfortunate, sick and suffering men who deserved protection. When these prisoners offended against the regulations, the cause for the most part lay in their miserable condition. Such men in such conditions were not likely to be really refractory. The accused should have avoided being unduly severe; and above all he ought not to have indulged in such reprehensible means of punishment as blows, kicks, tying-up and such like. Such conduct dishonors our army, and is singularly unfitting in a man of his education and military as well as civilian position.

Therefore it seems to the court that detention in a fortress is too light a sentence to follow such an accumulation of offences.

The most grievous mistake of the accused, having regard to the lamentable health conditions in the camp, is considered to be his compelling of sick men to work (under IV, 4). For this there must be a sentence of 2 months' imprisonment. For the other offences there will be:

Under I, 2 and 3, 5, 6, e , . Under II, 1 and under IV, 3 e Under I, 1, 4, 7 and 8 each one weeks' arrest: Under I, 9, two weeks' arrest, these cases being considered as less grievous: Under III, 1 and 2, and under IV, 2, each one week's arrest: and Under IV, 1, two weeks' arrest.

Out of these separate sentences there will be a total sentence of 6 months' imprisonment in accordance with Section 74 of the Penal Code and Section 54 of the Military Penal Code. In respect of the other charges the accused is acquitted.

The costs are regulated in accordance with Sections 497, 498, para. 1, in conjunction with Section 4 of the Imperial Law for the Prosecution of War Crimes and Offences of 24th AMarch 1920.

(Signed) SCHMIDT, SABARTH, DR. PAUL, BACKS, SCHULTZ, KLEINE, HAGEMANN.

The present copy agrees with the original document. The Clerk of the Court of the 2nd Criminal Senate of the Imperial Court of Justice. (Seal of the Court.)

YAMASHITA CASE

TRIAL OF GENERAL TOMOYUKI YAMASHITA
UNITED STATES MILITARY COMMISSION, MANILA,
(8TH OCTOBER-7TH DECEMBER, 1945)

JUDGMENTS DELIVERED ON 4 FEBRUARY 1946

Responsibility of a Military Commander for offences committed by his troops. The sources and nature of the authority to create military commissions to conduct War Crime Trials, Non-applicability in War Crime Trials of the United States Articles of War and of the provisions of the Geneva Convention relating to Judicial Proceedings. Extent of review permissible to the Supreme Court over War Crime Trials.

Tomoyuki Yamashita, formerly Commanding General of the Fourteenth Army Group of the Imperial Japanese Army in the Philippine Islands, was arraigned before a United States Military Commission and charged with unlawfully disregarding and failing to discharge his duty as commander to control the acts of members of his command by permitting them to commit war crimes. The essence of the case for the Prosecution was that the accused knew or must have known of, and permitted, the widespread crimes committed in the Philippines by troops under his command (which included murder, plunder, devastation, rape, lack of provision for prisoners of war and shooting of guerrillas without trial), and/or that he did not take the steps required of him by international law to find out the state of discipline maintained by his men and the conditions prevailing in the prisoner-of-war and civilian internee camps under his command. The Defence argued, *inter alia*, that what was alleged against , Yamashita did not constitute a war crime, that the Commission was without jurisdiction to try the case, that there was no proof that the accused even knew of the offences which were being perpetrated and that no war crime could therefore be said to have been committed by him, that no kind of plan was discernible in the atrocities. committed, and that the conditions under which Yamashita had had to work, caused in large part by the United States military offensive and by guerrilla activities, had prevented him from maintaining any adequate overall supervision even over the acts of such troops in the islands as were actually under his command.

The evidence before the Commission regarding the accused's knowledge of, acquiescence in, or approval of the crimes committed by his troops was conflicting, but of the crimes themselves, many and widespread both in space and time, there was abundant evidence, which in general the Defence did not attempt to deny.

The Commission sentenced Yamashita to death and its findings and sentence were confirmed by higher military authority. When the matter came before the Supreme Court of the United States on a petition for certiorari and an application for leave to file a petition for writs of habeas corpus and prohibition, the majority of that Court, in a judgment delivered by Chief Justice Stone, ruled that the order convening the Commission which tried Yamashita was a lawful order under both United States and International Law, that the Commission was lawfully constituted, that the offence of which Yamashita was charged constituted a violation of the laws of war, and that the procedural safeguards of the United States Articles of War and of the provisions of the Geneva Prisoners of War Convention relating to Judicial Proceedings had no application to war crime trials.

Mr. Justice Murphy and Mr. Justice Rutledge dissented. Questions other than those already mentioned which were touched upon either in the majority judgment or in the two minority judgments were the following : the applicability or non-applicability to such proceedings as those taken against Yamashita of the safeguards provided by the United States Constitution and particularly of the Fifth Amendment thereto ; the extent of review permissible to the Supreme Court over war crimes trials ; and the alleged denial of adequate opportunity for the preparation of Yamashita's defence. Yamashita was executed on 23rd February 1946.

A. OUTLINE OF THE PROCEEDINGS

1. THE APPOINTMENT OF THE COMMISSION

The Court which tried Yamashita was a United States Military Commission established under, and subject to, the provisions of the Pacific Regulations of 24th September, 1945, Governing the Trial of War Criminals. (Footnote 1: See Volume III of these Reports, p. 105.) Acting under authority from General MacArthur, Commander-in-Chief,

United States Army Forces, Pacific Theatre, General Styer, Commanding General, United States Army Forces, Western Pacific, appointed the Commission, and instructed it to meet in the City of Manila, Philippine Islands, " at the call of the President thereof." The Commission was convened on 8th October, 1945, at the High Commissioner's Residence in Manila.

2. AN INTENDED DEFENCE WITNESS PERMITTED TO ACT AS DEFENCE COUNSEL

In addition to the six officers appointed by Lt.-General Styer to defend the accused, the latter requested that his former Chief-of-Staff, Lieutenant-General Muto, and his former Assistant Chief or Deputy Chief-of-Staff, Major-General Utsunomiya, should act as additional counsel. There were, he explained, a number of records and facts with which they alone were conversant. He needed their advice and assistance.

In view of the fact that the accused was proposing to call one of the men named as a Defence witness, however, the Prosecution submitted that, in a criminal proceeding, it would be entirely irregular for a witness for the Defence also to represent the accused as counsel. Even if his intention was not to serve as counsel, it would be equally irregular to allow the witnesses for a person accused as a criminal to sit in Court through the proceedings. He should be allowed to enter the court-room only if and when counsel proposed to call him as witness. On a Defending Officer stating that the proposed new Counsel would be in the court room only during the hearing of the Prosecution's evidence and that he would leave the court-room before the opening of the Defence, Counsel for the Prosecution pointed out that the damage would be done when the witnesses were in the courtroom during the Prosecution's case and not during the hearing of the evidence for the defence.

The President ruled that, since it was the desire of the Commission to conduct a fair trial, the request of the Defence would be granted.

Lt.-General Muto subsequently appeared as a defence witness.

3. THE ACCUSED AND THE CHARGE

Prior to 3rd September, 1945, the accused, Tomoyuki Yamashita, was Commanding General of the Fourteenth Army Group of the Imperial Japanese Army in the Philippine Islands. On that date he surrendered to and became a prisoner-of-war of the United States Army Forces in

Baguio, 1 Philippine Islands. On 25th September, by order of Lieutenant-General Wilhehn D. Styer, Commanding General of the United States Army Forces, Western Pacific, which command embraced the Philippine Islands, Yamashita was served with a charge prepared by the Judge Advocate General's Department of the Army which alleged that he, " Tomoyuki Yamashita, General Imperial Japanese Army, between 9th October, 1944 and 2nd September, 1945, at Manila and at other places in the Philippine Islands, while a commander of armed forces of Japan at war with the United States of America and its allies, unlawfully disregarded and failed to discharge his duty as commander to control the operations of the members of his command, permitting them to commit brutal atrocities and other high

crimes against people of the United States and of its allies and dependencies, particularly the Philippines ; and he, General Tomoyuki Yamashita, thereby violated the laws pf war."

On 8th October, 1945, the accused was arraigned before the Military Commission already described.

4. THE BILL OF PARTICULARS AND SUPPLEMENTAL BILL OF PARTICULARS

On 8th October, 1945, as a result of a motion put forward by the Defence, (Footnote 1: see p. 8) the Prosecution filed a Bill of Particulars making 64 separate allegations, under a general introductory sentence which claimed that : " Between 9th October, 1944, and 2nd September, 1945, at Manila and other places in the Philippine Islands, members of Armed Forces of Japan under the command of the accused committed the following : " On 29th October, after a recess during which the Defence was to prepare its case, the Prosecution filed a Supplemental Bill of Particulars claiming that : " members of the armed forces of Japan, under the command of the accused, were permitted to commit . . . during the period from 9th October, 1944, to 2nd September, 1945, at Manila and other places in the Philippine Islands " a further 59 offences or groups of offences. The Defence claimed that the' Supplemental Bill made a completely new type of allegation, but this view was not shared by the Commission. (Footnote 2: See pp. 8-9.)

The classification of alleged offences made by the President of the Commission in delivering judgment may be reproduced at this point. He pointed out that : " The crimes alleged to have been permitted by the accused in violation of the laws of war may be grouped into three categories :

(1) Starvation, execution or massacre without trial and maladministration generally of civilian internees and prisoners of war ;

(2) Torture, rape, murder and mass execution of very large numbers of residents of the Philippines, including women and children and members of religious orders, by starvation, beheading, bayoneting, clubbing, hanging, burning alive, and destruction by explosives ;

(3) Burning and demolition without adequate military necessity of large numbers of homes, places of business, places of religious worship, hospitals, public buildings, and educational institutions. In point of time, the offences extended throughout the period the accused was in command of Japanese troops in the Philippines. In point of area, the crimes extended throughout the Philippine Archipelago, although by far the most of the incredible acts occurred on Luzon."

Nearly all of the 123 paragraphs contained in the two Bills of Particulars alleged the commission of a number of separate illegal acts ; nearly all of them also charged the perpetration of more than one crime, of which " mistreating " and " killing " appeared most frequently. An attempt was clearly made to arrange under each paragraph offences alleged to have been committed in one locality during one period of time or at the same approximate date.

Thus, in the first paragraph of the Bill of Particulars, appear a number of different categories of crimes, committed against thousands of persons and against property :

" 1. During the period from 9th October, 1944, to 1st May, 1945, undertaking and putting into execution a deliberate plan and purpose to massacre and exterminate a large part of the civilian population of Batangas Province, and to devastate and destroy public, private and religious property therein, as a result of which more than 25,000 men, women and children, all unarmed non-combatant civilians, were brutally mistreated and killed, without cause or trial, and entire settlements were devastated and destroyed wantonly and without military necessity."

The fifth paragraph provides an example of one offence allegedly committed against a plurality of persons :

" 5. During November 1944, in northern Cebu Province, massacre, without cause or trial, of more than 1,000 unarmed non-combatant civilians." .

Paragraph 122, which appeared in the Supplemental Bill, alleged the commission of one offence against one person, the killing, on about 20th January, 1945, at Los Banos Internment Camp, Laguna Province, without cause or trial, of a named non-combatant civilian citizen of the United States of America, then and there interned by armed forces of Japan.

While many paragraphs simply alleged, for instance, the " killing of patients and civilian refugees by shellfire " (12), the " rape of civilian women " (14), or " brutally mistreating and killing two unarmed non-combatant male civilians " (16), others set out the names of the victims. Paragraph 22 alleged the brutal killing without cause or trial of three named persons, an Austrian citizen, a German citizen and a Russian citizen, all unarmed and non-combatant civilians.

The offences against persons alleged in the two Bills were largely described in the following terms, often with the addition of the words, " without cause or trial " : mistreating, beating, wounding, torturing, mutilating, maiming, raping, attempting to rape, killing, attempting to kill, executing, burning alive, massacring and exterminating.

Other such alleged offences were the unjustified failure or refusal to provide prisoners of war or civilian internees with adequate shelter, food, water, clothing, sanitation, medical care, and other essentials it being sometimes stated specifically that such omission caused malnutrition and death ; abandoning, without care or attention helplessly sick, wounded or starved prisoners of war and internees ; and deliberately profaning the bodies of dead prisoners of war and internees ; compelling non-combatant civilians to construct fortifications and entrenchments and otherwise take part in the operations of armed forces of Japan against the country of those civilians ; deliberately and unnecessarily exposing prisoners of war and civilian internees to gunfire and other hazards; and deliberately contaminating and poisoning a well of water, the sole source of potable drinking water for a large number of civilians. A breach of the Geneva Prisoners of War Convention was implied by paragraph 89, which alleged that, during the month of December 1944, at Manila, the crimes were committed against various prisoners of war, named and unnamed, of " subjecting to trial without prior notice to a representative of the protecting power, without opportunity to defend, and without counsel ; denying opportunity to appeal from the sentence pronounced ; and executing a death sentence without communicating to the representative of the protecting power the nature and circumstances of the offence charged."

The Bills of Particulars also alleged many offences against property, again often of a mass and indiscriminate nature, on the part of the accused's troops. There were many allegations of the devastation, destruction and pillage, unjustified by military necessity, of public, private or religious property. For instance, paragraph 15 enumerates : " During the period from 1st January, 1945, to 1st March, 1945, both dates inclusive, deliberately, wantonly and without justification or military necessity, devastating, destroying and pillaging and looting of large areas of the city of Manila, including public, private and religious buildings and other property, and committing widespread theft of money, valuables, food and other private property in that city." Paragraphs 70 and 72 allege, *inter alia*, the destruction of property devoted exclusively to religious, hospital, or educational purposes. Paragraph 6 includes an allegation relating to, ". . . looting and stealing the contents of, and wilfully falling to deliver or make available, Red Cross packages and supplies intended for such prisoners of war."

Those stated to have been the victims of these atrocities were unarmed non-combatant civilians, civilian internees and prisoners of war ; and unspecified hospital patients. The civilians included Austrian, French, Russian, Chinese and German nationals as well as United States citizens.

The allegation that atrocities were committed according to a plan was made not only in paragraph 1, already quoted, (Footnote 1: See p.5) but also in paragraph 25, which sets out the following offences : " During the period from 1st January, 1945, to 1st March, 1945, deliberately planning and undertaking, without cause or trial, the extermination, massacre and wanton, indiscriminate killing of large numbers of unarmed non-combatant civilian men, women and children, inhabitants of the city of Manila and its environs, brutally mistreating, wounding, mutilating, killing and attempting to kill, without cause or trial, large numbers of such inhabitants, and raping or attempting to rape large numbers of civilian women and female children in that city."

In his opening address, the Prosecutor said that, in calling his witnesses, the number of the paragraph to which each piece of evidence related would be indicated. The legal significance of the Bills of Particulars was never defined by the Commission, and the brief analysis of their contents, which has been set out above, is intended simply to show the range of the offences for which the Prosecution held the accused responsible.

5. DEFENCE PLEAS AND MOTIONS RELATING TO THE CHARGE AND THE BILLS OF PARTICULARS

Apart from the plea of not guilty, a number of motions were entered by the accused and his Counsel concerning various aspects of the Charge and the Bills of Particulars. These are described in the following ten paragraphs. It will be noticed that, while the first nine paragraphs set out arguments which took place before the beginning of the hearing of the evidence, and the rulings of the Commission on the matters in dispute, the last paragraph deals with certain events which took place during the hearing of the evidence but which are most conveniently dealt with in this part of the Report.

(i) *Claim of the Accused that a Copy of the Specifications was not Properly Served on Him*

On 8th October, 1945, the accused pleaded that no copy of the specifications had been sent to him in accordance with paragraph 14 (a) of the letter dated 24th September, 1945, General Headquarters, United States Forces, Pacific, entitled " Regulations Governing the Trial of War Criminals " :

" 14. RIGHTS OF THE ACCUSED. The accused shall be entitled :

" (a) To have in advance of trial a copy of the charges and specifications, so worded as clearly to apprise the accused of each offence charged."

The Prosecution claimed that the Charge which was served upon the accused included both what was ordinarily known as a Charge and also the specifications. In court-martial procedure, he went on, the Charge Sheet contained the Charge proper, as for instance the violation of the 86th Article of War. Underneath that, in a separate paragraph, would appear what was known as a specification, alleging that the accused, on a certain time, at a certain place, did certain things. If the Commission would examine the Charge which had been served upon the accused it would note that it did include both of those elements. He submitted that since court-martial procedure was much more strict in its provisions than the procedure followed before Military Commissions, it followed that the Charge against the accused was adequately drafted.

On finding that Defence Counsel were in agreement with the Prosecution on this point, the Commission ruled that the Charge and specifications had been properly served upon the accused.

(ii) *The First Motion to Dismiss the Case*

Later during the same sitting of the Commission, however, Defence Counsel moved that the Charge in hearing be stricken on the ground that it failed to state a violation, in so far as General Yamashita was concerned, of the laws of war. The Prosecution pointed out that the Commission had been ordered to try General Yamashita. If the Defence were seeking to raise a point of law, the appropriate time to do so was at the conclusion of the Prosecution's case, when they could move for a judgment of acquittal.

He submitted, however, that there was no provision in the Commission's procedure for a motion such as Defence Counsel was now interposing. The objection of Counsel for the Defence was not sustained by the Court.

(iii) *Motion for the Filing of a Bill of Particulars*

Thereupon, Counsel for the Defence claimed that the language in which the Charge and specifications .had been drafted was uncertain and indefinite and did not fairly apprise the accused of that with which he stood charged. The Defence therefore moved that the Charge and cause in hearing be made more definite and certain, by specifying the time, place and dates of the accused's disregarding and failing to discharge his duty as Commander to control the operations of the members of his command. Details as to time, place and date should also be furnished as to the alleged offences and as to the persons who were allegedly permitted to commit them. The Prosecution, however, stressed that, although a motion such as this might be permissible in a court of law, the regulations the Defence was putting forward governing the Commission made no provision for such a motion. If the accused desired a Bill of Particulars, the Prosecution had no objection to supplying one ; what they objected to was an attempt to apply to the proceedings of the

Commission " the technical objections and rules of evidence, pleadings and procedure which might apply in a court of law." Defence Counsel admitted that the Commission was not bound by the rules of a court of law, and based its application on principles of justice and fairness to the accused. Until they had received a Bill of Particulars, the Defence did not know what was charged and could not in fairness plead to the general issue of guilty or not guilty. The Prosecution then agreed to file a Bill of Particulars which they had already drafted, provided that they should have at a later date the privilege of serving and filing a Supplemental Bill of Particulars ; certain new information was expected from the United States, and other material had arrived too late for incorporation in the first Bill.

The Court granted the Defence motion for a Bill of Particulars and ruled that a Supplemental Bill of Particulars might be filed later, subject to such conditions as the Commission might then specify. The Court would judge these additional charges on their merits when the Prosecution presented them. Whereupon, the Bill of Particulars was received into evidence. (Footnote 1: See p.4)

(iv) *Plea of Not Guilty*

The accused was then asked for his plea to the Charge, and pleaded not guilty. The Commission then went into recess for three weeks to enable the Defence to prepare their case and the Prosecution to complete theirs.

(v) *Objection to the Filing of a Second Bill of Particulars*

On 29th October, the Commission was reconvened, and the Prosecution requested that there should be incorporated into the record of the proceedings the Prosecution's Supplemental Bill of Particulars. To this procedure the Defence objected.

Defence Counsel began his argument on this point by claiming that on 8th October, 1945, the Defence had successfully objected to the granting to the Prosecution of the right to file a Supplemental Bill of Particulars, on the grounds that it was unprecedented and against ordinary principles of law and justice to allow the Prosecution, after a case had begun, to continue to file additional specifications. Counsel for the Defence submitted that any normal, intelligent person would assume that when the Prosecution, after filing sixty-four separate specifications, stated that they wished to file a Supplemental Bill of Particulars, that Supplemental Bill would probably contain one, two, three, four or perhaps even half a dozen additional particulars. Yet the Supplemental Bill of Particulars contained fifty-nine new, separate and distinct alleged offences. These fifty-nine offences were new in so far as the persons involved were concerned, in so far as the times were concerned, and for the most part in so far as the places were concerned. The Defence urged that it was " unconscionable in a case of this type practically to double at the last minute the list of offences charged."

In the second place, the Defence pointed out that whereas the first Bill had commenced with the words : " Between 9th October, 1944, and 2nd September, 1945, at Manila and other places in the Philippine Islands, members of Armed Forces of Japan under the command of the Accused committed the following : . . ." the opening words of the Supplemental Bill stated that ". . . members of the Armed Forces of Japan, under the command of the Accused, were permitted to commit " certain acts which were then set out. The new Bill alleged the granting of " permission " for 59 acts, and in no single case did it provide any details as to that " permission." It was not said who permitted any one of these acts, or how or in what circumstances.

The Prosecution first reminded the Commission that it had indeed given the former permission to file a Supplemental Bill of Particulars, then went on to say that there was no significance in the different opening wording contained in the two Bills. The purpose of the so-called Bill of Particulars was simply to specify the instances which were referred to generally in the Charge, and whether the Bill of Particulars said that the acts alleged were " permitted " or whether it claimed that they were " committed " by members of the command of the accused was immaterial. There was no provision in the regulations governing the procedure of such Commissions as the present for the production of a Bill of Particulars or for a motion to make the Charge more definite and certain. It was purely a matter of discretion for the Commission as to whether or not it would require a Bill of Particulars. The document had been termed a " Bill of Particulars " for lack of any more appropriate term, but it was not in fact a bill of the kind signified when that term was used in courts of law in the United States. Its sole purpose was to specify the instances when the members of the command of the accused were permitted to commit acts contrary to the Laws of War. In other words, it referred back to and-must be construed in the light of the Charge itself.

The Defence thereupon pointed out that the Commission, in allowing the Bill of Particulars to be filed, had stated that a Supplemental Bill might be filed later, " subject to such conditions as the Commission may then specify." Counsel submitted that the normal, natural condition that would be specified in the filing of any Supplemental Bill of Particulars was that it should stay within the bounds of reason. The filing of nearly as many particulars as were contained in the first Bill he described as unconscionable. Defence Counsel could not agree that the two sets of opening words were materially the same, and claimed that the very essence of the case was the question of what must be established to prove an offence against the Laws of War, the four possible requirements being to show simply that an act was committed by someone under the command of a certain General, or that somebody permitted those acts, or that someone authorised them, or that someone ordered them.

The Commission rejected the Defence motion.

(vi) *Motion that the Prosecution Amplify the Particulars in Certain Ways*

The Defence next moved that particulars be furnished by the Prosecution, regarding each of the 59 new paragraphs, as to who granted permission to commit the alleged offences, to whom such permission was granted, the form of expression of the permission, and the times, places and dates of the giving of permission.

The Prosecutor replied that the Charge stated specifically that it was the accused who permitted these acts to be committed. Even in a United States Civil Court, the Prosecution would not be required to disclose their evidence through the medium of a Bill of Particulars, as was shown by the following passage from the judgment in the case of *Commonwealth v. Jordan*, 207 Massachusetts Reports 259 :

" The office of a Bill of Particulars is not to compel the Commonwealth to disclose its evidence but to give the defendant such information in addition to that contained in the complaint or indictment in regard to the crime with which he is charged, as law and justice require that he should have in order to safeguard his constitutional rights and to enable him to fully understand the crime with which he is charged and to prepare his defence."

The Prosecutor pointed out that the mention of " constitutional rights " made in this dictum constituted a reference to the Constitution of the United States, which in any case conferred no rights on the accused, an enemy alien. He thought that the details already provided in the Bills of Particulars met all of the requirements of justice and fair trial.

Defence Counsel's answer was that the Fifth Amendment of the Constitution of the United States applied to " any person," not " any citizen. " Nevertheless, the Commission rejected the Defence motion.

(vii) *The First Motion for a Continuance*

The Defence then entered a motion requesting a recess of two weeks in order to enable the preparation of a case in answer to the 59 new allegations, to allow the Defence, for instance, so to acquaint themselves with the new accusations as to place them in a position properly to cross-examine the Prosecution's witnesses. Counsel reminded the Commission that the Prosecution had expressed surprise when the Defence had stated, on 8th October, 1945, that they could properly prepare a defence in two weeks. Surely, if the Prosecution was surprised that the Defence could prepare a defence on 64 specifications in two weeks, Counsel did not think that they could now object to a recess of two weeks to prepare a defence for a similar number of specifications based on new facts, new places, new names and a new theory of the case.

Defence Counsel quoted the passage from paragraph 14 of the Commission's rules of procedure to which reference had already been made : " The accused shall be entitled . . . to have in advance of trial a copy of the Charges and specifications, so worded as clearly to apprise the accused of each offence charged." Counsel interpreted the action of the Commission on 8th October, in requiring the Prosecution to furnish a Bill of Particulars, as signifying that a Supplemental Bill should also be furnished " in advance of trial," and claimed that this phrase signified : " Sufficient time to allow the Defence a chance to prepare its defence."

The Prosecutor at this point began to urge again that the specifications were incorporated in the original charge, as he had claimed when the accused himself insisted that he had not been served with specifications ; but the President interrupted the Prosecutor and said that this point had been adequately discussed.

The Defence motion was rejected by the Commission, but the latter added that if, at the end of the presentation by the Prosecution of evidence concerning the Bill of Particulars as presented during the arraignment, Defence Counsel should believe that they required additional time to prepare their case, the Commission would consider such a motion at that time.

Defence Counsel then indicated, but without further result, that time was desired at once " as much, if not more " to prepare for cross-examination " as the Prosecutor's case goes in " as to prepare an affirmative defence.

(viii) *The Second Motion to Dismiss the Case*

The Defence then entered a motion to dismiss the case. Counsel first reminded the Commission that the previous motion to dismiss, made on the ground that the charge failed to state a violation of the Laws of War by the accused, was denied. The present motion was addressed to the Charge as supplemented by the original Bill of Particulars and by the Supplemental Bill of Particulars, and the claim was again made that it failed to set forth a violation of the Laws of War by the accused and that the Commission did not have jurisdiction to try the cause. It was the contention of Defence that the Bill of Particulars did not cure the defects of the Charge. On the contrary, it provided further reasons for allowing the motion.

The Bill of Particulars detailed sixty-four instances in which members of the accused's command ,were alleged to have committed. war crimes. In no instance was it alleged that the accused committed or aided in the commission of a crime or crimes, In no instance was it alleged that the accused issued an order, expressly or impliedly, for the perpetration of the crime or crimes charged. Nor was it alleged that the accused authorised the crimes prior to their commission or condoned them thereafter.

The Charge alleged that the accused failed in his duty to control his troops, permitting them to commit certain alleged crimes. The Bill of Particulars, however, set forth no instance of neglect of duty by the accused. Nor did it set forth any acts of commission or omission by the accused as amounting to a " permitting " of the crimes in question. What then was the substance of the Charge against the accused ? It was submitted by the Defence that, on the three documents now before the

Commission, the Charge and the two Bills of Particulars, the accused was not accused of having done something or having failed to do something, but solely of having been something, namely commander of the Japanese forces. It was being claimed that, by virtue of that fact alone, he was guilty of every crime committed by every soldier assigned to his command.

American jurisprudence recognised no such principle so far as its own military personnel was concerned. The Articles of War denounced and punished improper conduct by military personnel, but they did not hold a commanding officer responsible for the crimes committed by his subordinates. No one would even suggest that the Commanding General of an American occupation force became a criminal every time an American soldier violated the law. It was submitted that neither the Laws of War nor the conscience of the world upon which they were founded would countenance any such charge. It was the basic premise of all civilised criminal justice that it punished not according to status but according to fault, and that one man was not held to answer for the crime of another.

It was an incontrovertible fact that the branding of military personnel as war criminals did not rest upon the mere fact of the command of troops, but rather upon the improper exercise of that command. This point was recognised officially by the War Department in its publication, *Rules of Land Warfare* (FM 27-10, Section 345, l), which provided as follows : " Liability of Offending Individuals. Individuals and organisations who violate the accepted laws and customs of war may be punished therefor. However, the fact that the acts complained of were done pursuant to order of a superior or government sanction may be taken into consideration in determining culpability, either by way of defence or in mitigation of punishment. The person giving such orders may also be punished."

There was nothing said in that provision concerning the Commanding General of a force being responsible, under the Laws of War, for any offences committed by members of his command without his sanction. Liability for war crimes was imposed on the persons who committed the crimes and on the officers who ordered the commission thereof. The war crime of a subordinate, committed without the order, authority or knowledge of his superior, was not a war crime on the part of the superior. The pleadings now before the Commission did not allege that the accused ordered, authorised or had knowledge of the commission of any of the alleged atrocities or war crimes. Without such an allegation, it was submitted, the cause must be dismissed as not stating an offence under the Laws of War.

The Defence claimed that if a violation of the Laws of War was not alleged, the Military Commission had no jurisdiction to hear the cause. In the " case of the saboteurs," *Ex Parte Quirin* [Outline details of the case], decided in 1942, the judgment of the Supreme Court stated that : " Congress . . . has exercised its authority to define and punish offences against the law of nations by sanctioning, within constitutional limitations, the jurisdiction of military commissions to try persons and offences which, according to the rules and precepts of the law of nations, and more particularly the Law of War, are cognisable by such tribunals. . . . We are concerned only with the question of whether it is within the constitutional power of the national government to place petitioners on trial before a military commission for the offences with which they are charged. We must therefore first inquire whether any of the acts charged is an offence against the Law of War cognisable before a military tribunal, and if so, whether the Constitution prohibits the trial."(Footnote 1: *Ex Parte Quirin et al*, 317 U.S.l, 1942.) *Ex Parte Quirin et al*, 317 U.S.l, 1942.

The Supreme Court found that the allegations contained in the charges against Quirin and his associates were offences within the Laws of War. Defence Counsel submitted that, had they found these allegations not related to offences against the Laws of War, the Supreme Court would have ruled that the military commission had no jurisdiction.

Defence Counsel maintained that there were two other grounds for the proposition that the Commission had no jurisdiction to try the case. The Commission was appointed by the Commanding General of Army Forces, Western Pacific, pursuant to authority delegated to him by the Commander-in-Chief, Army Forces, Pacific. The record did not, however, said Counsel, show any grant of authority from the President of the United States to the Commander-in-Chief, Army Forces, Pacific. Neither the Commander-in-Chief, Army Forces, Pacific, nor the Commanding General, Army Forces, Western Pacific, in the submission of the Defence, had authority to take the above-mentioned action. It was well settled that, in the absence of express statutory authority, a military commander had power to appoint a military commission only (a) as an exercise of martial law, (b) as an exercise of military government in occupied territory, or (c) as an incident of military operations during a period of hostilities. This principle was stated in Winthrop, *Military Law and Precedents*, on page 936.

There existed, said Counsel, neither martial law nor military government in the Philippines, and hostilities had ceased on or about 2nd September, 1945. There was no justification in law for the exercise by the Commander-in-Chief of the Army Forces, Pacific, of the extraordinary power by virtue of which the Commission was set up. The fundamental principle involved was apparently within the contemplation of the Commander-in-Chief, Army Forces, Pacific, when he issued the letter of 24th September, 1945, upon which the Commission based its authority, because paragraph 3 of his letter read as follows : " The Military Commissions established hereunder shall have jurisdiction over all Japan and all other areas occupied by the armed forces commanded by the Commander-in-Chief, Army Forces, Pacific." The Philippine Islands, Counsel pointed out, were not areas occupied by the armed forces. The above-mentioned letter, consequently, did not grant authority to set up military commissions in the Philippine Islands ; and Special Orders No. 112, Headquarters, United States Army Forces, Western Pacific, dated 1st October, 1945, was therefore without authority.

Paragraph 271 of the War Department Basic Field Manual, *Rules of Land Warfare*, in its reprint of Article 42 of the Annex of the Hague Convention No. IV of 1907, said that : " A territory is considered occupied when it is actually placed under the authority of the hostile army." The United States was not and never had been a hostile army with respect to the Philippine Islands. The re-entry into the Philippine Islands in 1944 and 1945 had constituted a recovery of territory, not an occupation. From the date of re-entry on Philippine soil, General MacArthur had consistently affirmed and recognised the full governmental responsibility of the Philippine Commonwealth. This was evidenced by publications in the *Official Gazette*, April 1945, page 86 ; May 1945, pages 145 to 148 ; and September 1945, page 494. On 22nd August, 1945, General MacArthur issued the following proclamation : " Effective on 1st September, 1945, United States Army Forces in the Pacific shall cease from further participation in the self-administration of the Philippines, as such is no longer necessary.

" Counsel claimed that if the projected trial should result in the conviction and sentence of the accused, such action would be subject to reversal, and made the following statement : " As officers of the United

States Army, and as lawyers appointed to defend the accused, Defence Counsel are charged with a duty to the accused, to the Army, and to the people of the United States to pursue all proper legal remedies open to the Defence, including, if warranted, recourse to the Federal courts, and more particularly, the Supreme Court of the United States-citing again the Quirin case.

" In his reply, the Prosecutor submitted that there was no reason for the Commission to reverse its previous decision of 8th October, 1945, to deny the motion to dismiss. The mere fact that a Bill of Particulars and a Supplemental Bill of Particulars had subsequently been presented to the Commission had no bearing upon the issue. In any case, it was beyond question that the Commission had no authority to dismiss this proceeding, It was under direct orders of the Commanding General, Army Forces, Western Pacific, to proceed with the trial of Tomoyuki Yamashita. The Letter Order of General MacArthur, as Commander-in-Chief of the United States Army Forces, Pacific, dated 24th September, 1945, and addressed to the Commanding General, United States Army Forces, Western Pacific, stated : " It is desired that you proceed immediately with the trial of General Tomoyuki Yamashita, now in your custody, for the crimes indicated in the attached charge." Special Orders No. 112, dated 1st October, 1945, being the Order of the Commanding General, Army Forces, Western Pacific, establishing the Military Commission and directing its proceedings, required that it should follow the provisions of the above-mentioned letter. The Prosecutor concluded, therefore, that the Commission had no authority to dismiss the case at this stage. It must try Tomoyuki Yamashita and, in order to accomplish that task, it must hear the Prosecution's case.

Called upon to offer his arguments in rebuttal, Defence Counsel claimed that, if the officer who gave the direction to try Tomoyuki Yamashita had no jurisdiction to appoint a commission, he had no jurisdiction to order the trial of General Yamashita. The courts of the Commonwealth were open for any crimes which were committed by any member of the Japanese forces while they were in occupation of the Philippine Islands. He added that the present motion was not based on the Charge alone as had been the original motion to dismiss ; it was based on the Bill of Particulars and the Supplemental Bill, which did not state an offence against the Laws of War. The Defence had understood that the Bill of Particulars would cure the defects in the Charge but this had not been so.

The Commission rejected the second Defence motion to dismiss the case.

(ix) *A Question relating to the Status of the Accused*

The final motion put forward by the Defence before the Prosecutor's opening speech was one to cause the Prosecution to state for the record whether or not any notice had been given to the protecting power of the Japanese government concerning the trial of the case now before the Commission, in accordance with Article 60 of the Geneva Convention and paragraph 133 of Field Manual 27-10. The Prosecutor pointed out that Defence Counsel was basing his inquiry on the assumption that the accused was a prisoner-of-war. He claimed, however, that Yamashita was not before the Commission as a prisoner-of-war but as an alleged war criminal. The Prosecutor had therefore no objection to stating, for the benefit of the record, that so far as he knew, the United States of America had not given any notification, official notification, to the Government of Spain, the protecting power of Japan, that Tomoyuki Yamashita was being tried as a prisoner-of-war, for the reason that he was not being so tried. The Geneva Convention had no application to the case.

The President of the Commission then ruled that the request of the Defence Counsel had been adequately discussed by the Prosecution, within the limits of the information which would ordinarily be available, and requested the Prosecution to open its case.

(x) *Some Later Events Relating to the Preparation of the Defence*

This appears to be the most appropriate place to set out certain further requests for a continuance made by the Defence, and related events, which were referred to by Mr. Justice Rutledge in the course of his dissenting judgment on the motion and petition which Yamashita brought before the Supreme Court of the United States. (Footnote 1: See p.62)

On 29th October, 1945, near the end of the day's sittings, the President of the Commission interrupted the Prosecutor, who was about to call certain evidence relating to an item contained in the Supplemental Bill of Particulars, and stated that the Commission would not at that time listen to testimony or discussion on the item in question. In response to an inquiry by the Prosecution, the Defence indicated that it would require two weeks before it could proceed on the Supplemental Bill.

On 2nd November, 1945, after the Commission had received an affirmative answer to its inquiry whether the Defence was ready to proceed with an item in the Supplemental Bill which the Prosecution proposed to prove, the President said to the Defence Counsel : " Hereafter, then, unless there is no (*sic*) objection by the Defence, the Commission will assume that you are prepared to proceed with any items in the Supplemental Bill." On 6th November, 1945, the Prosecution enquired when the Defence would be ready to proceed on certain further items in the Supplemental Bill, and the Prosecutor added : " Frankly, sir, it took the War Crimes Commission some three months to investigate these matters and I cannot conceive of the Defence undertaking a similar investigation with any less period of time." At this point, the President stated : " Let the Commission answer that. We realise the tremendous task which we placed upon the Defence and with which they are faced and it is our determination to give them the time they require. We ask that no time be wasted and we feel confident that you will not waste any, and we will see to it that you get time to prepare your defence."

On 12th November, 1945, the Commission announced that it would grant a continuance " only for the most urgent and unavoidable reasons." The Commission went on to question the need for all of the six officers representing the defence to be present during presentation of all the case, suggested that one or two would be adequate and others should be out of the court-room engaged in performing specific missions for Senior Counsel, and suggested bringing in additional Counsel, that " need to request continuance may not arise."

Finally, on 20th November, at the end of the presentation of the evidence for the Prosecution, the Defence moved for " a reasonable continuance." Counsel stated that during the time the court had been in' session, the Defence had had no time " to prepare any affirmative defence," since they had had to work " day and night to keep up with the new Bill of Particulars."

The Commission denied the motion ; in announcing its decision the President stated that in open session and in chambers the Commission had cautioned both Prosecution and Defence to so plan their preparation as to avoid the necessity of asking for a continuance, recalled the words used by the Commission on 12th November, and repeated that the Commission had, from an early point in the trial, from time to time invited the Defence to apply for the appointment of additional Counsel.

Counsel for the Defence then asked for " a short recess of a day." The Commission suggested a recess until 1.30 in the afternoon. Counsel responded this would not suffice. The Commission stated it felt " that the Defence should be prepared at least on its opening statement," to which Senior Counsel answered : " We haven't had time to do that, sir." The Commission then recessed until 8.30 the following morning.

6. THE OPENING ADDRESS FOR THE PROSECUTION

After repeating the Charge facing the accused and emphasising that the former alleged a disregard of his duty to control the members of his command, the Prosecution made the following claim regarding General Yamashita's command :

" We will open our case with proof that the accused, Yamashita, was Commander of the Army Forces in the Philippines during the period stated in the charge-that is to say, from 9th October, 1944, to the time of surrender, September 1945 ; that in addition he commanded, as a part of those forces, or attached thereto, the so-called ' Kempei Tai ', or military police. We will show also that he had overall command of the prisoner-of-war camps and civilian internment camps, labour camps, and other installations containing prisoners of war and other internees in all the Philippine Islands.

" We will show that his area or territory of command included all of the Philippine Islands, the entire area so known. We will show that at times he also commanded Navy forces and air forces, particularly when engaged as ground troops."

The Prosecutor then set out the essence of the case against the accused, in the following words :

" We will then show that various elements, individuals, units, organisations, officers, being a part of those forces under the command of the accused, did commit a wide pattern of widespread, notorious, repeated, constant atrocities of the most violent character ; that those atrocities were spread from the northern portion of the Philippine Islands to the southern portion ; that they continued, as I say, repeatedly throughout the period of Yamashita's command ; that they were so notorious and so flagrant and so enormous, both as to the scope of their operation and as to the inhumanity, the bestiality involved, that they must have been known to the accused if he were making any effort whatever to meet the responsibilities of his command or his position ; and that if he did not know of those acts, notorious, wide-spread, repeated, constant as they were, it was simply because he took affirmative action not to know. That is our case."

The Prosecutor made the following statement on the legal nature of the Commission and on the question of the applicability of the United States Articles of War (Footnote 1: See pp. 44-6 and 63-9.) to its proceedings :

" Furthermore, sir, the Articles of War do not apply to this Commission in any particular. It is so ruled by the Judge Advocate-General, and if the Commission or Defence so desires I will be glad to supply a copy of that recent ruling. The Articles of War are not binding upon, do not apply to this Commission.

" This Commission, sir, is not a judicial body ; it is an executive tribunal set up by, the Commander-in-Chief-more specifically, the Commanding General, AFWESPAC-for the purpose of hearing the evidence on this charge, and of advising him, along with the Commander-in-Chief of the Army Forces of the Pacific, as to the punishment, in the event that the Commission finds the charge to be sustained. It is an executive body, and not a judicial body."

7. THE OPENING ADDRESS FOR THE DEFENCE

Before introducing evidence, the Defence made a short opening statement summarising the facts which they hoped to prove, and making the following claims in particular :

" Defence will show that the accused never ordered the commission of any crime or atrocity ; that the accused never gave permission to anyone to commit any crimes or atrocities ; that the accused had no knowledge of the commission of the alleged crimes or atrocities ; that the accused had no actual control of the perpetrators of the atrocities at any time that they occurred, and that the accused did not then and does not now condone, excuse or justify any atrocities or violation of the laws of war.

" On the matter of control we shall elaborate upon a number of facts that have already been suggested to the Commission in our cross-examination of the Prosecution's witnesses :

1. That widespread, devastating guerilla activities created an atmosphere in which control of troops by high ranking officers became difficult or impossible

2. That guerilla activities and American air and combat activities disrupted communications and in many areas destroyed them altogether, making control by the accused a meaningless concept. And

3. That in many of the atrocities alleged in the Bill of Particulars there was not even paper control ; the chain of command did not channel through the accused at all. . . . "

You will see the picture of a General working under terrific pressure and difficulty, subject to last-minute changes in tactical plans ordered from higher headquarters, and a man who when he arrived in Luzon actually had command over less than half of the ground troops in the Island."

8. THE EVIDENCE BEFORE THE COMMISSION

As the President of the Commission pointed out, (Footnote 1: See p.33-4.) the latter heard 286 witnesses and also accepted as evidence 423 exhibits of various kinds.

(i) *The Evidence for the Prosecution*

The evidence brought before the Commission established hundreds of incidents which included the withholding of medical attention from, and starvation of, prisoners of war and civilian internees, pillage, the burning and destruction of homes and public buildings without military necessity, torture by burning and otherwise, individual and mass execution without trial, rape and murder, all committed by members of the Japanese forces under the command of accused. These offences were widespread as regards both space and time.

By and large, the Defence did not deny that troops under the command of the accused had committed these various atrocities, and it is not therefore proposed to summarise in these pages the testimony and documents which were placed before the Commission regarding these offences.

By stipulation, it was agreed that the accused was from 9th October, 1944, to 3rd September, 1945, Commanding General of Japanese 14th Army Group, including the Kempei Tei, or Military Police in the Philippine Islands ; this stipulation was received in evidence.

Apart from claiming that the widespread nature of the offences described above must lead inevitably to the conclusion that they were planned by Yamashita, in view of his position of command, the Prosecution also produced evidence purporting more directly to show that the accused was implicated in the offences charged. This evidence is summarised in the following paragraphs.

Colonel Masatoski Fujishige, of the Japanese Army, testified that troops under. his command had operated in the Batangas Islands and part of the Laguna Province after 1st January, 1945. His commander was Lt.-General Yokoyama ; the latter, stated the witness, probably " might have " come under Yamashita's command. Masatoski admitted having instructed certain officers and non-commissioned officers under his orders to kill all who oppose the Emperor with arms, even women and children ; he had had orders to expedite the clearing of his area of guerrillas.

Narciso Lapus stated that he had been private secretary to the Philippine General Artemio Ricarte, who had supported and worked for the Japanese during their occupation of the Philippine Islands. During the period from October 1944 and 31st December, 1944, Ricarte maintained contact with Yamashita as Commander-in Chief of the Japanese forces in the Philippines. Ricarte told the witness that Yamashita, as the highest commander of the Japanese forces in the Philippines, had control over the army the navy and the air force. Four or five days after Yamashita arrived in the Philippines, Ricarte had a conversation with him, and on returning to his house, the latter told Lapus that Yamashita had issued a general order to all the commanders of the military posts in the Philippine Islands " to wipe out the whole Philippines, if possible," and to destroy Manila, since everyone in the Islands were either guerrillas or active supporters of the guerrillas ;

wherever the population gave signs of favouring the Americans the whole population of that area should be exterminated. Yamashita subsequently rejected Ricarte's plea that he should withdraw these orders.

Joaquin Galang, who claimed to have been a friend of Ricarte, stated that in December 1944, Yamashita visited Ricarte, and the former rejected Ricarte's request that the order to kill all Philippine inhabitants and destroy Manila be revoked ; speaking through Ricarte's grandson as interpreter, Yamashita said : " An order is an order, it is my order, and because of that it should not be broken or disobeyed."

Hideo Nishiharu, who had been head of the Judge Advocate Section in the Headquarters of Yamashita in the Philippines, stated that on 14th December, 1944, he advised the accused that a large number of persons suspected of being guerrillas were in custody and that there was no time for trial. He suggested that the question of their punishment be left to military tribunal officers co-operating with the Military Police. Yamashita, said the witness, " offered no suggestions. He just nodded " and Nishiharu took this to signify assent. About 600 persons were thereupon executed without trial other than investigation by two officers.

Richard Sakakida stated that he had been an interpreter in the office of Yamashita's Judge Advocate. He testified that in the case of offences by Filipino civilians and Americans, an investigation was made by the Japanese Military Police (Kempei Tai) and the record thereof was sent to the Court Martial Department ; the Judge Advocate assigned to the case and the Chief Judge Advocate would then decide on the verdict and sentence in advance of the trial. During December 1944, trial consisted merely in the accused signing his name and giving his thumb-print, in reading the charge to him and in sentencing him. In the event of death sentence being passed, the victim was not informed of this until arrival at the cemetery. In one week in December 1944, cases involving about 2,000 Filipinos accused of being guerrillas were so handled in Yamashita's headquarters. If Japanese soldiers were tried, however, witnesses for the accused were allowed to testify, and the accused was told of any death sentence at the time of trial. Japanese soldiers were tried and convicted of rape, but the witness could remember no convictions after October 1944.

Fermin Miyasaki, a Filipino citizen who had been employed by the Japanese Military Police as an interpreter, described the various methods of torture used by the " Cortabitarte Garrison " (the Southern Manila Branch of the Militarjr Police) during the period October to December 1944, on civilians suspected of being guerrillas or guerrilla sympathisers ; the witness then went on to state that in December 1944, Yamashita commended the Garrison in writing for their work " in suppressing guerrilla activities."

The Prosecution put in as evidence a certificate signed by Mr. James F. Bymes, Secretary of State of the United States of America, under date of 26th October, 1945, which included the following words:

" I further certify that, in response to proposals made by the Government of the United States through the Swiss Minister in Tokyo, the Swiss Minister telegraphed on 30th January, 1942, that the ' Japanese Government has informed me : ". . . Although not bound by the Convention relative treatment prisoners of war Japan will apply *mutatis mutandis* provisions of that Convention to American prisoners of war in its power." ' "

Filemon Castillejos, a Filipino, after describing the killing of three American prisoners of war by Japanese troops belonging to General Tajima's garrison, said that a Japanese Captain, a lieutenant and two soldiers had told him that the victims were killed because there was a telegram from Yamashita to General Tajima ordering that all the American prisoners in the Philippines be killed.

Paul Herinesen, a United States national who had been a prisoner of war in the Philippines, described how an American civilian internee, at the prison camp commandant's order, had been shot without trial while lying wounded on the guard-house floor. When protest was made by the internees, the commandant stated that he had had orders from Imperial Headquarters in Manila to shoot persons attempting to escape.

(ii) *The Evidence for the Defence*

The following paragraphs set out the essential facts placed before the Commission by the Defence.

Denhichi Okoochi, who had been Supreme Commander of the naval forces in the Philippines, stated that he transferred to Yamashita tactical command of the navy and troops in Manila on 5th January, 1945, and that the accused retained this command until 24th August, 1945. The witness retained " administrative control " over these forces, that is to say control over " such things as personnel, supplies and so forth " but not the operational control, which was in Yamashita's hands.

Bislumino Romero, grandson of General Ricarte, stated that Galang was not stating the truth when he testified that Romero interpreted a conversation between Ricarte and Yamashita in the former's house ; he never interpreted any statement of the accused that " all Filipinos are guerrillas and even the people who are supposed to be under Ricarte," and the witness's grandfather had never made to Yamashita in the witness's presence any request that Yamashita should revoke an order to kill all Filipinos and destroy Manila.

Shizus Yokoyma, previously a Lieutenant-General in the Japanese Army under Yamashita, stated that the latter had issued no orders to him for the .killing of Filipino citizens or the destruction of property in Manila. The accused had warned him to be fair in all his dealings with the Filipino people. Yamashita had no power to discipline, promote, demote or remove members of the naval land forces.

Photostatic copies of parts of the issues of Manila Tribune for 4th, 17th and 26th November, 1944, and 31st January, 1945, which were put in as evidence by the Defence, showed that General Ricarte was active in assisting the Japanese and urging the Filipinos to resist the Americans. Official documents were put in as tending to prove that the Prosecution witnesses Lapus and Galang had been collaborators during the Japanese occupation of the Philippines.

Lieutenant-General Muto, Chief of Staff for Yamashita, appeared for the Defence. He stated that Yamashita had commanded the 11th Area Army with the duty to defend the entire Philippine Islands. Morale in the army was low and preparations for the defence were inadequate when the accused took over this task. Lack of knowledge of the Islands and the separation of commands prohibited the correction of deficiencies, and efforts to bring the independent commands under Yamashita's control required several months of negotiation. The accused had wanted to withdraw from Manila altogether and to fight in the mountains, but lack of transportation and reluctance on the part of certain of his officers had prevented him from taking this step, despite the orders which he gave that evacuation should take place. Only 1,500 to 1,600 of Yamashita's troops were in Manila at the time of the battle ; they had orders to maintain order and to protect supplies. Yamashita had no authority over the others. The witness had never heard of any order by Yamashita that non-combatant civilians be killed and Manila destroyed. Yamashita never visited any of the prisoner-of- war camps in the Philippines, but his policy was that prisoners should be treated in accordance with the Geneva Convention. Prisoners were to be fed according to the same standards as Japanese soldiers, but reduced rations were inevitable due to food shortages. After complaints had been made to Yamashita concerning Japanese military police methods, he succeeded in having the Military Police Commander removed by the authorities in Tokyo. The witness denied that Colonel Nishiharu, Yamashita's Judge Advocate, had reported that there were one thousand guerrillas in custody and that there was no time to try them. In December, 1944, the Shimbu Army had power to try all suspected guerrillas and impose death sentences.

Lieutenant-Colonel Ishikawa of Yamashita's headquarters staff, who had been in charge of supply after 27th September, 1944, and inspected prisoner and internee camps, also stated that the prisoners' food was similar to that of the Japanese soldiers. An order from Tokyo, that prisoners be treated in a friendly manner and that as much food as possible be left behind for them should the Americans approach, was passed on by Yamashita. The witness, on his trips to the camps at Santo Tomas, Bilibid and Fort McKinley, had heard no reports of cruelty or ill-treatment. The accused required that any complaints filed by American prisoners of war and civilian internees should be brought to his attention.

Lieutenant-General Koh, who had been Commanding General of Prison and Internment Camps in the Philippines under Yamashita, also claimed that prison camps were operated under orders from Tokyo in accordance with the provisions of the Geneva Convention. The food given to prisoners of war and internees was inadequate, but the Japanese were likewise on reduced rations. Yamashita did not inspect the camps.

This witness gave evidence regarding conditions in the camps tending to show that they were as high as they could be in the circumstances. Lieutenant-General Shiyoku Kou, who had been in charge of two prisoner-of- war camps and three civilian internment camps, and John

Shizuo Ohaski, an employee in one of the camps, were also called and gave similar evidence for the Defence.

The accused himself gave sworn evidence. He stated that, on his assuming command of the 14th Area Army on 9th October, 1944, he had but few experienced officers and he was short of all supplies, including food and transport. At first there were over 30,000 troops in the Islands who were not under his orders. These included the naval land forces in Manila, and when he did achieve control over these it was for operational and not for disciplinary purposes. He had unsuccessfully ordered the evacuation of Manila. He denied issuing orders for ill-treatment or torture of captives or having had reports of such offences, and his policy was to treat prisoners of war in the same way as his own troops in matters such as food. He had ordered that armed guerrillas be suppressed and had left the methods to be used to the discretion of his commanders. He denied that his Judge Advocate had ever told him that a large number of guerrillas would have to be disposed of without trial, for lack of time. The Commanding Generals of the 35th and Shimbu Armies had authority to pass death sentences on American prisoners of war tried in their areas without referring the matter to the accused. The accused admitted, nevertheless, that he was responsible to the Southern Army for seeing that the proper procedure was followed ; communications were cut, however, and he did not always know about details.

The accused admitted that prisoner-of-war and civilian internment camps were under his command and claimed that all death sentences passed in the 14th Army required his approval ; the death sentences passed on guerrillas which he had approved in the Philippines were not more than 44 in number.

9. THE TYPES OF EVIDENCE ADMITTED

As was indicated by the President of the Commission (Footnote 1:see pp. 33-4), a wide variety of types of evidence was admitted during the course of the trial. A large number of objections were made by the Defence, not always unsuccessfully, to the admission of items of evidence, in particular to pieces of documentary evidence and to hearsay evidence.

When the case eventually came before the Supreme Court of the United States, Mr. Justice Rutledge, in his dissenting opinion (Footnote 2:See pp.

60-l and 62-3.), referred to a series of events which it would be appropriate to describe at this point. On 1st November, 1945, the President of the Commission ruled that the latter was unwilling to receive affidavits without corroboration by witnesses on any item in the Bills of Particulars. On 5th November, however, the Commission reversed this ruling and affirmed its prerogative of receiving and considering affidavits or depositions, if it chose to do so, " for whatever probative value the Commission believes they may have, without regard to the presentation of some partially corroborative oral testimony."

10. THE CLOSING ADDRESS FOR THE DEFENCE

Defence Counsel attacked the evidence of the Prosecution concerning some few of the alleged offences, but in general the Defence did not deny that the atrocities alleged by the Prosecution had actually taken place, and the principal aim of Counsel was to show that the accused was not legally responsible for these offences.

Great stress was placed on the' difficulties which had faced the accused on his taking command of the 14th Army Group on 9th October, 1944. It was claimed that :

" The 14th Army Group was subordinate to the Supreme Southern Command under Count Terauchi, whose headquarters was in Manila. The navy was under a separate and distinct command, subordinate only to the naval command in Tokyo. Subordinate to Count Terauchi's command, but parallel with the 14th Army Group, were the 4th Air Army, the 3rd Transport Command, and the Southern Army Communications Unit. Therefore, out of approximately 300,000 troops in

Luzon, only 120,000 were under General Yamashita's command. An acute shortage of food existed, and the Japanese army was exceedingly short in both motor transport and gasolene. The accused found that the general state of affairs in the 14th Army Group was very unsatisfactory. The Chief of Staff was ill, there were only three members of Kuroda's staff left in the headquarters, and the new members were not familiar with the conditions that existed in Luzon. The 14th Army Group was of insufficient strength to carry out the accused's mission, inasmuch as it was, in his opinion, about five divisions short of what would be required. His troops were of poor calibre and not physically up to standard requirements. The morale of his men was poor. In addition, a strong anti-Japanese feeling existed among the Filipino population. Preparations for defence were practically non-existent. . . .

" To unify the 14th Command, General Yamashita requested that 30,000 troops under the Southern Command be transferred to him. This was accomplished in the early part of December. The 4th Air Army came under his command on 1st January, 1945, the 3rd Maritime Transport Command came under his command during the period 15th January to 15th February of this year. The navy never came under his command, but the naval troops in the City of Manila came under the command of the 14th Army Group on 6th January for tactical purposes during landing operations only.

" This limited command . . . involved the right to order naval troops to advance or to retreat, but did not include the command of such things as personnel, discipline, billeting or supply. . . .

" **After th**e American victory on Leyte, the Japanese situation on Luzon became extremely precarious. The American blockade became more and more effective ; the shortage of food became critical. The American air force continually strafed and bombed the Japanese transportation facilities and military positions. General Yamashita, charged specifically with the duty of defending the Philippines, a task that called for the best in men and equipment, of which he had neither, continued to resist our army from 9th October to 2nd September of this year, at which time he surrendered on orders from Tokyo.

" The history of General Yamashita's command in the Philippines is one of preoccupation and harassment from the beginning to the end."

The Defence maintained that the Manila atrocities were committed by the naval troops, and that these troops were not under General Yamashita's command. How, it was asked, could he be held accountable for the actions of troops which had passed into his command only one month before, at a time when he was 150 miles away-troops whom he had never seen, trained or inspected, whose commanding officers he could not change or designate, and over whose actions he had only the most nominal control ?

In the submission of the Defence no kind of plan was discernible in the Manila atrocities : " We see only wild, unaccountable looting, murder and rape. If there be an explanation of the Manila story, we believe it lies in this : Trapped in the doomed city, knowing that they had only a few days at best to live, the Japanese went berserk, unloosed their pent-up fears and passions in one last orgy of abandon."

It was pointed out that General Yamashita arrived in Manila on 9th October and left on 26th December. Until 17th November, General Yamashita was not even the highest commander in the City of Manila since his immediate superior, Count Terauchi, was there and in charge. It was Count Terauchi and not General Yamashita who was handling affairs concerning the civilian population, relations with the civil government and the discouragement and suppression of anti-Japanese activities. The crucial period, therefore, was from 17th November to 26th December, a matter of a mere five weeks, during which General Yamashita was in Manila and in charge of civilian affairs. Could it be seriously contended that a commander who was beset and harassed by the enemy and was staggering under a successful enemy invasion to the south and expecting at any moment another invasion in the north could in such a short period gather in all the strings of administration ? Even so, the accused took some steps in an attempt to curb the activities of the Japanese military police who were terrorising the civilian population.

Regarding the charges alleging the killings of prisoners of war, the submission of the Defence, in essence, was that Yamashita had not been shown to have known of, condoned, excused, permitted or ordered them ; sometimes there was no proof even of them having been committed by troops under his command.

The rest of the allegations as to prisoner-of-war camps had to do with treatment and, for the most part, the question of insufficient food. The Defence rested their argument in this connection on the seriousness of the general food situation in the Philippine Islands, which was aggravated by the United States offensive. The Defence claimed that the evidence had shown that, despite this situation, the prisoners of war got rations equal to those of the Japanese soldiers. The accused had done all he could to alleviate the food situation in the civilian internee and prisoner-of-war camps, and far from ordering all American prisoners of war executed, or ordering any prisoners of war executed, General Yamashita's orders were to turn them over to the American forces at the earliest available time.

The main submissions of the Defence relating to the military police and guerrilla situation in Manila were : first, that guerrillas were, in the eyes of International Law, subject to trial and execution if caught ; second, that International Law did not prescribe the manner or form of trial which must be given ; third, that the suspected guerrillas held in Manila in December, 1944, were tried in accordance with the provisions of Japanese military law and regulations ; fourth, that General Yamashita never ordered or authorised any deviation from the provisions of Japanese military law and regulations ; fifth, that the fact that the method of trial prescribed by Japanese military law and regulations is a summary one and not in accord with Anglo-Saxon conceptions of justice was immaterial, since International Law did not prescribe any special method of trial, and in no event were Japanese methods of trial provided by Japanese law the fault or responsibility of the accused.

The explanation for many of the atrocities alleged by the Prosecution was to be found in the activities of the Philippine guerrilla movement which did great damage to the Japanese position. However admirable its members i might be as fearless fighters, they were, in Japanese eyes, criminals, and the Japanese had every right under International Law to try and execute them as such. Any civilian who took up arms against the Japanese was, in the eyes of International Law, guilty of war treason, just as any Japanese in Tokyo who might now take up arms against the United States would be a war traitor and subject to the death sentence. The evidence regarding the treatment of the Philippine guerrillas on capture was confused but it seemed that there was first an investigation by a military police investigating officer ; then a consultation or conference by the judge advocate's department ; and finally a form of trial, which had much less importance and formality than the hearing in the judge advocate's department. The evidence indicated that Japanese methods of trial and procedure were foreign to the American standards of justice. It had been shown in the witness box, however, that these methods were used not only in the case of civilians accused of guerrilla activities, but also in the case of Japanese soldiers accused of purely military offences. In neither case was there a right to counsel ; in neither case were witnesses called. In both cases the decision of the court was based on the facts developed in the military police investigation held before trial. Furthermore, the methods of trial used were substantially those required by Japanese military law and regulations. As war criminals, guerrillas were liable to execution and there was an equal right on the part of the occupant to take stern methods to exterminate them. If captured, they were not entitled to any of the rights of a prisoner of war. There would certainly have to be proof that the person captured was a guerrilla, or was aiding the guerrillas, and this implied the holding of a trial. The Prosecution had alleged many executions without trial, but the Defence submitted that in practically all of these cases there was at least a semblance of an investigation. The Defence had claimed that because General Yamashita was a prisoner of war, his trial should follow at least the rules laid down by the *Manual for Courts Martial*, but the Prosecution had taken the position that General Yamashita, as an" accused war criminal, was not entitled to the rights of a prisoner of war and that those rules need not apply. The same should apply, *a fortiori*, to guerrillas, argued the Defence, because a guerrilla was never a prisoner of war.

The allegations concerning punitive expeditions that included the execution of small children or other persons who were not guerrillas were a different matter, but there had been no testimony that General Yamashita ever ordered or permitted or condoned or justified or excused in any way these atrocities. All of the testimony had been to the contrary. In relation to the guerrillas, however, the Defence submitted that General Yamashita did precisely what he should have done under the circumstances. He issued an order in which he directed action against armed guerrillas, but was careful to say " armed", and at the same time he informed his chiefs-of-staff " to handle the Filipinos carefully, to co-operate with them and to get as much co-operation as possible from the Filipino people."

The Defence anticipated that the Prosecution would claim that there were so many of these atrocities, that they covered so large a territory, that General Yamashita must have known about them. The reply of the Defence was that, in the first place, a man was not convicted on the basis of what someone thought he must have known but on what he has been proved beyond reasonable doubt to have known ; and in the second place, General Yamashita did not know and could not have known about any of these atrocities.

Practically all of the atrocities took place at times when and in areas where the communication of news of such matters was practically impossible. Further, the accused's orders were clear : to attack armed guerrillas and to befriend and win the co-operation of other civilians. When atrocities occurred, they were committed in violation of General Yamashita's orders, and it was quite natural that those who violated these orders would not inform him of their acts.

The accused had himself explained why he knew nothing of the various alleged atrocities. He had pointed out that he was constantly under attack by large American forces, and had said :

" Under these circumstances I had to plan, study and carry out plans of how to combat superior American forces, and it took all of my time and effort.
" At the time of my arrival I was unfamiliar with the Philippine situation, and nine days after my arrival I was confronted with a superior American force. Another thing was that I was not able to make a personal inspection and to co-ordinate the units under my command. . . . It was impossible to unify my command, and my duties were extremely complicated.
" Another matter was that the troops were scattered about a great deal and the communications would of necessity have to be good, but the Japanese communications were very poor. . . .

" Reorganisation of the military force takes quite a while, and these various troops, which were not under my command, such as the Air Force and the Third Maritime Command . . . were gradually entering the command one at a time, and it created a very complicated situation. . . .

Under the circumstances I was forced to confront the superior U.S. forces with subordinates whom I did not know and with whose character and ability I was unfamiliar.

" Besides this I put all my effort to get the maximum efficiency and the best methods in the training of troops and the maintaining of discipline, and even during combat I demanded training and main: tenance of discipline. However, they were inferior troops, and there simply wasn't enough time to bring them up to my expectations. . . .
" We managed to maintain some liaison, but it was gradually cut off, and I found myself completely out of touch with the situation. I believe that under the foregoing conditions I did the best possible job I could have done. However, due to the above circumstances, my plans and my strength were not sufficient to the situation, and if these things happened they were absolutely unavoidable."

The Defence submitted that General Yamashita's problem was not easy. He was harassed by American troops, by the guerrillas, and even by conflicting and unreasonable demands of his superiors. He had no time to inspect prisoners ; all he could do about the guerrilla situation was to give orders to suppress armed combatant guerrillas and befriend and co-operate with other civilians, and to trust his subordinates to carry out his orders.

Defence Counsel pointed out that the evidence of the Prosecution related almost exclusively to the proof of the atrocities alleged in the Bills of Particulars. A minute fraction thereof attempted to impute to General Yamashita the knowledge of the commission of the atrocities and, in a few instances, the ordering of the commission of the atrocities.

The evidence of Lapus (Footnote 1: See p.19), a collaborator during the Japanese occupation, had tended to show General Yamashita as having ordered the massacre of civilians and the destruction of the City of Manila, but his evidence had been full of inconsistencies. Galang, (Footnote 2: See p.19) another collaborator, testified that in a conversation General Ricarte said to General Yamashita, through Ricarte's grandson as interpreter : " I would like to take this occasion to ask you again to revoke the order to kill all of the Filipinos and to destroy all of the city," and that General Yamashita answered : " An order is an order ; it is my order. It should not be broken or disobeyed." Yet the grandson (Footnote 3: See p.21.) had testified that he had not interpreted the conversation alleged to have taken place between his grandfather and General Yamashita in the presence of Galang. The evidence of Castillegos (Footnote 4: See p.20) was valueless hearsay. Counsel for the Defence submitted that there was no credible testimony in the entire record of trial which in any manner supported any contention that General Yamashita had ordered or had actual knowledge of the commission of any of the atrocities set forth in the Bills of Particulars. Without knowledge of the commission or the contemplated commission of the offences, General Yamashita could not have permitted the commission of the atrocities. The Defence did not deny the commission of atrocities by Japanese troops, but the fact that atrocities were committed did not prove that General Yamashita had knowledge of the commission thereof ; nor could knowledge be inferred therefrom under the conditions which existed during the period in which the atrocities were committed.

Under adverse combat conditions, with the myriad of problems which had to be solved in fighting a losing battle, neither General Yamashita or the members of his staff could or would have time for any duties other than those of an operational nature and could not, and did not, know of the commission of the acts set forth in the Bills of Particulars by troops whose imminent and inevitable death turned them into battle-crazed savages. Nor was General Yamashita or the members of his staff chargeable with any dereliction of duty in not learning of these occurrences.

The evidence adduced by the Prosecution, therefore, did not establish that either General Yamashita or his headquarters issued orders directing the commission of the atrocities set forth in the Bills of Particulars ; nor did it establish that General Yamashita or his headquarters had any knowledge thereof, permitted the commission thereof, or that under the circumstances then existing General Yamashita unlawfully disregarded and failed to discharge his duty as the Commanding General of the 14th Area Army in controlling the operations of the members of his command, thereby permitting them to commit the atrocities alleged.

The only possible basis for imputing to General Yamashita any criminal responsibility for the commission of these atrocities was provided by his status as the Commanding General of some of the troops involved in the commission thereof. The United States did not recognise a criminal responsibility based upon the status of an individual as a Commanding General of troops, but did recognise the criminal liability attached to a Commanding General for the improper exercise of that command. The United States had defined the criminal liability of individuals offending against the Laws of War in the War Department Publication, *Rules of Land Warfare*, FM 27-10, Section 345. 1, wherein criminal liability was defined and limited to individuals and organisations who violated the accepted laws and customs of war.

Under this section, the liability for war crimes was imposed on the persons who committed them and on the officers who ordered the commission thereof. The war crime of a subordinate, committed without the order authority or knowledge of the superior officer, was not the war crime of the superior officer.

Not only was there no proof of the criminal responsibility of General Yamashita for the alleged offences ; witnesses for the Defence had testified that no orders directing or authorising the commission of the alleged acts were issued by General Yamashita or by his headquarters, that no reports of any of the acts were received by General Yamashita or his headquarters, that under the circumstances General Yamashita and the members of his staff were absorbed in the duties incident to combat to the exclusion of other duties normally performed by an army headquarters, and that the proper functioning of General Yamashita and his staff officers was complicated by enemy action, disabling and destruction of supply lines, lines of communication and motor equipment, the lack of gas and oil for the operation of the vehicles which were not damaged, and the consequent impossibility to keep advised of the administrative functioning of his command.

General Yamashita, testifying as a witness in his own behalf, had denied that he issued any orders directing the commission of any act of atrocity, that he received any report of the commission of such acts, that he had any knowledge whatsoever of the commission of such acts, that he permitted such acts to be perpetrated, or that he condoned the commission of such acts.

11. *THE CLOSING ADDRESS FOR THE PROSECUTION*

The Prosecution claimed that the principal contentions as between the Defence and the Prosecution were as to whether or not the accused failed to perform a duty which he owed as commander of armed forces in the Philippines, and as to whether or not such a failure would constitute a violation of the Laws of War.

The accused had acknowledged that he was under a duty under International Law to control his troops so that they would not commit wrongful acts, that if commanding officer ordered, permitted or condoned the crime which was committed by his troops or his subordinate, then that commanding officer would be subject to criminal punishment under the military law of Japan, and that if he took all possible means to prevent the crime committed by his troops or his subordinate, and yet that crime was committed, then the commanding officer, despite all of the efforts which he made, would bear administrative responsibility to his superiors.

The Prosecution underlined the fact that so far as the Laws of War were concerned there was no such distinction between criminal responsibility and administrative responsibility. If an act constituted a violation of the laws of war the death penalty might be assessed irrespective of whether or not under the military laws of the nation involved or in civil law there would or would not be a criminal responsibility.

The evidence had shown that the accused became to all intents and purposes after the 17th November, 1944, the military governor of the Philippine Islands. He was the highest military commander in this area. It was his duty, in addition to his duty as a military commander, to protect the civilian population. Whereas Defence Counsel had referred to the atrocities as having been committed by " battle-crazed men under the stress and strain of battle," there was in fact evidence that in many instances those acts were committed under the leadership of commissioned officers. That is quite a far cry from the sudden breaking of bounds of restraint by individuals on their own initiative. The submission of the Prosecution was that the evidence showed that these atrocities were carefully planned, carefully supervised ; they were in fact commanded.

The Prosecution recalled that the accused had asserted that he had no knowledge of these acts, and that if he had had knowledge or any reason to forsee these acts he would have taken affirmative steps to prevent them. In explanation of his claim that he had no knowledge he had asserted that his communications were faulty. The Prosecution submitted however that there was nothing in the record to the effect that the accused did have adequate communications. For instance, the accused had acknowledged that reports from Batangas concerning guerrilla activity were received from time to time. Even if it were accepted that the accused did not know of what was going on in Batangas, the fact remained that he did not make an adequate effort to find out. It was his duty to know what was being done by his troops under his orders. The accused had pleaded that he was too hard pressed by the enemy to find out what was the state of discipline among his troops. The Prosecution claimed however that the performance of the responsibility of the commanding officer toward the civilian populations is as heavy a responsibility as the combating of the enemy. And if he chose to ignore one and devote all of his attention to the other he did so at his own risk.

The accused had made no special attempt to find what the prevailing conditions were in the prison camps under his control, and many of the atrocities against the civilian population were committed very close to his headquarters. The accused had testified that he did not inquire as to the methods being pursued by the military police. He issued orders for the release of certain unfortunate captives upon the approach of United States troops, but only because he knew he was defeated and wanted to improve his record.

He had also acknowledged that he knew that prisoners of war were being made to work on airfields or on airfield installation. In response to questions he had stated that, in his opinion, airfield work was entirely in accordance with International Law, so long as the airfield was not under attack. The Prosecution claimed, however, that it was a violation of the Geneva Convention for those men to work on that airfield at all.

Turning to the food situation, the Prosecutor claimed that the evidence showed that according to the observation and the personal knowledge of internees the Japanese garrison at each of those camps actually were getting better food and more food than were the internees.

There was no evidence that the accused ordered the executions of certain prisoners of war which had been proved. The executions were, however, carried out by men under his command. The very method by which those executions were accomplished, the complete disregard of the prescribed procedure, showed that those men were acting under approval. Otherwise they would never have dared tp be so arbitrary.

Many thousands of unarmed women and children had been butchered in Manila and in Batangas, and they could not be considered guerrillas. They were given no trial, and their killing was carried out by military men acting as military units, and led by officers, non-commissioned and commissioned. These massacres were not done in the heat of battle. More than 25,000 people, over a period of more than a month, were massacred in a methodical obviously planned way and, as the evidence indicated very strongly, under the orders of General Fujisige, the Commanding Officer in the Batangas area. The Prosecution claimed that the accused must be held responsible for these atrocities in view of the wide and general nature of the order which he issued for the prompt subjugation of armed guerrillas. The Prosecutor claimed that : " He knew the guerrilla activity. He knew that his troops were being harassed. He gave them an order which naturally under the circumstances would result in excesses, in massacres, in devastation, unless the order were properly supervised. He unleashed the fury of his men upon the helpless population, and apparently, according to the record, made no subsequent effort to see what was happening or to take steps to see to it that the obvious results would not occur-not a direct order, but contributing necessarily, naturally and directly to the ultimate result."

Whatever the procedures of the courts martial under Yamashita may have been, he had acknowledged that he made no effort to determine what those courts martial were doing. He had stated that no American prisoner of war was tried by court martial. But he could not possibly know one way or the other because, as he had said, he received no reports from them. The same applied with respect to trials by military tribunals of civilian internees.

A suspected guerrilla was not afforded any particular type of trial under International Law. There must, however, be a trial, and the minimum requirements of a trial would be knowledge of the charges, an opportunity to defend, and a judicial determination of guilty or innocence on the basis of the evidence. In fact, if the Military Police saw fit to decide that a person was to be killed, that person did not go to a court martial ; he was executed by the Military Police. General Yamashita had denied that he had ever given the Military Police authority to carry out death sentences, or authority to try and assess death sentences ; and yet, according to the testimony of the interpreter at the Cortabitarte garrison headquarters that was the practice of the Military Police. If Yamashita did not know of it, that was his fault. There was no question that the Military Police were directly under the command of Yamashita ; he had acknowledged that to be so.

Yamashita had claimed that the naval troops in Manila were only under his tactical command, but General Muto had acknowledged that any officer having command of troops of another branch under him did have the authority and duty of restraining those men from committing wrongful acts. The atrocities committed by these naval troops were not the acts of irresponsible individuals, acting according to a whim or while in a drunken orgy ; nor were they usually committed in the heat of battle. They were acting under officers, sometimes in concert with officers. Obviously, their acts constituted a deliberate, planned enterprise.

The Prosecutor admitted that the application of the Laws of War to a commanding officer who fails to control his troops had not frequently been attempted. Nevertheless, he submitted that it was well recognised in International Law, even under the international conventions, that a commanding officer did have a duty to control his troops in such a way that they did not commit widespread, flagrant, notorious violations of the laws of war. He repeated that since there had existed in the Philippines a wide-spread pattern of atrocities over a period of time, necessarily notorious and committed by organised military units led by officers, there must have been a failure on the part of the ultimate commander of those troops to perform his duty so to control those troops that they would not commit such acts.

The Prosecutor argued that, since Yamashita had acknowledged that he did command an army composed of lawful belligerents, then Article 1 of the Hague Convention made him responsible for the acts of his subordinates. (Footnote 1: " The laws, rights and duties of war apply not only to armies, but also to militia and volunteer corps fulfilling the following conditions : " 1. To be commanded by a person responsible for his subordinates." ") This was true also under the common usages of war. Further, claimed the Prosecutor : " The criminal laws, the customs, the laws generally of civilised nations, are construed to apply in the international field as a part of the Laws of War as well, wherever they bear any relation at all," and " under laws generally, any man who, having the control of the operation of a dangerous instrumentality, fails to exercise that degree of care which under the circumstances should be exercised to protect third persons, is responsible for the consequences of his dereliction of duty. We say, apply that in this case ! Apply that in the field of military law. It is applied by international tribunals or claims commissions with respect to claims for pecuniary damages by individuals or governments against individuals of another government, or against other governments, arising out of illegal acts. There are many cases where, under International Law, a government of one nation - or let us say a nation has been held financially responsible because of the wrongful acts of its agents or representatives, military or otherwise, with consequent injuries to the nationals of other countries. There is nothing to prevent the application of that same principle in the law of war on a criminal basis."

The Prosecution regarded the present case to be a clear case, in the international field, of criminal negligence. Wharton's *Criminal Evidence*, Volume I, Section 88, stated that a person " is not supposed to have known the facts of which it appears he was ignorant ; but if his ignorance is negligent or culpable . . . then his ignorance is no defence." A similar principle had been applied in the field of International Law. For instance, Borchard, *Diplomatic Protection*, page 217, stated that : ". . . the failure of a government to use due diligence to prevent a private injury is a well recognised ground of international responsibility." The Prosecutor continued : " Now, if it is proper and permissible under International Law and the Laws of War to apply to an entire government, an entire nation, civil responsibility in the form of damages for wrongful actions, violations of Laws of War by the agents or the representatives of that nation, is there any reason under the sun why a responsibility, criminal or civil, under the Laws of War, might not properly be applied under the proper circumstances in the proper case to an individual. The Defence cries that Yamashita was too far away from the scene of battle, too far removed from the actual perpetrators, justly to be charged and punished for the crimes of those under him. Yet, his very government, his entire nation may legally be held responsible - even farther removed from the perpetrators and from the scene of the crime." The analogy of liability under municipal law for the specific crime of manslaughter was also used by the Prosecution.

Moore's *International Law Digest*, Volume VI, page 919, stated that " . . . It is true that soldiers sometimes commit excesses which their officers cannot prevent ; but in general, a commanding officer is responsible for the acts of those under his orders. Unless he can control his soldiers, he is unfit to command them." The Prosecution concluded that if Yamashita could not control his troops, it was his duty to mankind, to say nothing of his duty to his country to inform his superiors of that fact so that they might have taken steps to relieve him. There was no evidence that he did that.

12. THE VERDICT AND SENTENCE

The findings of the Commission were delivered on 7th December, 1945.

The President of the Commission, after repeating the charge and summarising the offences contained in the Bills of Particulars, (Footnote 1: See p.4.) pointed out that it was "noteworthy that the accused made no attempt to deny that the crimes were committed, although some deaths were attributed by Defence Counsel to legal execution of armed guerrillas, hazards of battle and action of guerrilla troops favourable to Japan."

The President made the following remarks concerning the evidence which had been received :

" The Commission has heard 286 persons during the course of this trial, most of whom have given eye-witness accounts of what they endured or what they saw. They included doctors and nurses ; lawyers, teachers, businessmen ;men and women of religious orders ; prisoners of war and

civilian internees ; officers of the United States Army officers of the Japanese Army and Navy ; Japanese civilians ; a large number of men, women and children of the Philippines ; and the accused. Testimony has been given in eleven languages or dialects. Many of the witnesses displayed incredible scars of wounds which they testified were inflicted by Japanese from whom they made miraculous escapes followed by remarkable physical recovery. For the most part, we have been impressed by the candour, honesty and sjncerity of the witnesses whose testimony is contained in 4055 pages in the record of trial.
" We have received for analysis and evaluation 423 exhibits consisting of official documents of the United States Army, the United States State Department, and the Commonwealth of the Philippines ; affidavits ; captured enemy documents or translations thereof ; diaries taken from Japanese personnel, photographs, motion picture films, and Manila newspapers."

The President then went on to set out what may be regarded as the essential facts of the case as follows :

" The Prosecution presented evidence to show that the crimes were so extensive and widespread, both as to time and area, that they must either have been wilfully permitted by the accused, or secretly ordered by the accused. Captured orders issued by subordinate officers of the accused were presented as proof that they, at least, ordered certain acts leading directly to exterminations of civilians under the guise of eliminating the activities of guerrillas hostile to Japan. With respect to civilian internees and prisoners of war, the proof offered to the Commission alleged criminal neglect, especially with respect to food and medical supplies, as well as complete failure by the higher echelons of command to detect and prevent cruel and inhuman treatment accorded by local commanders and guards. The Commission considered evidence that the provisions of the Geneva Convention received scant compliance or attention, and that the International Red Cross was unable to render any sustained help. The cruelties and arrogance of the Japanese Military Police, prison camp guards and officials, with like action by local subordinate commanders were presented at length by the Prosecution.

" The Defence established the difficulties faced by the accused with respect not only to the swift and overpowering advance of American forces, but also to the errors of his predecessors, weaknesses in organisation, equipment, supply with especial reference to food and gasolene, train communication, discipline and morale of his troops. It was alleged that the sudden assignment of Naval and Air Forces to his tactical command presented almost insurmountable difficulties. This situation was followed, the Defence contended, by failure to obey his orders to withdraw troops from Manila, and the subsequent massacre of unarmed civilians, particularly by Naval forces. Prior to the Luzon Campaign, Naval forces had reported to a separate ministry in the Japanese Government and Naval Commanders may not have been receptive or experienced in this instance with respect to a joint land operation under a single commander who was designated from the Army Service. As to the crimes themselves, complete ignorance that they had occurred was stoutly maintained by the accused, his principal staff officers and subordinate commanders, further, that all such acts, if committed, were directly contrary to the announced policies, wishes and orders of the accused. The Japanese Commanders testified that they did not make personal inspections or independent checks during the Philippine campaign to determine for themselves the established procedures by which their subordinates accomplish their missions. Taken at full face value, the testimony indicates that Japanese senior commanders operate in a vacuum, almost in another world with respect to their troops, compared with standards American Generals take for granted. "

The Judgment of the Commission was delivered by the President in the following words :

" This accused is an officer of long years of experience, broad in its scope, who has had extensive command and staff duty in the Imperial Japanese Army in peace as well as war in Asia, Malaya, Europe, and the Japanese Home Islands. Clearly, assignment to command military troops is accompanied by broad authority and heavy responsibility. This has been true in all armies throughout recorded history. It is absurd, however, to consider a commander a murderer or rapist because one of his soldiers commits a murder or a rape. Nevertheless, where murder and rape and vicious, revengeful actions are widespread offences, and there is no effective attempt by a commander to discover and control the criminal acts, such a commander may be held responsible, even criminally liable, for the lawless acts of his troops, depending upon their nature and the circumstances surrounding them. Should a commander issue orders which lead directly to lawless acts, the criminal responsibility is definite and has always been so understood. The *Rules of Land Warfare*, Field Manual 27-10, United States Army, are clear on these points. It is for the purpose of maintaining discipline and control, among other reasons, that military commanders are given broad powers of administering military justice. The tactical situation, the character, training and capacity of staff officers and subordinate commanders as well as the traits of character, and training of his troops are other important factors in such cases. These matters have been the principal considerations of the Commission during its deliberations.

" General Yamashita : The Commission concludes : (1) That a series of atrocities and other high crimes have been committed by members of the Japanese armed forces under your command against people of the United States, their allies and dependencies throughout the Philippine Islands ; that they were not sporadic in nature but in many cases were methodically supervised by Japanese officers and non-commissioned officers ; (2) That during the period in question you failed to provide effective control of your troops as was required by the circumstances.

" Accordingly upon secret written ballot, two-thirds or more of the members concurring, the Commission finds you guilty as charged and sentences you to death by hanging."

ABBAYE ARDENNE CASE

TRIAL OF S.S. BRIGADEFUHRER KURT MEYER
CANADIAN MILITARY COURT, AURICH, GERMANY

10TH-28TH, DECEMBER, 1945

Incitement by Regimental Commander to his men to deny quarter to opposing troops. Extent of his responsibility for shooting of prisoners of war by men under his command.

Kurt Meyer was accused of having, as Commander of the 25th S.S. Panzer Grenadier Regiment of the 12th S.S. Panzer Division, incited and counselled his men to deny quarter to allied troops ; ordered (or alternatively been responsible for) the shooting of prisoners of war at his headquarters ; and been responsible for other such shootings both at his headquarters and during the fighting nearby. He pleaded not guilty. In connection with the last set of charges and with the alternative charge, the Prosecution referred to the presumptions contained in Regulations 10 (3), (4) and (5) of the War Crimes Regulations (Canada). The accused was found guilty of the incitement and counselling, and was held responsible for the shootings at his headquarters, though not guilty of ordering them, and was found not to be responsible for the shootings outside his headquarters. A charge contained in a second Charge Sheet was abandoned. The sentence of death passed against him was commuted by the Convening Authority to one of life imprisonment.

A. OUTLINE OF THE PROCEEDINGS

1. THE COURT

The Court was convened by the General Officer Commanding the Canadian Occupation Force, 3rd Canadian Infantry Division, Major-General C. Vokes, C.B., C.B.E., D.S.O., pursuant to the War Crimes Regulations (Canada).

It consisted of Major-General H. W. Foster, C.B.E., D.S.O., G.O.C. 4 Cdn. Armd. Div., as President, and, as members, Brig. I. S. Johnston, D.S.O., E.D., T./G.O.C., 5 Cdn. Armd. Div. ; Brig. H. A. Sparling, D.S.O., C.R.A., 3 Cdn. Inf. Div. C.A.O.F. ; Brig. H. P. Bell-Irving, D.S.O., O.B.E.,

Comd. 10 Cdn. Inf. Bde., and Brig. J. A. Roberts, D.S.O., Comd. 8 Cdn. Inf. Bde. Lt.-Col. W. B. Bredin, D.J.A.G. 3 Increment " B " (C.A.O.F.), Canadian J.A.G. Overseas, was Judge Advocate. The Prosecutor was Lt.-Col. B. J. S.

Macdonald, O.B.E., E.D., O.C. 1 Cdn. War Crimes Investigation Unit, and the Defending Officer was Lt.Col. M. W. Andrew, D.S.O., O.C. The Perth Regt.

2. THE CHARGE

The Convening Officer directed that the accused be tried on two Charge Sheets. Pursuant to sub-section (1) of Section 4 of the War Crimes 1 Regulations (Canada), Brigadier R. J. Orde, Judge Advocate-General, certified the case as approved for trial on the charges set out therein. At the conclusion of the trial on the first Charge Sheet, however, the approval of the Convening Officer was asked, and given, not to proceed with the second.

The accused pleaded not guilty to all the charges.

The following are the texts of the two Charge Sheets :

FIRST CHARGE SHEET

The Accused, *BRIGADEFUHRER KURT MEYER,* an *Offcer in the former Waffen S.S., then a part of the Armed Forces of the German Reich, now in the charge of 4 Battalion, Royal Winnipeg Rifles, Canadian Army Occupation Force, Canadian Army Overseas, is Charged With :*

FIRST CHARGE: COMMITTING A WAR CRIME

in that he in the Kingdom of Belgium and Republic of France during the year 1943 and prior to the 7th day of June, 1944, when Commander of 25 S.S. Panzer Grenadier Regiment, in violation of the laws and usages of war, incited and counselled troops under his command deny quarter to Allied troops.

SECOND CHARGE: COMMITTING A WAR CRIME

in that he in the Province of Normandy and Republic of France on or about the 7th day of June, 1944, as Commander of 25 S.S. Panzer

Grenadier Regiment, was responsible for the killing of prisoners of war, in violation of the laws and usages of war, when troops under his command killed twenty-three Canadian prisoners of war at or near the Villages of BURON and AUTHIE.

THIRD CHARGE : COMMITTING A WAR CRIME

in that he at his Headquarters at L'Ancienne Abbaye, Ardenne in the Province of Normandy and Republic of France on or about the 8th day of June, 1944, when Commander of 25 S.S. Panzer Grenadier Regiment, in violation of the laws and usages of war gave orders to troops under his command to kill seven Canadian prisoners of war, and as a result of such orders the said prisoners of war were thereupon shot and killed.

FOURTH CHARGE : COMMITTING A WAR CRIME

(Alternative to Third Charge)

in that he in the Province of Normandy and Republic of France on or about the 8th day of June, 1944, as Commander of 25 S.S. Panzer Grenadier Regiment, was responsible for the killing of prisoners of war in violation of the laws and usages of war, when troops under his command shot and killed seven Canadian prisoners of war at his Headquarters at L'Ancienne Abbaye Ardenne.

FIFTH CHARGE : COMMITTING A WAR CRIME

in that he in the Province of Normandy and Republic of France on or about the 7th day of June, 1944, as Commander of 25 S.S. Panzer Grenadier Regiment, was responsible for the killing of prisoners of war in violation of the laws and usages of war, when troops under his command killed eleven Canadian prisoners of war (other than those referred to in the Third and Fourth Charges) at his Headquarters at L'Ancienne Abbaye Ardenne.

SECOND CHARGE SHEET

The Accused, *BRIGADEFUHRER KURT MEYER, an Officer in the former Waffen SS., then a part of the Armed Forces of the German Reich, now in the charge of 4 Battalion, Royal Winnipeg Riffles, Canadian Army Occupation Force, Canadian Army Overseas, is Charged With :*

CHARGE : COMMITTING A WAR CRIME

in that he in the Province of Normandy and Republic of France on or about the 17th day of June, 1944, as Commander of 12 S.S. Panzer Division (Hitler-Jugend), was responsible for the killing of prisoners of war in violation of the laws and usages of war, when troops under his command killed seven Canadian prisoners of war at or near the Village of MOUEN.

3. THE OPENING OF THE CASE FOR THE PROSECUTION

The Prosecutor rested his case upon Articles 23 (c) and (d) of the Hague Convention of 1907 concerning the Laws and Customs of War on Land, Articles 2 and 5 of the Geneva Convention of 1929 relative to the Treatment of Prisoners of War, and Articles 1 and 2 of the Geneva Convention for the Amelioration of the Condition of the Wounded and Sick in Armies in the Field. He referred also to Amendment No. 12 (1929) of the *Manual of Military Law*. The last, he said, contained a number of relevant provisions, many of which were simply restatements of the Hague and Geneva Conventions ; Paragraph 51, however, in dealing with the prohibition of the killing or wounding of an enemy who has laid down his arms and has no longer means of defence, stated that, " This prohibition is clear and distinct ; there is no question of the moment up to which acts of violence may be continued without disentitling the enemy to be ultimately admitted to the benefit of quarter. War is for the purpose of overcoming armed resistance and no vengeance can be taken because an individual has done his duty to the last but escaped injury."

The Prosecution contended that Meyer was responsible, either directly or due to" wilful or criminal negligence and failure of the accused to perform his duties as commander of the troops concerned," for the offences alleged in the first Charge Sheet.

Dealing with the first charge, the Prosecutor stated his opinion that there was sufficient evidence to show that Meyer had ordered his troops to deny quarter, but, he observed, " We have, however, to avoid any argument on that point, confined our charge to one simply of inciting and counselling, which of course, in any event, is a war crime."

Turning to the second charge, he pointed out that it was believed that at least one officer had participated in the mass shootings alleged to have taken place at Buron and Authie, and stated : " Apart from regulation'(4), which makes this participation *prima facie* evidence of Meyer's responsibility, (Footnote: By " regulation (4)," Counsel intended to signify number 10 (4) of the War Crimes Regulations (Canada). Regarding this provision, he himself has admitted that he took an active part in leading this battle, and was well forward, as was his usual practice, in an effort to ' draw on ' his young troops in this, their first engagement. It will be submitted that because of this the court can reasonably infer that the accused must share directly in the responsibility for what occurred. . . . The ferocity of this treatment of prisoners, its widespread character, and the large number of separate crimes, conveys a definite impression that there must have been preliminary incitement and approval given, or orders issued, and is therefore of assistance to the court in determining the responsibility of the accused on this particular charge."

The Prosecutor indicated that whether the Court accepted the third or the fourth charge, which were alternatives, might turn in part on the weight which they placed on the evidence of a Polish youth named Jesionek. On these, and on the fifth charge, he summarised the evidence which he proposed to call.

4. THE EVIDENCE FOR THE PROSECUTION

Twenty-nine witnesses were called by the Prosecution. Further evidence included various pre-trial statements and affidavits and a considerable number of extracts from the proceedings of a SHAEF Court of Enquiry which had made a preliminary investigation of the case.

The evidence against the accused may be divided into four parts, comprising respectively that intended to prove, first the inciting and counselling alleged in the first Charge, secondly the shooting of prisoners of war by troops under his command in or near Buron and Authie alleged in Charge 2 and a connection between Meyer and these offences sufficient to make him responsible for them, thirdly the shootings at the headquarters alleged in Charges 3-5, and fourthly the giving of the orders by the accused alleged in third Charge.

In connection with the first charge, evidence was provided by four ex-members of the 25th S.S. Panzer Grenadier Regiment which had been under Meyer's command. (Footnote: Acting under No. 10 (8) of the War Crimes Regulations (Canada), the President of the Court ruled that the names of the German witnesses should not be released to the press, in order to protect them against possible retaliation. In deference to this decision, the names of German witnesses are not given in these pages.)

The first, in a statement made previously before the SHAEF Court of Enquiry, which was read to the court, said that in April 1944, a Company Sergeant Major had read to him and the rest of the .H.Q. Company, while on parade, certain secret orders, which the Company had had to sign, to signify that they understood them, and which included instructions that if prisoners were taken they were to be shot after interrogation.

The second witness acknowledged a pre-trial statement made to a war crimes investigation unit, in which he said that he had heard Meyer utter words to the effect that his regiment took no prisoners. On being questioned by the President of the Court, the witness said that in February or March 1944, orders that no prisoners should be taken had been read to his company by the same Company Sergeant Major as has previously been mentioned.

The third witness said that on 6th June, 1944, his platoon had heard a speech from a Company Commander to the effect that no prisoners should be taken and that he had been present when Meyer in a speech made late in 1943, at Beverloo, had said, " my regiment takes no prisoners." On being asked by defending counsel, however, whether Meyer had not actually said " I do not want any of my troops to be made prisoners," the witness replied that he was no longer able to give an answer to that question. He could not remember ever being told by any officer or N.C.O. to shoot prisoners. He remembered. an order offering leave to soldiers who did take prisoners, and he thought that no punishment was meted out to those who took them. The speech at Beverloo was forgotten by himself and his comrades when they went into action.'

The fourth of the witnesses referred to, Jan Jesionek, a Polish youth who had been conscripted into the 12th S.S. Panzer Division, told how the accused had made a speech at Le Sap, in which he had said that the German soldiers should take reprisals on prisoners of war. (Under cross-examination, however, the witness confessed that the accused used the word " Englishman " not " prisoners," but he claimed that the speech was so worded. that it was understood that no prisoners were to be taken, but should be shot.) The witness said that von Buettner, the accused's Adjutant, whom the accused had described as his best officer, had at about Whitsun, 1944, issued a company instruction in which he said, " our company takes no prisoners."

Much of the evidence for the Prosecution fell within the second category and was intended to show that the shooting of prisoners of war alleged in Charge 2 had taken place, and in circumstances which would make Meyer legally responsible for these offences. For the most part, testimony was given by members and ex-members of the Canadian Army, who had themselves been taken prisoners during the action around Authie and the Abbaye Ardenne in the first days of the Allied invasion ; but corroborating evidence was provided by French civilians.

An extract from the evidence given at the SHAEF Court of Enquiry by Major Learmont, whose company had been in the vanguard of the fighting, indicated that he and a group of other prisoners had been lined against a wall at Buron, and covered by machine guns. It seemed clear that they were to be shot. A German soldier, whom the Major took to be an N.C.O., appeared and from his actions seemed to prevent the shootings from taking place. Similar stories of such interventions by individual Germans were told by two other witnesses. Major Learmont, however, also saw a fellow prisoner shot because he had been wounded and could not march. The witness was able to state that the particular group of prisoners of which he formed a part were, from the time of their arrival at the Abbaye Ardenne, escorted by Feldgendarmerie of the 12th S.S. Division.

The evidence which Lt.-Col. Petch, who had commanded the North Nova Scotia Highlanders in the fighting, had given the SHAEF Court of Enquiry, in which he described the military situation around Authie on 7th June, included a statement that the enemy personnel in the area had included elements of two infantry regiments belonging to the static defences of the area. Furthermore, a prisoner of the 21st S.S. Panzer Division had been captured near Buron on that day. .

As part of the evidence of the shootings at Meyer's headquarters, alleged in Charges 3-5, the testimony of a French national named M. Vico, of various members of Canadian and British Concentration Units and of a Canadian Army Pathologist showed that eighteen bodies of Canadian soldiers had been disinterred from concealed graves in the garden of the Abbaye and had been identified by the discs which they wore. All bore fatal head wounds ; eight had evidently been shot while the others appeared to have been killed with a blunt instrument.

Evidence was brought to show that these prisoners were missing from their unit on 7th June, and that several of them had been interrogated at the Abbaye headquarters on that day. It was shown that at the relevant times, the accused had been at the Abbaye, and that it had been his Regimental Headquarters.

Cpl. Macleod of the Canadian Army (along with three other witnesses) stated that, when the pay books which had been taken away from certain of the prisoners at the Abbaye were later returned, they were not all distributed, because some of the prisoners were no longer present to claim them.

The evidence falling within the fourth category was given by Jan Jesionek, who said that, at the Abbaye on 8th June, 1944, he had seen a guard announce to the accused that seven Canadian prisoners had been taken. Whereupon Meyer had said, " what should we do with these prisoners ; they only eat our rations." (The witness later confessed under cross-examination that he could not remember the accused's exact words, but their meaning was, " what can we do with these men ; their only purpose is to eat our rations.") The accused had then said, for all those present to hear, " In future no more prisoners are to be taken." After that the prisoners had been conducted into a park attached to the Abbaye and as each one went into the park the witness heard a shot. He could only assume that Meyer had given orders that they should be shot. Jesionek had then entered the park and had seen seven Canadian dead bodies. He and several other German soldiers had stood in a big semi-circle around the bodies, because the spot where the bodies lay was full of blood.

5. THE EVIDENCE FOR THE DEFENCE

The accused, giving evidence on oath, denied ever saying that his unit took or would take no prisoners, and emphasised that during the entire Normandy Campaign he gave no orders to shoot prisoners. Describing the speech which he had delivered to the 15th Company at Le Sap, he said that Jesionek's statement that he had instructed the soldiers to take reprisals against prisoners of war was untrue. He also denied knowing, on 7th June, that any Canadian prisoners were shot at the Abbaye, and claimed that on the morning of the 10th June, two officers had reported that a number of dead Canadians had been found lying in a garden inside the headquarters. They had the impression that the Canadians had been shot. He went to the garden and when he found that their report was true he had been incensed. He gave instructions to his Adjutant to find out who had done the deed, and ordered that the Canadians should be buried.

In surveying the operations of 7th June, he mentioned that, in a village near the Abbaye Ardenne called Cussy, he had found the Commander of the Grenadier Regiment of the 21^{st}Panzer Division, who had his headquarters there. The accused also stated that there had been Feldgendarmerie at his headquarters at the Abbaye Ardenne.

The second witness for the Defence, an officer of the 12th S.S. Panzer Division, said that during training and during the first days of the invasion an instruction had been circulated that all prisoners should be sent " back to Division " as quickly as possible, except those taken by Reconnaissance missions, who had permission to question them. He had heard no reports that the accused had said that his unit took no prisoners. The witness stated that during July 1944, the accused had ordered that 150 prisoners should be sheltered in the buildings of his own headquarters because of the bad weather. He had never heard of prisoners being shot at the Abbaye at any time.

When asked whether there were other troops north-west of Caen on the 7th of June, besides the 12th Panzer Division, he replied that Caen itself was in the billeting area of the 21^{st}Panzer Division, that a battle group of the latter Division had been put into action north-west of Caen on the 6th, and that other units in the area had comprised Coastal Defence personnel, Air Force Units and a heavy anti-tank battalion.

In connection with the disposition of troops in the Caen area, the third witness for the Defence, the Regimental Commander of the 21st S.S. Panzer Regiment, said that the headquarters of that Division and of the 716th Coastal Division were situated in a quarry north-west of Caen on the 8th June. In the same area on the same day he could remember parts of the 202 Anti-tank Battalion of the 21st Panzer Division and some Air Force personnel.

A further Defence witness, an Adjutant of the l2th S.S. Panzer Division, said that he had received orders three or four days after the beginning of the invasion that prisoners of war should be evacuated " back to Division " as soon as possible.

As witnesses for the character of the accused, the Defence produced his wife, his Senior Commanding General, an ex-officer of Meyer's battalion and a Canadian Captain who had gained a favourable impression of Meyer when a prisoner in his hands.

6. THE EVIDENCE FOR THE REBUTTAL .

The Prosecution called several witnesses for the rebuttal. One of these, a youth named Daniel Lachevre, said that in the evening of the 8th June, 1944, he had gone into the garden of the Abbaye with about four friends in order to play games. While he was there he noticed that the Germans had built a shelter, the position of which he indicated. He returned on the 9th and 10th in the evening and apart from the shelter he saw nothing unusual : in particular, he saw no dead bodies. Under cross-examination the witness said that he was very familiar with the garden and that he would have noticed if anyone had been digging there.

7. THE CASE FOR THE DEFENCE

Counsel for the Defence chose not to make any opening address before calling witnesses, but delivered a closing address.

He began by asking the Court to place little weight on the evidence of the first Prosecution witness, who had not been present for cross-examination by the Defence and questioning by the Court. He submitted that the witness's story, according to which an N.C.O. had read secret orders in the street of a town, no doubt with civilians present, in the absence of any officer on parade, was contrary to common sense and from a military point of view ridiculous. He also doubted whether a witness could possibly have memorised accurately a document which he had once heard read.

Counsel pointed out that Jesionek had said that it had only been understood from Meyer's speech (the exact words of which he could not remember) that reference was actually being made to prisoners. Meyer on the other hand, while his account of his speech was the same as that of Jesionek in so far as it had stressed the need for self-reliance, denied that retaliation against prisoners had been intended. Three Prosecution witnesses, as well as Meyer, had said that there were standing orders that prisoners should be taken ; and exercises on the interrogation of such prisoners had been mentioned.

Counsel's submission was that Meyer never gave any order that prisoners should not be taken and that if any such statement had been made no weight was placed on it by the men in his command. The first charge therefore remained unproved.

Regarding the second charge, Counsel made three submissions for the consideration of the Court. The first was that there were not only 25th Panzer Regiment troops around Buron and Authie on 7th June, 1944, but troops of the 21st Panzer Division, too. Secondly, the Defence claimed that if Canadian prisoners were killed in the area of Authie and Buron on 7th June, 1944, there was no evidence as to the formation to which those responsible belonged. To rebut the presumption that there was a general plan, sponsored by Meyer, to shoot prisoners was the evidence of Major Learment and Sgt. Dudka, who both told of an N.C.O. or officer who had stopped any intended shooting by the guards of Canadians. Other witnesses had described how they had been accorded the normal treatment of prisoners of war. In the third place, there was evidence that Meyer had given shelter of 150 prisoners in his own headquarters. Furthermore, 200 Canadians had been captured on 7th June, 1944. They had survived, although they could not all be needed for interrogation. There could therefore be no general plan for shooting prisoners.

Counsel concluded his treatment of the second charge by submitting that once a Brigade Commander had sent his men to the attack he had no control over their individual actions.

Turning to the third and fourth charges, Counsel spent some time in attempting to discredit Jesionek's evidence by contrasting his statements in court on a number of details not connected or only indirectly connected with the alleged offences with his words spoken during his interrogations by a war crimes investigating team, and with the evidence of other witnesses on the same subjects. With more particular reference to the alleged shootings, Counsel claimed that Jesionek's story conflicted with the evidence of Lachevre. Counsel asked how the garden at the Abbaye could be completely undisturbed and unmarked if graves had recently been dug and if there had been a large pool of blood where the bodies had been ? Finally, as there was no evidence as to who shot the seven Canadians, even as to their regiment, Counsel submitted that the Court could not rightly find anyone guilty of the act.

With regard to the fifth charge, Counsel pointed out that there was considerable evidence that the German military police had had charge of the prisoners in question, and submitted that any suspicion should be directed in their direction. He expressed the opinion that, had any person in authority ordered the shootings, it was unlikely in the first place that the pay books of the victims would have been openly produced later, instead of being destroyed, and in the second place that marks of identification would have been left on the bodies.

8. THE PROSECUTOR'S CLOSING ADDRESS

Dealing in the course of his closing remarks with the first charge, Counsel for the Prosecution asked whether it was likely that a Company Sergeant Major would have undertaken to read orders of the kind alleged, unless he had a superior order to do so. He maintained further that this officer had adopted the only possible means of conveying secret orders to his troops, when he gathered them together in tight formation and conveyed to them orally the contents of the written instructions which he held in his hand. Counsel pointed out the wealth of evidence which must be weighed against the word of the accused that he had given no orders that prisoners were to be shot. As proof of the accuracy of Jesionek's words, Counsel asked the Court to compare the bulk of his account of Meyer's speech at Le Sap with that of the accused himself.

If the Court still had any doubt as to the first charge, Counsel asked them to consider the evidence as to the actual shootings and to ask themselves whether these could have happened without incitement or counsel. Furthermore, there was practically no evidence that they had resulted in the punishment of the offenders.

Whether the accused were found guilty on either the third or the fourth charge would depend almost exclusively on the weight placed by the Court on his evidence and on that of Jesionek. The latter was a Pole who had deserted from the German Army ; his father had been imprisoned by the S.S. for a period. Nevertheless, there was no reason why he should act out of spite against Meyer personally. His evidence had not been shaken in any material respect by cross-examination. Taking it as firmly established that the shooting did occur, the only explanation would be that someone at the headquarters, with Meyer's knowledge or approval, carried it out, within a hundred metres of his command post, in broad daylight, and at a time when he could have been and probably was there. This presupposed either that the persons committing the deed felt secure in the knowledge that the Regimental Commander had ordered the shooting or had approved it, or that the perpetrators had no fear of disciplinary consequences if they should be found out. The Court had heard of the accused's reputation as a strict disciplinarian.

By contrast with Jesionek's account, which he characterised as honest and convincing, Counsel drew attention to the fact that Meyer, in previous examinations, had denied all knowledge of the shootings, even after being informed of the evidence obtained from Jesionek. On being told that he was to be tried he had subsequently made a statement, which Counsel regarded as untrue, admitting that he knew of the shooting of eighteen prisoners, and saying that it was reported to him on 10th or 11th June. Despite the recent nature of the shootings, he had told the Court that he had not been able to find the perpetrators. Was it probable, asked Counsel, that the bodies were left for several days with civilians in the vicinity ? Would they have been buried in five separate graves had they all been shot at the same time? Furthermore, Mm. Vico and Lachevre had shown that no bodies were there on the evenings of the 8th, 9th, or 10th June, or on the 11th. Again, the shelter which had been constructed by the Germans was in such a position as to make it improbable that the accused had entered the garden by the way he had described, or seen the bodies from the position which he had indicated while in the witness box.

While he would not claim that there definitely were no other troops in the neighbourhood, Counsel maintained that there was no positive evidence that the prisoners were killed by troops other than the Meyer's Regiment. Though most of the troops involved in the killings were wearing camouflage uniform, he claimed that they were all under Meyer's command. He pointed out that the offer of leave to soldiers who took prisoners only came later, when the flow of prisoners had diminished.

Even if the shootings alleged in the fifth charge were committed by the Military Police serving at Meyer's headquarters, the former, were clearly under the latter's disciplinary control.

Regarding the question of the handing back of the prisoners' pay books, Counsel for the Prosecution thought that the Defence was expecting a little too much efficiency in suggesting that any person in authority would have destroyed those of the shot prisoners.

9. SUMMING UP OF THE JUDGE ADVOCATE

The Judge Advocate pointed out that the killing of prisoners was a war crime, not only under international custom and usage, but also under the Hague Convention No. IV of 1907 and the Geneva Prisoners of War Convention of 1929.

If an officer, though not a participant in or present at the commission of a war crime incited, counselled, instigated or procured the commission of a war crime, and *a fortiori*, if he ordered its commission, he might be punished as a war criminal. The first and third charges fell within this category of offences. In the second, fourth and fifth charges, however, Meyer was alleged to have been " responsible for " the crimes set out therein. In this connection, the Judge Advocate pointed out that Regulations 10 (3) (4) and (5) of the War Crimes Regulations (Canada) stated that when certain evidence was adduced, that evidence might be received by the Court as *prima facie* evidence of responsibility. By virtue of these Regulations, it was unnecessary, as far as the second, fourth and fifth charges were concerned, for the Prosecution to establish by evidence that the accused ordered the commission of a war crime, or verbally or tacitly acquiesced in its commission, or knowingly failed to prevent its commission. The facts proved by the Prosecution must, however, be such as to establish the responsibility of the accused for the crime in question or to justify the Court in inferring such responsibility. The secondary onus, the burden of adducing evidence to show that he was not in fact responsible for any particular war crime then shifted to the accused. All the facts and circumstances must then be considered to determine whether the accused was in fact responsible for the killing of prisoners referred to in the various charges. The rank of the accused, the duties and responsibilities of the accused by virtue of the command he held, the training of the men under his command, their age and experience, anything relating to the question whether the accused either ordered, encouraged or verbally or tacitly acquiesced in the killing of prisoners, or wilfully failed in his duty as a military commander to prevent, or to take such action as the circumstances required to endeavour to prevent, the killing of prisoners, were matters affecting the question of the accused's responsibility.

Dealing with the third charge, the Judge Advocate said : " There is no evidence that anyone heard any particular words uttered by the accused which would constitute an order, but it is not essential that such evidence be adduced. The giving of the order may be proved circumstantially ; that is to say, you may consider the facts you find to be proved bearing upon the question whether the alleged order was given, and if you find that the only reasonable inference is that an order that the prisoners be killed was given by the accused at the time and place alleged, and that the prisoners were killed as a result of that order, you may properly find the accused guilty of the third charge." He drew attention, however, to paragraph 42 of Chapter VI of the *Manual of Military Law* regarding circumstantial evidence, which states : ". . . before the Court finds an accused person guilty on circumstantial evidence, it must be satisfied not only that the circumstances are consistent with the accused having committed the act " (that is, said the Judge Advocate, that he gave the order) " but that they are inconsistent with any other rational conclusion than that the accused was the guilty person.".

In connection with the fourth charge, he pointed out that Regulation 10 (5) provided that if the accused or an officer or N.C.O. of his regiment was present when members of his regiment shot the seven prisoners then the Court might accept that fact as *prima facie* evidence of the accused's responsibility for that crime.

10. THE VERDICT

Meyer was found guilty of the first, fourth and fifth charges, and not guilty of the second and third..

11. THE SENTENCE

Meyer was sentenced to death by shooting.

The Convening Authority, however, commuted the death sentence to one of life imprisonment, on the grounds that Meyer's degree of responsibility did not warrant the extreme penalty.

THE EICHMANN CASE
SENTENCING
29 MAY 1962

Presiding Judge:

After considering the appropriate sentence for the Accused with a deep feeling of the burden of responsibility borne by us, we reached the conclusion that in order to punish the Accused and deter others, the maximum penalty laid down in the law must be imposed on him. In the Judgment we described the crimes in which the Accused took part. They are of unparalleled horror in their nature and their scope. The objective of the crimes against the Jewish People of which the Accused was found guilty was to obliterate an entire people from the face of the earth. In this respect they differ from criminal acts perpetrated against persons as individuals. It may be said that such comprehensive crimes, as well as crimes against humanity which are directed against a group of persons as such, are even more heinous than the sum total of the criminal acts against individuals of which they consist.

But at the stage of passing sentence consideration must also, and perhaps primarily, be given to the injury inflicted on the victims as individuals, which was implicit in these crimes, and the immeasurable anguish which they and their families suffered and still suffer to this very day because of these crimes. For the des patch of each train by the Accused to Auschwitz, or to any other extermination site, carrying one thousand human beings, meant that the Accused was a direct accomplice in a thousand premeditated acts of murder, and the degree of his legal and moral responsibility for these acts of murder is not one less than the responsibility of the person who with his own hands pushed these human beings into the gas chambers.

Even if we had found that the Accused acted out of blind obedience, as he argued, we would still have said that a man who took part in crimes of such magnitude as these over years must pay the maximum penalty known to the law, and he cannot rely on any order even in mitigation of his punishment. But we have found that the Accused acted out of an inner identification with the orders that he was given and out of a fierce will to achieve the criminal objective, and in our opinion, it is irrelevant even for the purpose of imposing a punishment for such terrible crimes, how this identification and this will came about, and whether they were the outcome of the training which the Accused received under the regime which raised him, as his Counsel argues.

This Court sentences Adolf Eichmann to death, for the crimes against the Jewish People, the crimes against humanity and the war crimes of which he has been found guilty. We shall not impose a penalty on him for membership of a hostile organization, of which he was found guilty (see the Criminal Procedure (Trial Upon Information) Ordinance Section 30(2), last part, and Crim. App. 132/57, 11 *Piskei Din* , 1544,1552).

This is the Sentence. You are entitled to appeal against the Judgment and the Sentence, and if you wish to do so, you must submit the Statement of Appeal to the office of this Court within ten days from today and the grounds of appeal within fifteen days from today.

ALEKSOVSKI CASE

THE APPEALS CHAMBER INCREASES HIS SENTENCE

24 MARCH 2000

Today, Friday 24 March 2000, the Appeals Chamber of the International Criminal Tribunal for the former Yugoslavia (ICTY) rendered its reasoned written Judgement in the case of Zlatko Aleksovski.

As authorized by an Order of the Vice-President issued on 22 March 2000, the Judgement was delivered by Judge May (Presiding), Judge Mumba and Judge Hunt, in the absence of Judge Robinson and Judge Wang due to exceptional circumstances. Judge Robinson and Judge Wang participated in the hearing of the case, in deliberations and in the drafting of the Judgement.

The substance of the Appeals Chamber's Judgement:

the accused's four grounds of appeal against his conviction by Trial Chamber I on 7 May 1999 are denied: The submission by the Appellant that the Trial Chamber failed to establish his "discriminatory intent" was rejected. The Appeals Chamber ruled that *"a discriminatory intent or motive is not an element of offences under Article 3 of the Statute (violations of the laws or customs of war) nor of the offence of outrages upon personal dignity".* The Appeals Chamber *"could find no reason to doubt the seriousness of the crimes"* committed by Zlatko Aleksovski. It also rejected the defence of extreme necessity: "*The Appellant, faced with the actual choice of ill-treating the detainees or not, was convicted for choosing the former".* The Appeals Chamber is satisfied that the Trial Chamber "*did not err in the exercise of its discretion when it evaluated the testimony of various witnesses*" and thus "*applied the standard of proof correctly".* The Appeals Chamber found that "*the Appellant has failed to convince the Chamber that unreasonable conclusions were drawn by the Trial Chamber*" in respect of his role as a superior. the Prosecution's two grounds of appeal against the Judgement of 7 May 1999 are allowed in part: Upholding the Tadic Decision of 15 July 1999, the Appeals Chamber accepted the Prosecution's submissions that the conflict in this case was "*international*" and that "*the victims were protected persons under Article 4 of Geneva Conventions IV".* However it decided "*not to remit the case to the Trial Chamber*"and *"declined to reverse the acquittals"* because *"any additional sentence imposed would be concurrent on all counts and would not lead to any increase in sentence".* The Appeals Chamber overturned the Trial Chamber's finding that the accused was not responsible for the mistreatment of prisoners outside the prison compound. The Appeals Chamber found that Zlatko Aleksovski "*was responsible for the mistreatment by the HVO outside the prison*" and declared him "*guilty of aiding and abetting*" this mistreatment.

However the Appeals Chamber specified that it "*does not believe that the additional finding of itself warrants any heavier sentence*".

<u>the Prosecution's third ground of appeal against the initial sentence of two and a half years is allowed:</u> The Appeals Chamber found that the Trial Chamber "*erred in its imposition of sentence. In particular, the Appeals Chamber finds that the Trial Chamber erred in not having sufficient regard to the <u>gravity of the conduct</u> of the Appellant for the following reasons. His offences were not trivial. Instead of preventing it, the Appellant as a superior involved himself in violence against those whom he should have been protecting, and allowed them to be subjected to psychological terror. He also failed to punish those responsible. Most seriously, the Appellant, by participating in the selection of detainees to be used as human shields and for trench digging, as he must have known, was putting at risk the lives of those entrusted to his custody. With his direct participation as a commander he provided additional encouragement to his subordinates to commit similar acts. The combination of these factors should, therefore, have resulted in a longer sentence and should certainly not have provided grounds for mitigation*". The Appeals Chamber decided to revise the sentence in accordance with the finding in the Tadic Decision of 15 July 1999 in which the Appeals Chamber held that it should not intervene in the exercise of the Trial Chamber's discretion with regard to sentence unless there is a "discernable error". Applying that test, the Appeals Chamber found that "*there was a <u>discernable error</u> (...): that error consisted of giving insufficient weight to the gravity of the conduct of the Appellant and failing to treat his position as commander as an aggravating feature in relation to his responsibility under Article 7(1) of the Statute. The sentence imposed by the Trial Chamber was <u>manifestly inadequate</u>*". In imposing a revised sentence, the Appeals Chamber considered "*the element of double jeopardy in this process in that the Appellant has had to appear for sentence twice for the same conduct, suffering the consequent anxiety and distress, and also that he has been detained a second time after a period of*

release of nine months. Had it not been for these factors the sentence would have been considerably longer".

the accused's sentence is increased to 7 (seven) years.
This prison term is to run from today, Friday 24 March 2000. However the time already spent by Zlatko Aleksovski in custody, namely three (3) years and 12 days will be deducted.

BACKGROUND ON THE PROCEEDINGS

On 7 May 1999, Trial Chamber I found Aleksovski guilty of one count of violations of the laws or customs of war (Article 3 of the Statute), namely outrages upon personal dignity, committed in 1993 in a prison facility at Kaonik (central Bosnia). Aleksovski was the commander of this prison, and was convicted on the basis of his individual and superior responsibility.

He was sentenced to two years' and six months' imprisonment. However, applying sub-rule 101(D) of the Tribunal's Rules of Procedure and Evidence, the Trial Chamber considered that Aleksovski was entitled to credit for time served for a period of two years, 10 months and 29 days. The Trial Chamber therefore ordered his immediate release, notwithstanding any appeal.

Following the Trial Chambers' Judgement, both the accused and the Prosecution appealed against the Judgement and Sentence of 7 May 1999 (see press release 469).

On 9 February 2000, the Appeals Chamber heard the oral submissions by the Parties. At the conclusion of this hearing, the Appeals Chamber:

dismissed Aleksovski's appeal against conviction;

allowed the Prosecution's appeal against sentence, stating that a "*revised sentence*" would be considered, and ordered Aleksovski's immediate return to custody;

reserved its Judgement on the Prosecution's grounds of appeal against the Judgement of 7 May 1999 and announced that a written reasoned Judgement, including the revised sentence, would be issued in due course.

BACKGROUND ON THE ACCUSED

Zlatko Aleksovski was arrested on 8 June 1996 in the Republic of Croatia by the Croatian police acting pursuant to an arrest warrant issued by the Tribunal. He was transferred to the Tribunal's Detention Unit in The Hague on 28 April 1997.

According to the indictment issued against him on 10 November 1995, Aleksovski was the commander of the prison facility at Kaonik, near Busovaca, prior to becoming the Head of the District Croatian Defence Council (HVO) "Heliodrom" prison in Mostar. According to the indictment *"SfCrom January 1993 until at least the end of May 1993, Zlatko Aleksovski accepted hundreds of detained Bosnian Muslim civilians from the HVO or their agents into his custody at the detention facilities in Kaonik. The detainees were from a widespread area including, but not exclusive to, Vitez and Busovaca municipalities. Many of the detainees under his control were subjected to inhumane treatment, including, but not limited to, excessive and cruel interrogation, physical and psychological harm, forced labour (digging trenches), in hazardous circumstances, being used as human shields and some were murdered or otherwise killed".*

CELEBICI CASE

APPEAL JUDGEMENT

20 FEBRUARY 2001

Acquittal of Zejnil Delalic affirmed Dismissal for cumulative convictions of all counts charging Zdravko Mucic, Hazim Delic and Esad Landzo with violations of the laws or customs of war Remaining sentences of the convicted accused to be reconsidered by a Trial Chamber for possible adjustment

Please find below the full text of the summary of the conclusions of the Appeals Chamber, read out by presiding Judge David Hunt at today's Judgement hearing

"The Appeals Chamber is sitting today to deliver judgment in the appeal from a judgment of a Trial Chamber, given in a case which has been known as the *Celebici* Case. The Trial Chamber was constituted by Judge Karibi-Whyte, who presided, Judge Odio Benito and Judge Jan.

The trial

The trial related to events which took place in 1992 in a prison camp near the town of Celebici, in central Bosnia and Herzegovina. The four accused in this case, Zejnil Delalic, Zdravko Mucic, Hazim Delic and Esad Landzo, were charged with numerous counts of grave breaches of the Geneva Conventions of 1949 under Article 2 of the Tribunal's Statute and of violations of the laws or customs of war under Article 3. The victims were the Bosnian Serb detainees in the Celebici camp.

Delalic was alleged to have co-ordinated the activities of the Bosnian Muslim and Bosnian Croat forces in the area and later to have been the Commander of the First Tactical Group of the Bosnian Army. He was alleged in that capacity to have had authority over the Celebici camp. The Trial Chamber found him not guilty on all counts, on the basis that he did not have sufficient command and control over the Celebici camp and its guards to found his criminal responsibility as a superior for the crimes which they committed in the camp.

Mucic was found by the Trial Chamber to be the Commander of the Celebici camp, and he was found guilty under the principles of superior responsibility for crimes committed by his subordinates, including murder, torture and inhuman treatment. He was also found guilty of personal responsibility for the unlawful confinement of civilians. Mucic was given a total sentence of seven years.

Delic was found by the Trial Chamber to have acted as the Deputy Commander of the camp, and he was found guilty on the basis of personal responsibility for crimes including murder, torture and inhuman treatment. He was given a total sentence of twenty years.

Landzo was found by the Trial Chamber to have been a guard at the camp, and he was found guilty of committing offences including murder, torture and cruel treatment. He was given a total sentence of fifteen years imprisonment.

The appeal

The three convicted accused, Mucic, Delic and Landzo, filed appeals against the Trial Chamber's judgment. The prosecution also filed an appeal against the judgment on a number of grounds, including grounds of appeal relating to the acquittal of Delalic. The four appellants between them filed a total of forty-eight grounds of appeal. Certain of the grounds of appeal of the three convicted appellants related to the same subject matter, and they were therefore dealt with together in the hearing of oral submissions and in the written judgment delivered today.

For the purposes of this hearing, I propose to summarise briefly the conclusions of the Appeals Chamber on the various grounds of appeal, grouped in the same order as they are dealt with in the judgment. I emphasise that this is a *summary* only, and that it forms no part of the judgment which is delivered. The only authoritative account of the Appeals Chamber's conclusions, and of its reasons for those conclusions, is to be found in the written judgment, copies of which will be made available to the parties at the conclusion of this hearing.

Article 2 of the Statute

The convicted appellants raised three issues in relation to the legal conditions for the application of Article 2 of the Statute, which gives to the Tribunal jurisdiction over grave breaches of the Geneva Conventions of 1949.

It is established in the Tribunal's jurisprudence that the prosecution must prove the existence of an international armed conflict in relation to any offences charged under Article 2. The Trial Chamber found that the armed conflict in Bosnia and Herzegovina at the relevant time was international, as the Bosnian Serb forces fighting in Bosnia and Herzegovina were under the control of the Federal Republic of Yugoslavia. The Appeals Chamber has re-affirmed its *Tadic* Conviction Appeal Judgment, which had been followed in its *Aleksovski* Appeal Judgment, and which held that what must be established by the prosecution is that the foreign intervening party was in "*overall* control" of the local forces.

The Appeals Chamber has reiterated that it will follow the *ratio decidendi* of its previous decisions unless there are "cogent reasons in the interests of justice to depart from them." It considers that there is no reason to depart from the decision in its*Tadic* Conviction Appeal Judgment as to the relevant standard of control for this purpose. The Appeals Chamber has expressed additional reasons as to why that interpretation was correct, and it is satisfied that the Trial Chamber's factual determination on this issue was consistent with the overall control standard which had been stated.

The appellants also challenged the Trial Chamber's finding that, for the purposes of Article 2 of the Statute, the victims were persons protected under the relevant Geneva Convention. In the Tadic Conviction Appeal Judgment, the Appeals Chamber held that "a person may be accorded protected person status, notwithstanding the fact that he is of the same nationality as his captors", a ruling subsequently endorsed by the Appeals Chamber in Aleksovski. The Appeals Chamber has concluded that there is no reason to depart from this interpretation, and it has confirmed that "the nationality of the victims for the purpose of the application of Geneva Convention IV should not be determined on the basis of formal national characterisations", but that the nationality should take into account the differing ethnicities of the victims and the perpetrators and their bonds with a foreign intervening State. The Appeals Chamber is satisfied that the Trial Chamber's findings were consistent with this interpretation. Delic also challenged the Tribunal's jurisdiction to prosecute grave breaches of the Geneva Conventions because, it was submitted, Bosnia and Herzegovina was not a party to the Conventions until after the relevant events, having acceded to them subsequently. The Appeals Chamber has held that Bosnia and Herzegovina succeeded to the Geneva Conventions, with the effect that it is considered to be a party to the treaty from the date of its succession or independence, which was prior to the relevant events. The Appeals Chamber has also stated that, even without a formal act of succession, Bosnia and Herzegovina would automatically have succeeded to the Geneva Conventions, as they are treaties of a universal multilateral character relating to fundamental human rights.

Common Article 3 and Article 3 of the Statute

The appellants also challenged the jurisdiction of the Tribunal to prosecute violations of Article 3 common to the Geneva Conventions under Article 3 of the Statute. The Appeals Chamber has concluded that there is no reason to depart from its *Tadic* Jurisdiction Decision, which held that the violations of the laws or customs of war which may fall within Article 3 of the Statute of the Tribunal include violations of common Article 3, that these violations give rise to individual criminal responsibility, and that they may be prosecuted whether committed in internal or international conflicts. It has expressed additional reasons as to why that decision was correct.

Command responsibility

Mucic was convicted under Article 7.1 for his superior authority as commander of the Celebici camp for the crimes committed there. He argued that command responsibility is limited to de jure commanders, or those superiors with control over subordinates equivalent to such de jure authority. The Appeals Chamber has rejected that argument, accepting that a position of de facto command may be sufficient to establish the necessary superior-subordinate relationship, as long as the relevant degree of control over subordinates is established. The relevant superior-subordinate relationship is established where the superior has effective control over the persons committing the underlying violations of international humanitarian law, in the sense of having the material ability to prevent or punish the commission of these offences. Mucic also challenged the sufficiency of the evidence to establish that he was a de facto commander. The Appeals Chamber has held that, on the evidence before the Trial Chamber, it was open to a reasonable tribunal of fact to find that Mucic exercised powers of control sufficient to constitute the exercise of de facto authority over the camp, and therefore that no basis for reviewing the Trial Chamber's findings of fact had been made out. The prosecution appealed against the Trial Chamber's interpretation of the requirement, in Article 7.3, that a superior "knew or had reason to know" that a subordinate is about to commit crimes or had done so. The Appeals Chamber has concluded that the phrase "reason to know" in Article 7.3 means that a superior will be charged with knowledge of subordinates' offences if information of a general nature was available to him which would have put him on notice of those offences. The Appeals Chamber is satisfied that the Trial Chamber's conclusions on this issue were consistent with that interpretation. The prosecution also contended that the ability of an accused to exercise forms of influence should suffice to establish the relevant superior-subordinate relationship. The Appeals Chamber has concluded that, whilst indirect as well as direct relationships of subordination will suffice, the relevant standard of effective control over subordinates must be established, and that any forms of influence which fall short of such control would not suffice. The Appeals Chamber is satisfied that, on the evidence before the Trial Chamber, it was open to a reasonable tribunal of fact to acquit Delalic on the basis that he was not a superior in relation to the Celebici camp and those working there.

Unlawful confinement of civilians

Both Mucic and the prosecution filed grounds of appeal relating to the charges of unlawful confinement of civilians. Mucic challenged his conviction for that offence, and the prosecution challenged the acquittal of Delalic and Delic of those offences.

The Trial Chamber concluded that the offence of unlawful confinement of civilians is committed:

- first, when civilians are involuntarily confined in breach of Article 42 of Geneva Convention IV, which provides that civilians may only be detained where there are reasonable grounds to believe that the security of the Detaining Power makes it absolutely necessary, and

- secondly, when civilians are detained without compliance with Article 43 of the Geneva Convention, which provides that their detention must be reviewed by an appropriate court or administrative board.

The Appeals Chamber has confirmed the Trial Chamber's definition of the offence, and it has accepted that, on the evidence before the Trial Chamber, it was open to a reasonable tribunal of fact to find that the detainees in the Celebici camp were unlawfully detained.

The Appeals Chamber has also confirmed that the prosecution does not have to establish that a person is in a position of superior authority before he can be found guilty of direct responsibility for this offence under Article 7.1 of the Statute, but that a prison guard with no authority to release prisoners will not be guilty of the offence by virtue only of his failure to take unauthorised steps to release them. The Appeals Chamber has dismissed the prosecution appeal against the acquittal of Delalic and Delic on this charge, on the basis that the prosecution has failed to identify any evidence before the Trial Chamber which demonstrated that a finding of guilty was the only reasonable conclusion to be drawn. As to the appeal by Mucic against his conviction on this charge, the Appeals Chamber has held that, on the evidence before the Trial Chamber, it was open to a reasonable tribunal of fact to find that he had some authority to release prisoners, that he had failed to release those civilians whom he knew to be unlawfully detained because they had not received the necessary procedural review of their detention, and that he was therefore guilty of this offence.

Cumulative convictions

Delic and Mucic challenged their convictions upon charges based upon the same conduct and alleging both grave breaches of the Geneva Conventions under Article 2 of the Statute and violations of the laws or customs of war under Article 3. This was the first time that the issue of cumulative convictions has arisen for the express consideration of the Appeals Chamber.

The Appeals Chamber has concluded that reasons of fairness to the accused, and the consideration that only distinct crimes justify cumulative convictions, require that cumulative convictions are permissible only if each statutory provision involved has a materially distinct element not contained in the other. The Appeals Chamber has concluded, by majority, that this assessment of the elements of the offences must take into account all of the elements of the offences, including the *chapeaux*(or legal pre-requisite elements) of each Article of the Statute.

Where this test is not met, a decision must be made in relation to which offence it will enter a conviction, on the basis that the conviction must be for the offence containing the more specific provision. Where, as in the present case, the evidence establishes the guilt of an accused based upon the same conduct under both Article 2 and Article 3 of the Statute, the conviction must be entered for the offence under Article 2.

The challenge by Delic and Mucic has therefore been upheld, and the charges against them under Article 3 have been dismissed. As Landzo similarly received cumulative convictions under Articles 2 and 3, the charges against him under Article 3 have also been dismissed, notwithstanding that he did not challenge them.

In a separate and dissenting opinion, Judge Hunt and Judge Bennouna have agreed with the majority that cumulative convictions should be permissible only where each offence has a materially different element not contained in the other, but they have proposed different tests for determining whether this was so in the particular case and, where cumulative convictions are not permissible, for determining which offence should carry the conviction. These tests would in some cases have produced a different result. As the sentencing outcome in respect of each of the three convicted accused may have been different had the Trial Chamber not imposed multiple convictions, the issue of re-sentencing has been remitted to a new Trial Chamber to be designated by the President of the Tribunal.

Delic - factual issues

Delic challenged his convictions upon ten of the counts against him, involving five separate incidents, on the basis that the Trial Chamber had erred in its relevant factual findings.

In relation to the murder of Šcepo Gotovac, one of the detainees in the Celebici camp, the Appeals Chamber has concluded that the Trial Chamber's conclusion that Delic participated in the beating which was responsible for Mr Gotovac's death was not open on the evidence before it. The convictions relating to this incident have been quashed, and verdicts of not guilty entered. In relation to the other four incidents, the Appeals Chamber has concluded that, on the evidence before the Trial Chamber, it was open to a reasonable tribunal of fact to find him guilty of the offences charged.

The prosecution interviews with Mucic

Mucic challenged the admission into evidence of interviews conducted with him by investigators from the Office of the Prosecutor following his arrest. He submitted that the Trial Chamber should have found that he had not voluntarily waived his right to counsel under the Tribunal's Statute and Rules, and that it should therefore have excluded the evidence obtained as a result of the interviews. Mucic also claimed that the Trial Chamber erred in refusing to issue a subpoena to the interpreter present at these interviews to give evidence of any conversation between the investigators and himself which took place before the interviews started and which may have led to the waiver.

The Appeals Chamber is not satisfied that any error has been demonstrated in the Trial Chamber's refusal to issue a subpoena to the interpreter to give evidence. It has stated that a *voir dire* procedure could be of assistance, in appropriate cases, in determining any factual issues relating to the admissibility of evidence such as these, but that the Trial Chamber committed no error in the exercise of its discretion in not adopting that procedure in the absence of any clear indication that the accused would give evidence in relation to those issues.

The Appeals Chamber is satisfied that, on the evidence before the Trial Chamber, it was open to a reasonable tribunal of fact to find that Mucic had expressed the wish to be interviewed without counsel, and that the Trial Chamber had accordingly not erred in the exercise of its discretion to allow the evidence to be tendered on that basis.

Diminished mental responsibility

Before the trial, Landzo gave notice under the Tribunal's Rules of Procedure and Evidence that he would be relying upon the "special defence" of diminished mental responsibility, and he submitted that such a defence amounted to a complete defence to the offences with which he had been charged, leading to an acquittal.

Landzo argued that the Trial Chamber erred by refusing to define the "special defence" in advance of evidence being given in support of it. The Appeals Chamber has held that it is no part of a Trial Chamber's obligation to define such issues in advance, and that in any event no prejudice had been established as resulting from that refusal.

Landzo also challenged the Trial Chamber's rejection of the "special defence" as having been "inconsistent with the great weight of the evidence". The Appeals Chamber has held that an accused's diminished mental responsibility is relevant to the sentence to be imposed, but it is not a defence to offences charged under the Tribunal's Statute. Rule 67(A)(ii)(b) must therefore be interpreted as referring to diminished mental responsibility where it is raised by the defendant as a matter in mitigation of sentence. The Appeals Chamber has also held that, in any event, on the evidence before the Trial Chamber it was open to a reasonable tribunal of fact to reject the evidence of Landzo as to his state of mind upon which his psychiatrist witnesses relied, and therefore – as the Trial Chamber did – to reject their opinion that he had suffered from a diminished mental responsibility.

Selective prosecution

Landzo challenged his conviction upon the basis that he was the victim of selective prosecution based on discriminatory grounds.
In 1998, the Office of the Prosecutor withdrew indictments against a number of low ranking accused as a result of a changed prosecutorial strategy. Landzo alleged that the continued maintenance of the charges against him was discriminatory, as he was a young Muslim camp guard and the others against whom indictments had been withdrawn were all non-Muslims of Serb ethnicity. He contends that he was prosecuted as a "representative" of the Bosnian Muslims.

The Appeals Chamber has held that, whilst the Prosecutor has a wide discretion in relation to prosecutorial strategy, this discretion is not unlimited. However, Landzo has not discharged his burden of establishing any abuse of the prosecutorial discretion. He has not demonstrated that his prosecution was continued for any impermissible motive, or that other accused, similarly situated to himself, were not prosecuted. At the time of the dismissal of the indictments against other accused, none of whom was in the custody of the Tribunal, Landzo's trial was well underway. The continuation of the proceedings against him was consistent with the policy of the Prosecutor to prosecute not only those holding higher levels of responsibility, but also those "personally responsible for exceptionally brutal or otherwise extremely serious offences".

Judge Karibi-Whyte

Landzo challenged the fairness of his trial upon the basis that the Presiding Judge, Judge Karibi-Whyte, had been "asleep during substantial portions of the trial". At a late stage of the appellate proceedings, Delic and Mucic adopted this ground of appeal. The burden of the argument, however, was left to Landzo. The parties agreed that the relevant principle was that proof that a judge slept through part of the proceedings, or was otherwise not completely attentive to them, is a matter which, if it causes actual prejudice to a party, may affect the fairness of the proceedings to such a degree as to give rise to a right to a new trial or other adequate remedy.

Both Landzo and the prosecution selected, from the audio-visual records of the trial produced by the courtroom cameras generally focussed on the judges' bench, those portions of the records upon which they relied in support of this ground of appeal, and in opposition to it. The written submissions filed by Landzo contained extensive and detailed descriptions of what was said to be seen and heard on the videotapes. Before the oral hearing, the Appeals Chamber viewed those portions upon which the parties relied. The Appeals Chamber has concluded that the descriptions given were both highly coloured and gravely exaggerated, and that they appeared to have been given with a reckless indifference to the truth.

The Appeals Chamber has found that the appellants have manifestly failed to establish the allegation that Judge Karibi-Whyte was "asleep during substantial portions of the trial", but that the portions of the videotapes relied upon by Landzo nevertheless demonstrated a recurring pattern of behaviour where the judge appears not to have been fully conscious of the proceedings for short periods of time. These periods were usually five to ten seconds long, and sometimes up to thirty seconds – but they were repeated over extended periods of ten to fifteen minutes. On one occasion only, the judge appeared to be asleep for approximately thirty minutes. The Appeals Chamber has proceeded to consider whether, notwithstanding their failure to establish the factual basis of these grounds of appeal, the appellants nevertheless have a valid cause for complaint as to the fairness of the trial.

The Appeals Chamber has stated, firmly, that Judge Karibi-Whyte's conduct cannot be accepted as appropriate conduct for a judge. It has also said that, if a judge suffers from some condition which prevents him or her from giving full attention during the trial, then it is the duty of that judge to seek medical assistance and, if that does not help, to withdraw from the case. However, before a judgment will be quashed upon this basis, it must be established that some identifiable prejudice was caused by that conduct to the appellant, and the failure of counsel to object at the trial to the conduct in question is relevant to whether such prejudice has been established. The requirement that the issue be raised during the proceedings is not simply an application of a formal doctrine of waiver, but a matter indispensable to the grant of fair and appropriate relief.

The Appeals Chamber has not been satisfied that any specific prejudice was suffered by Landzo or the other appellants. In the absence of any actual prejudice, the Appeals Chamber has rejected the ground of appeal.

Judge Odio Benito and Vice-Presidency of Costa Rica

During the course of the trial, Judge Odio Benito was elected Vice-President of Costa Rica, and she took an oath of office as such. All three convicted accused challenged her qualifications to remain as a judge of the Tribunal during the rest of the trial, and they alleged that, in any event, she should have disqualified herself as a judge by reason of those facts because she was no longer independent.

The Appeals Chamber has held that, because the judges of the Tribunal must necessarily come from a wide variety of legal systems, the requirement of Article 13 in the Tribunal's Statute (as it was at the relevant time) that the judges of the Tribunal "possess the qualifications required in their respective countries for appointment to the highest judicial offices" was intended to ensure that the *essential* qualifications did not differ from judge to judge, and that it was not intended to include within the required *legal* qualifications any constitutional disqualifications peculiar to a particular country. The Appeals Chamber has in any event rejected the argument that, by virtue of her election as Vice-President of Costa Rica, Judge Odio Benito was constitutionally disqualified for election as a magistrate of the Supreme Court of Justice under the constitution of that country.

The Appeals Chamber has also rejected the argument that Judge Odio Benito should nevertheless have disqualified herself as a judge because she was no longer independent. The Appeals Chamber has not accepted that the judge exercised any executive functions in Costa Rica during the time she was also a judge of the Tribunal. The appellants have failed to establish that the reaction of the hypothetical observer (with sufficient knowledge of the circumstances to make a reasonable judgment) would be that she might not bring an impartial and unprejudiced mind to the issues arising in the *Celebici* case.

Judge Odio Benito and the Victims of Torture

All three convicted accused also alleged that Judge Odio Benito was automatically disqualified as a judge of the Tribunal because she was, at the time this case was heard, a member of the Board of Trustees of the United Nations Voluntary Fund for Victims of Torture. They contended that, since the indictment in this case included allegations of torture, there was a strong appearance of bias on the part of the judge against those accused who were the subject of those allegations.

The Appeals Chamber has held that the same hypothetical observer would be aware that the objects of this fund are solely focussed on fundraising to enable material assistance to be given to the victims of torture – through the receipt and redistribution of donations for humanitarian, legal and financial aid to victims of torture and their relatives – and would not expect judges to be morally neutral about torture. Rather, such an observer would expect judges to hold the view that persons*responsible* for torture should be punished. It has accepted the statement that "it is S...C important that judicial officers discharge their duty to sit and do not, by acceding too readily to suggestions of apparent bias, encourage parties to believe that, by seeking the disqualification of a judge, they will have their case tried by someone thought to be more likely to decide the case in their favour".

Sentencing

All of the parties, with the exception of Delalic, filed grounds of appeal in relation to sentencing. The **Prosecution** challenged the sentences imposed on Mucic of seven years, to be served concurrently, as "manifestly inadequate". **Mucic** challenged his sentence as too long in all the circumstances.

The Appeals Chamber has concluded that the Trial Chamber failed to take adequate account of the gravity of offences for which Mucic was convicted and that, in a number of respects, it failed to take into account, or gave inadequate weight to, various matters in aggravation. The Appeals Chamber has rejected one complaint by the prosecution, that the Trial Chamber erred when it did not take into account criminal conduct which was not specifically alleged in the indictment and in relation to which the prosecution had not requested the Trial Chamber to make specific findings. The Appeals Chamber has accepted one complaint by Mucic, that the Trial Chamber erred in making an adverse reference in its sentencing considerations to the fact that Mucic had declined to give oral testimony at the trial, but it has otherwise rejected his complaints.

The Appeals Chamber has indicated that, taking into account the various considerations relating to the gravity of his offences, all the aggravating circumstances, the mitigating circumstances to which the Trial Chamber referred, and the "double jeopardy" element involved in re-sentencing, it would have imposed on Mucic a heavier sentence, of a total of around ten years' imprisonment. This is a figure to which the new Trial Chamber to consider sentencing issues may have regard in its own determination.

Delic challenged his sentence on the basis that the Trial Chamber contravened the principles of legality, by imposing sentences on him which were greater than the sentences which would have been permitted at the relevant time under the sentencing laws and practice of the former Yugoslavia. The Appeals Chamber has rejected that challenge. It has also stated that, whilst Trial Chambers must, as required by Article 24.1 of the Statute, have *recourse to* the general practice regarding sentencing in the courts of the former Yugoslavia, they are not *bound* by that practice. The Appeals Chamber has also concluded that the sentences imposed on Delic have not been shown to be excessive or in any way outside of the Trial Chamber's sentencing discretion.

Landzo challenged his sentence on the basis that it was manifestly excessive. He sought to show a disparity between his sentence and sentences imposed on persons convicted in other cases before the Tribunal. The Appeals Chamber has not accepted that the comparisons made by him are valid. It has also concluded that the Trial Chamber adequately considered the mitigating factors applicable to Landzo.

Disposition

The formal orders made by the Appeals Chamber in the Disposition section of the judgment are as follows:

In relation to Counts 1 and 2 of the Indictment, the Appeals Chamber ALLOWS the ninth and tenth grounds of appeal filed by Hazim Delic, it QUASHES the verdict of the Trial Chamber accordingly, and it enters a verdict that Hazim Delic is NOT GUILTY upon those counts.
In relation to the grounds of appeal relating to cumulative convictions, the Appeals Chamber ALLOWS the twenty-first ground of appeal filed by Hazim Delic and the seventh ground of appeal filed by Zdravko Mucic; it DISMISSES Counts 14, 34, 39, 45 and 47 against Zdravko Mucic; it DISMISSES Counts 4, 12, 19, 22, 43 and 47 against Hazim Delic, and it DISMISSES Counts 2, 6, 8, 12, 16, 25, 31, 37, and 47 against Esad Landzo. It REMITS to a Trial Chamber to be nominated by the President of the Tribunal the issue of what adjustment, if any, should be made to the sentences imposed on Hazim Delic, Zdravko Mucic, and Esad Landzo to take account of the dismissal of these counts.

In relation to the eleventh ground of appeal filed by Zdravko Mucic, the Appeals Chamber FINDS that the Trial Chamber erred in making adverse reference when imposing sentence to the fact that he had not given oral evidence in the trial, and it DIRECTS the Reconstituted Trial Chamber to consider the effect, if any, of that error on the sentence to be imposed on Mucic.

The Appeals Chamber ALLOWS the fourth ground of appeal filed by the Prosecution alleging that the sentence of seven years imposed on

Zdravko Mucic was inadequate, and it REMITS the matter of the imposition of an appropriate revised sentence for Zdravko Mucic to the Reconstituted Trial Chamber, with the indication that, had it not been necessary to take into account a possible adjustment in sentence because of the dismissal of the counts referred to, it would have imposed a sentence of around ten years.

The Appeals Chamber DISMISSES each of the remaining grounds of appeal filed by each of the appellants.
The Appeals Chamber's reasons for these orders are now published.

The accused are to remain in custody in the Detention Unit until further order".

BLASKIC CASE

APPEALS CHAMBER JUDGEMENT IN THE CASE THE PROSECUTOR V. TIHOMIR BLASKIC: SUMMARY OF JUDGEMENT

29 JULY 2004

The Appeals Chamber is here today to deliver its judgement on appeal in the case of the Prosecutor against Tihomir Blaskic. The trial in this case commenced on 24 June 1997, and Trial Chamber I of this Tribunal delivered its Judgement on 3 March 2000. The Appellant Tihomir Blaskic appealed on 17 March 2000.

This case relates to crimes that were perpetrated during the conflict between the Croatian Defense Council and the Bosnian Muslim Army in the Lašva Valley region of Central Bosnia from May 1992 until January 1994. The Appellant, Tihomir Blaskic, was the Commander of the HVO Armed Forces in Central Bosnia at the time the crimes at issue were committed.

The Trial Chamber convicted the Appellant on the basis of nineteen counts set forth in the Second Amended Indictment, for crimes that occurred in the Vitez, Busovaca, and Kiseljak municipalities. These counts encompassed violations of Articles 2, 3, and 5 of the Statute of the International Tribunal. The Appellant was convicted on the basis of Article 7(1) of the Statute for ordering the crimes. The Trial Chamber also stated in the disposition of the judgement that "in any event, as a commander, he failed to take the necessary and reasonable measures which would have allowed these crimes to be prevented or the perpetrators thereof to be punished." Therefore, the Trial Chamber also convicted the Appellant under Article 7(3) of the Statute. The Trial Chamber imposed a single sentence of 45 years' imprisonment.

Following the practice of the Tribunal, I will not read out the text of the Appeal Judgement except for the disposition. Before doing that, I will first summarise the issues on appeal and the reasoning and findings of the Appeals Chamber so that you, Tihomir Blaskic, together with the public, will know the reasons for the Appeals Chamber's decision. I emphasise, however, that this is only a summary, and that it does not in any way form part of the Judgement of the Appeals Chamber. The only authoritative account of the findings of the Appeals Chamber is in the written Judgement which will be available today at the end of these proceedings.

Because of the complexity of this Appeal, the summary of the Judgement which I will now read is longer than our customary practice.

The Additional Evidence Issue

This appeal has been characterized by the filing of an enormous amount of additional evidence. This was due *inter alia* to the lack of co-operation on the part of the Republic of Croatia at that time, and to the delay in the opening of the Republic of Croatia's archives, which only occurred following the death of former president Franjo Tuđjman on 10 December 1999, thus preventing the parties to this case from availing themselves of these materials at the trial. During the appeal proceedings, the Appellant filed four motions pursuant to Rule 115 of the Rules of the International Tribunal. In these motions, he sought to admit over 8,000 pages of material as additional evidence. The first of these additional evidence motions was filed on 19 January 2001, and the last, on 12 May 2003.

Following the filing of the fourth and final Rule 115 motion by the Appellant, and rebuttal material by the Prosecution in relation to this motion, the Appeals Chamber rendered its decisions on additional evidence on 31 October 2003. It found that in the circumstances of this case, a re-trial was not warranted. It decided to admit a total of 108 items, and as a consequence, several witnesses were heard in the evidentiary portion of the hearing on appeal, which took place from 8-11 December 2003, which was followed by final arguments on 16-17 December 2003.

The Appeals Chamber has duly considered the evidence before it, including evidence on the trial record, additional evidence submitted by the Appellant, and rebuttal material presented by the Prosecution.

Grounds of Appeal

The Appellant Blaskic has brought several grounds of appeal in this case. In relation to the applicable law, he alleges errors of law concerning Articles 2, 5, and 7 of the Statute. He also alleges a denial of due process of law, by virtue of the Second Amended Indictment and Rule 68 violations. In relation to the factual findings of the Trial Chamber, he alleges errors concerning his responsibility for crimes committed in Ahmici, parts of the Vitez Municipality other than Ahmici, the Busovaca Municipality, and the Kiseljak Municipality. He also alleges factual errors concerning his responsibility for detention-related crimes. The Appellant also appeals against his sentence.

Standard of Review

The Appeals Chamber may consider appeals on grounds of an error of law invalidating the decision of a Trial Chamber, or an error of fact occasioning a miscarriage of justice. In this case, the Appeals Chamber has had cause to consider the standard of review on appeal in relation to findings challenged only by the Defence, in the absence of a Prosecution appeal.

If the Appeals Chamber finds that an alleged error of law arises from the application of a wrong legal standard by a Trial Chamber, it is open to the Appeals Chamber to articulate the correct legal standard and to review the relevant findings of the Trial Chamber accordingly. In doing so, the Appeals Chamber not only corrects a legal error, but applies the correct legal standard to the evidence contained in the trial record, in the absence of additional evidence, and must determine whether it is itself convinced beyond reasonable doubt as to the factual finding challenged by the Defense, before that finding is confirmed on appeal.

As to errors of fact, the standard applied by the Appeals Chamber has been that of reasonableness, namely, whether the conclusion of guilt beyond reasonable doubt is one which no reasonable trier of fact could have reached. The Appeals Chamber bears in mind that in determining whether or not a Trial Chamber's finding was reasonable, it will not lightly disturb findings of fact by a Trial Chamber.

The Appeals Chamber concurs with the Kupreskic Appeal Judgement's finding that:

...where the Appeals Chamber is satisfied that the Trial Chamber returned a conviction on the basis of evidence that could not have been accepted by any reasonable tribunal or where the evaluation of the evidence was "wholly erroneous", it will overturn the conviction since, under such circumstances, no reasonable tribunal of fact could be satisfied beyond reasonable doubt that the accused had participated in the criminal conduct.

The Appeals Chamber considers that there are no reasons to depart from the standard set out above, in relation to grounds of appeal alleging pure errors of fact and when no additional evidence has been admitted on appeal. That standard shall be applied where appropriate in the present Judgement.

When factual errors are alleged on the basis of additional evidence proffered during the appellate proceedings, Rule 117 of the Rules provides that the Appeals Chamber shall pronounce judgement "on the basis of the record on appeal together with such additional evidence as has been presented to it."

The Appeals Chamber in Kupreskic established the standard of review when additional evidence has been admitted on appeal, and held:

The test to be applied by the Appeals Chamber in deciding whether or not to uphold a conviction where additional evidence has been admitted before the Chamber is: has the appellant established that no reasonable tribunal of fact could have reached a conclusion of guilt based upon the evidence before the Trial Chamber together with the additional evidence admitted during the appellate proceedings.

The standard of review employed by the Appeals Chamber in that context was whether a reasonable trier of fact could have been satisfied beyond reasonable doubt as to the finding in question, a deferential standard. In that situation, the Appeals Chamber in Kupreskic did not determine whether it was satisfied itself, beyond reasonable doubt, as to the conclusion reached, and indeed, it did not need to do so, because the outcome in that situation was that no reasonable trier of fact could have reached a finding of guilt.

However, if in a given case, the outcome were that a reasonable trier of fact could reach a conclusion of guilt beyond reasonable doubt, the Appeals Chamber considers that, when the Appeals Chamber is itself seized of the task of evaluating trial evidence and additional evidence together, and in some instances in light of a newly articulated legal standard, it should, in the interests of justice, be convinced itself, beyond reasonable doubt, as to the guilt of the accused, before confirming a conviction on appeal. The Appeals Chamber underscores that in such cases, if it were to apply a lower standard, then the outcome would be that neither in the first instance, nor on appeal, would a conclusion of guilt based on the totality of evidence relied upon in the case, assessed in light of the correct legal standard, be reached by either Chamber beyond reasonable doubt.

In sum, when the Appeals Chamber is confronted with an error in the legal standard applied in relation to the factual finding and an alleged error of fact, and additional evidence has been admitted on appeal, there are two steps involved:

(i) The Appeals Chamber will apply the correct legal standard to the evidence contained in the trial record, and will determine whether it is itself convinced beyond reasonable doubt as to the finding of guilt, on the basis of the trial record. If it is not convinced, then no further examination of the matter is necessary as a matter of law.

(ii) If, however, the Appeals Chamber, applying the correct legal standard to the evidence contained in the trial record, is itself convinced beyond reasonable doubt as to the finding of guilt, it will then proceed to determine whether, in light of the trial evidence assessed together with the additional evidence admitted on appeal, it is itself still convinced beyond reasonable doubt as to the finding of guilt.

This standard of review supplements the standard of review employed by the Appeals Chamber in the *Kupreskic* case.

I will now set out in some detail the Appeals Chamber's findings in respect of each ground of appeal.

1. Alleged errors of law concerning Article 7 of the Statute

a) Article 7(1)

The Appellant challenges the standards set forth in the Trial Judgement concerning the forms of criminal participation in Article 7(1) of the Statute.

The Appellant was not convicted for planning or instigating crimes. The issue before the Appeals Chamber is whether a standard of *mens rea* that is lower than direct intent may apply in relation to ordering under Article 7(1) of the Statute.

In the present case, the Trial Chamber in paragraph 474 of the Trial Judgement articulated the following standard and I quote:

Any person who, in ordering an act, knows that there is a risk of crimes being committed and accepts that risk, shows the degree of intention necessary (recklessness) S*le dol éventuel* in the original French textC so as to incur responsibility for having ordered, planned or incited the commitment of the crimes.

Although the Trial Chamber indicated that this standard in paragraph 474 had already been explained earlier in the Trial Judgement, an examination of previous paragraphs pertaining to the legal elements of Article 7 demonstrates that the Trial Chamber did not actually do so. Other paragraphs in the Trial Judgement articulated the standard set out in paragraph 474 using different expressions.

Having examined the approaches of national systems as well as the International Tribunal precedents, the Appeals Chamber considers that the Trial Chamber's articulations of the *mens rea* for ordering under Article 7(1) of the Statute are incorrect. The knowledge of any kind of risk, however low, does not suffice for the imposition of criminal responsibility for serious violations of international humanitarian law. The Trial Chamber does not specify what degree of risk must be proven. Indeed, it appears that under the Trial Chamber's standard, any military commander who issues an order would be criminally responsible, because there is always a possibility that violations could occur.

The Appeals Chamber finds that a person who orders an act or omission with the awareness of the substantial likelihood that a crime will be committed in the execution of that order, has the requisite *mens rea* for establishing liability under Article 7(1) pursuant to ordering. Ordering with such awareness has to be regarded as accepting that crime.

The Appellant also challenges the Trial Chamber's findings in relation to the *actus reus* and *mens rea* requirements for aiding and abetting. In this case, the Trial Chamber correctly followed the standard set out in the *Furundžija* Trial Judgement in respect of the*actus reus* of aiding and abetting.

In relation to the *mens rea* of an aider and abettor, the Trial Chamber held that in addition to knowledge that his acts assist the commission of the crime, the aider and abettor needs to have intended to provide assistance, or as a minimum, accepted that such assistance would be a possible and foreseeable consequence of his conduct. As stated in the *Vasiljevic* Appeal Judgement, knowledge on the part of the aider and abettor that his acts assist in the commission of the principal perpetrator's crime suffices for the *mens rea* requirement of this mode of participation. In this respect, the Trial Chamber erred.

The Appeals Chamber therefore finds that the Trial Chamber was correct in part and erred in part in setting out the legal requirements of aiding and abetting. However, the Trial Chamber did not hold the Appellant responsible for aiding and abetting the crimes at issue. In addition, the Appeals Chamber considers that this form of participation was insufficiently litigated on appeal, and not fairly encompassed by the Second Amended Indictment and the Appeals Chamber declines to consider this form of participation any further.

b) Article 7(3)

The Appellant submits that the Trial Chamber erred in its interpretation of the knowledge requirement under Article 7(3). In respect of this requirement for commanders, the Trial Chamber "holds...that their role obliges them to be constantly informed of the way in which their subordinates carry out the tasks entrusted them, and to take the necessary measures for this purpose."

The Appeals Chamber considers that the *Celebici* Appeal Judgement has settled this issue, and that a superior will be criminally responsible under the principle of superior responsibility only if information was available to him which would have put him on notice of offences committed by subordinates. However, neglect of a duty to acquire such knowledge is not a separate offence under Article 7(3). A superior will not therefore be liable for such failures but only for failing to take necessary and reasonable measures to prevent or to punish. The Trial Judgement's interpretation of the standard is not consistent with the jurisprudence of the Appeals Chamber in this regard and is corrected accordingly.

The Appellant was charged in the Indictment under both Article 7(1) and Article 7(3) of the Statute. From the conclusions drawn by the Trial Chamber in relation to certain events and in view of the Disposition, it is clear that the Trial Chamber considered the merits of the case in terms of both Article 7(1) and Article 7(3) in relation to those events.

But the Appeals Chamber has to express concern at the Disposition of the Trial Judgement wherein the Trial Chamber, having found the Appellant guilty for *ordering* persecutions and for *having committed* other offences on the basis of the same factual findings, further finds that in any event, as a commander, he failed to take the necessary and reasonable measures which would have prevented these crimes or led to the perpetrators thereof to being punished. This statement, which refers to Article 7(3) responsibility, reveals a case of concurrent conviction pursuant to Article 7(1) and Article 7(3) of the Statute, in contradiction with the correct view expressed in paragraph 337 of the Trial Judgement which reads:.

It would be illogical to hold a commander criminally responsible for planning, instigating or ordering the commission of crimes and, at the same time, reproach him for not preventing or punishing them. However, as submitted by the Prosecution, the failure to punish past crimes , which entails the commander's responsibility under Article 7(3), may, pursuant to Article 7(1) and subject to the fulfilment of the respective *mens rea* and *actus reus* requirements, also be the basis for his liability for either aiding and abetting or instigating the commission of *further* crimes.

The provisions of Article 7(1) and Article 7(3) of the Statute connote distinct categories of criminal responsibility. It is not appropriate to convict under both Article 7(1) and Article 7(3) of the Statute in relation to a particular count. Where both Article 7(1) and Article 7(3) responsibility are alleged under the same count, and where the legal requirements pertaining to both of these heads of responsibility are met, a Trial Chamber should enter a conviction on the basis of Article 7(1) only, and consider the accused's superior position as an aggravating factor in sentencing.

The Appeals Chamber therefore considers that the concurrent conviction pursuant to Article 7(1) and Article 7(3) of the Statute in relation to the same counts based on the same facts, as reflected in the Disposition of the Trial Judgement, constitutes a legal error invalidating the Trial Judgement in this regard. Furthermore, where the Trial Chamber did not make any factual findings on the basis of Article 7(3) of the Statute, the Appeals Chamber has not considered this mode of responsibility, notwithstanding the sweeping statement concerning Article 7(3) responsibility contained in the Disposition of the Trial Judgement.

2. Alleged errors of law concerning Article 5 of the Statute

The Appellant submits that the Trial Chamber erred in several significant respects in construing and applying the legal requirements of Article 5, crimes against humanity. This ground of appeal has several elements.

As to the requirement of a widespread or systematic attack, the Appeals Chamber has considered the Trial Chamber's articulation of this element of crimes against humanity and concludes that the Trial Chamber was correct in its analysis of this element.

As to the requirement that the attack be directed against a civilian population, the relevant requirement was set out in the *Kunarac*Appeal Judgement: both the status of the victim as a civilian, and the scale on which the attack is committed or the level of organization involved, characterize a crime against humanity.

In determining the scope of the term "civilian population," the Appeals Chamber considers that the presence within a population of members of resistance groups, or former combatants, who have laid down their arms, does not alter its civilian characteristic. The Trial Chamber was correct in this regard. However, the Trial Chamber erred in part in its characterization of the civilian population and of civilians under Article 5 when it stated that the specific situation of the victim at the time the crimes were committed must be taken into account in determining his standing as a civilian. The victim's specific situation at the time the crimes are committed may not determine his civilian or non-civilian status. If he is indeed a member of an armed organization, the fact that he is not armed or in combat at the time of the commission of crimes, does not accord him civilian status.

The Appeals Chamber further considers that, in order to determine whether the presence of soldiers within a civilian population deprives the population of its civilian character, the number of soldiers, as well as whether they are on leave, must be examined, and that the Trial Chamber erred when it stated that the presence of soldiers within an intentionally targeted civilian population does not alter the civilian nature of that population

As to the requirement that the acts of the accused and the attack itself must have been committed in pursuance to a pre-existing criminal policy or plan, the Appeals Chamber reiterates what was stated in *Kunarac*, that a plan or policy is not a legal element of a crime against humanity, though it may be evidentially relevant in proving that an attack was directed against a civilian population and that it was widespread or systematic. The Trial Judgement was not clear on this point of law.

As to the requirement that the accused has knowledge that his acts formed part of the broader criminal attack, the Appeals Chamber considers that the *mens rea* of crimes against humanity is satisfied when the accused has the requisite intent to commit the underlying offense(s) with which he is charged, and when he knows that there is an attack on the civilian population and also knows that his acts comprise part of that attack. As set out in the Appeals Judgement, the Appeals Chamber finds that the Trial Chamber erred in part in its articulation of the *mens rea* applicable to crimes against humanity.

As to the *actus reus* element of Persecutions as a Crime against Humanity

The Appeals Chamber considers that persecutions as a crime against humanity has already been defined in the case-law of the International Tribunal. The Trial Judgement, however, set forth a definition of persecutions that characterizes the *actus reus* as encompassing infringements upon fundamental human rights. This analysis constituted a failure to assess whether the underlying acts amount to persecutions as a crime against humanity in international customary law. The Trial Chamber erred in this regard.

As set out in the Appeals Judgement, the Appeals Chamber considered each of the types of conduct considered by the Trial Chamber. They were: Killing (or Murder) and Causing Serious Injury; Destruction and Plunder of Property; Deportation, Forcible Transfer, and Forcible Displacement; Inhumane Treatment of Civilians; and Attacks on Cities, Towns, and Villages.

In conclusion, the Appeals Chamber considers that it is evident from the Trial Chamber's analysis of the applicable law on persecutions that it did not consider the requirement that acts of persecutions must be of an equal gravity or severity as the other acts enumerated under Article 5 of the Statute. The Appeals Chamber notes that it is not enough that the underlying acts be perpetrated with a discriminatory intent, and the Trial Chamber erred in this regard.

As to the *mens rea* element of Persecutions as a Crime against Humanity

The Appeals Chamber stresses that there is no requirement in law that the actor possess a "persecutory intent" over and above a discriminatory intent for persecution. The Appeals Chamber also emphasises that the *mens rea* of the perpetrator carrying out acts of persecutions requires evidence of a specific intent to discriminate on political, racial, or religious grounds. The Trial Chamber was correct when it held that the *mens rea* for persecutions "is the specific intent to cause injury to a human being because he belongs to a particular community or group."

Second, the Appeals Chamber is aware that in making its factual findings relating to the ordering of crimes under Article 7(1) of the Statute, the Trial Chamber frequently employed language such as "took the risk" or "deliberately ran the risk." The Appeals Chamber has articulated above, the *mens rea* applicable to ordering a crime in the absence of direct intent. Thus, an individual who orders an act with the awareness of a substantial likelihood that persecutions as a crime against humanity will be committed in the execution of the order, may be liable under Article 7(1) for the crime of persecutions. Ordering with such awareness has to be regarded as accepting that crime.

3. Alleged errors of law in application of Article 2 of the Statute

The offences covered by Article 2 of the Statute must be committed against persons or property protected under the provisions of the Geneva Conventions. Article 4(1) of Geneva Convention IV defines protected persons as "those who, at a given moment and in any manner whatsoever, find themselves, in case of a conflict or occupation, in the hands of a Party to the Conflict or Occupying Power of which they are not nationals." The *Tadic* Appeals Chamber concluded that this provision is directed to the protection of civilians to the maximum extent possible, and that even if in the circumstances of that case the perpetrators and the victims were to be regarded as possessing the same nationality, Article 4 would still be applicable.

Applying the same principles in the context of the conflict between the Bosnian Croats and the Bosnian Muslims, the Appeals Chamber in *Aleksovski* reasoned that since the conflict was international by reason of Croatia's participation, it would follow that the Bosnian Muslim victims were in the hands of a party to the conflict, Croatia, of which they were not nationals and that, therefore, Article 4 of Geneva Convention IV was applicable. The Appeals Chamber in *Celebici* reaffirmed and elaborated upon these principles when considering their implications for Bosnian Serbs held by Bosnian Muslims.

The Appeals Chamber finds that there is no merit in the Appellant's assertion that, under the "allegiance test," Bosnian Croats would not qualify as "protected" *vis-à-vis* Bosnian Muslim captors. The Appeals Chamber finds that there is no merit in the Appellant's assertion that the present case can be distinguished from the *Tadic* and *Celebici* cases on the basis that the Bosnian Serbs, unlike the Bosnian Croats, were attempting to secede from Bosnia-Herzegovina.

Arguments that the victims should be excluded from the status of "protected persons" according to a strict construction of the language of Article 4 of Geneva Convention IV, have already been rejected by the Appeals Chamber. The Appeals Chamber is satisfied, therefore, that the principle of legality has not been violated in this case. The Appeals Chamber sees no error in the Trial Chamber's determination in this respect.

The Appellant further submits that the "protected persons" requirement is based upon Article 4(2) of Geneva Convention IV, which provides that "nationals of a co-belligerent State, shall not be regarded as protected persons while the State of which they are nationals has normal diplomatic representation in the State in whose hands they are."

The Appeals Chamber considers that it is evident, both from the text of Article 4(2) of Geneva Convention IV and the accompanying Commentary, that for Article 4(2) to be relevant, it must be demonstrated, first, that the States were allies and second, that they enjoyed *effective* and *satisfactory* diplomatic representation with each other. The States of Croatia and Bosnia-Herzegovina were engaged in a conflict against each other. This, in itself, establishes that they were not co-belligerents within the meaning Article 4(2). This ground of appeal therefore fails.

4. Alleged errors concerning denial of due process of law

The Appellant claims that he was unfairly denied his right to a fair trial under Article 21 of the Statute of the International Tribunal in two principal ways: (i) he was tried and convicted on the basis of a "fatally vague" indictment; and (ii) the Prosecution failed to meet its disclosure obligations with respect to exculpatory evidence under Rule 68 of the Rules. The Appellant contends that this deprived him of the due process of law, and materially prejudiced his ability to prepare and present his defence.

a) Vagueness of the Indictment

On 21 November 1996, the first indictment was amended to charge the Appellant with 19 counts. On 4 April 1997, the Trial Chamber granted the Appellant's motion objecting to the amended indictment, and ordered the Prosecution to further amend the indictment. The Prosecution filed a Second Amended Indictment on 25 April 1997. The Appellant again challenged the Second Amended Indictment, and the Trial Chamber issued a second decision on 10 June 1997 whereby it ruled that the Second Amended indictment was defective; however, it decided to begin the trial without instructing the Prosecution to amend the Second Amended Indictment.

Having raised the issue twice before the Trial Chamber, and having received from the Trial Chamber a specific assurance that the Trial Chamber would *not fail* to draw all the legal consequences at trial of the possible total or partial failure to satisfy the obligations incumbent upon the Prosecution, insofar as that failure *inter alia* might not have permitted the accused to prepare his defence, the Appeals Chamber considers that the Appellant was entitled to assume that the Trial Chamber would adhere to its prior commitment, and concludes that the Appellant has not waived his right to raise the issue of the vagueness of the indictment on appeal.

Having analysed the Second Amended Indictment in accordance with the principles of pleading set out in this Judgement, the Appeals Chamber finds that the Second Amended Indictment failed to plead the material facts with sufficient particularity, and concludes that the Second Amended Indictment does not comply with the principles of pleading set out in the present Judgement.

The Appeals Chamber's review of the trial record however suggests that the Prosecution did clearly present the necessary information to put the Appellant on notice of the nature of its case against him during the trial. The Appeals Chamber concludes that defects in the Second Amended Indictment did not hamper the Appellant's ability to prepare his defence and thus render his trial unfair. As a result, the Appeals Chamber dismisses this aspect of the ground of appeal.

b) Alleged violations of Rule 68 of the Rules

The Appellant alleges that the Prosecution violated Rule 68 of the Rules by failing to disclose Exhibits 2, 16, and 25 to the Second Rule 115 Motion, and Exhibit H1.

The Appeals Chamber concludes as to Exhibit 2, the Prosecution did not violate Rule 68. With respect to Exhibits 16 and 25, the Appeals Chamber concludes that the Appellant has not suffered material prejudice. With respect to Exhibit H1, the Appeals Chamber considers the Prosecution's failure to disclose this exhibit constitutes a breach of its obligations under Rule 68. However, in light of the fact that the Appellant was able to call Witness Watkins to testify during the hearing on appeal, the Appeals Chamber concludes that the prejudice caused to the Appellant has been remedied.

Consequently, even though the Appeals Chamber considers that the Prosecution did violate Rule 68, in light of the absence of material prejudice to the Appellant in this case, dismisses this aspect of the appeal.

5. Alleged errors concerning the Appellant's responsibility for crimes committed in the Ahmici area

Appellant's Responsibility under Article 7(1)

The Trial Chamber convicted the Appellant pursuant to Article 7(1) for crimes that targeted the Muslim civilian population and were perpetrated as a result of his *ordering* the Viteska Brigade, the Nikola Subic Zrinski Brigade, the 4th Military Police Battalion, the D`okeri (Jokers), the Vitezovi and the Domobrani to offensively attack Ahmici and neighbouring villages. The Appeals Chamber considers that the

Appellant's conviction under Article 7(1) is based upon the following findings reached by the Trial Chamber: (i) that the attack was organised, planned at the highest level of the military hierarchy and targeted the Muslim civilian population in Ahmici; (ii) that the Military Police, the Jokers, the Domobrani, and regular HVO (including the Viteska Brigade) took part in the fighting, and no military objective justified the attacks; and (iii) that the Appellant had "command authority" over the Viteska Brigade, the Domobrani, the 4th MP Battalion, and the Jokers during the period in question.

In support of the Appellant's conviction pursuant to Article 7(1) of the Statute, the Trial Chamber found that exhibit D269 was "very clearly" an order to attack, addressed to the Viteska Brigade, the 4th MP Battalion, the forces of the Nikola Subic Zrinski Brigade and the forces of the civilian police which the Trial Chamber stated were recognised on the ground as being those which had carried out the attack.

The Appeals Chamber considers that the Trial Chamber's assessment of Exhibit D269 as reflected in the Trial Judgement, diverges significantly from that of the Appeals Chamber following its review. The Appeals Chamber considers that the Trial Chamber's assessment was wholly erroneous.

The Appeals Chamber considers that the trial evidence does not support the Trial Chamber's conclusion that the ABiH forces were not preparing for combat in the Ahmici area. In addition, the Appeals Chamber notes that additional evidence admitted on appeal, shows that there was a Muslim military presence in Ahmici, and that the Appellant had reason to believe that the ABiH intended to launch an attack along the Ahmici - Santici -Dubravica axis. Consequently, the Appeals Chamber considers that there was a military justification for the Appellant to issue D269.

In light of the analysis of the Trial Chamber's interpretation of D269 and on the basis of the relevant evidence before the Trial Chamber, the Appeals Chamber concludes that no reasonable trier of fact could have reached the conclusion that D269 was issued "with the clear intention that the massacre would be committed," or that it gave rise to the crimes committed in Ahmici on 16 April 1993.

The Trial Chamber found that in addition to the Military Police, and the Jokers, regular HVO units, in particular the Viteska Brigade, took part in the fighting in the Ahmici area on 16 April 1993, and concluded that the crimes committed were not the work of the Military Police alone but were also ascribable to the regular HVO units, in particular, the Viteska Brigade and the Domobrani.

The Appeals Chamber considers that the finding that the Viteska Brigade and the Domobrani took part in the commission of crimes during the attack on Ahmici and neighbouring villages, on the basis of the trial record, was a tenuous finding. The Appeals Chamber stresses that the additional evidence admitted on appeal fatally undermines the said finding and suggests that the crimes committed in the Ahmici area on 16 April 1993 were perpetrated by the Jokers and the 4th MP Battalion. For the foregoing reasons, the Appeals Chamber considers that the Trial Chamber's finding that the crimes committed in Ahmici "were also ascribable to the regular HVO units, in particular, the *Viteska* Brigade and the Domobrani," cannot be sustained on appeal.

The Appeals Chamber considers that some documents admitted as additional evidence on appeal, support the assertion that the 4th MP Battalion and the Jokers committed the crimes in the Ahmici area on 16 April 1993, and identify others as those responsible for planning and ordering the massacre.

The Trial Chamber concluded that since the Appellant knew that some of the troops engaged in the attack on Ahmici had previously participated in criminal acts against the Muslim population of Bosnia or had criminals within their ranks, when ordering those troops to launch an attack on the village of Ahmici pursuant to D269, the Appellant deliberately took the risk that crimes would be committed against the Muslim civilian population in Ahmici and their property.
The Appeals Chamber has articulated the *mens rea* applicable to ordering a crime under Article 7(1) of the Statute, in the absence of direct intent. The Trial Chamber did not apply this standard in relation to the Appellant's conviction under Article 7(1).

The analysis of the evidence relied upon by the Trial Chamber supports the conclusion that concrete measures had been taken to deter the occurrence of criminal activities, and for the removal of criminal elements once they had been identified. The Appeals Chamber considers that the orders and reports relied upon by the Trial Chamber do not constitute sufficient evidence to meet the legal standard articulated by the Appeals Chamber.

Therefore, the Appeals Chamber is not satisfied that the relevant trial evidence, assessed together with the additional evidence admitted on appeal prove beyond reasonable doubt that the Appellant is responsible under Article 7(1) of the Statute for ordering the crimes committed in Ahmici and neighbouring villages on 16 April 1993.

Appellant's Responsibility under Article 7(3)

The Appeals Chamber considers that besides finding the Appellant guilty under Article 7(1), the Trial Chamber also entered a conviction against the Appellant for his superior criminal responsibility under Article 7(3) of the Statute.

The Appeals Chamber concludes that on the basis of the relevant evidence before the Trial Chamber, and in particular the Appellant's admission that troops from the Military Police could be attached to him for *ad hoc* missions pursuant to specific requests, a reasonable trier of fact could have concluded, as the Trial Chamber did, that the Appellant had "command authority" over the Military Police.

The Appeals Chamber determined whether in light of the trial evidence assessed together with the additional evidence admitted on appeal, it is itself convinced beyond reasonable doubt as to whether the Appellant had effective control over the Military Police.

The Appeals Chamber considers that evidence admitted on appeal shows that: (a) members of the Military Police were involved in criminal activities; (b) suggests that the Military Police enjoyed the protection of, and often acted on orders of others; and (c) bolsters the conclusion that the Appellant's authority was not recognized by the members of the Military Police, and that his orders were not carried out. The Appeals Chamber also heard evidence on appeal which reveals that the Military Police units, including the Jokers, were not *de facto* commanded by the Appellant.

The Appeals Chamber finds that the Trial Chamber erred in its interpretation of the mental element "had reason to know." Its analysis of the evidence underlying the Trial Chamber's finding that the Appellant knew that crimes had been or were about to be committed, reveals no evidence that the Appellant *had information* which put him on notice that crimes had been committed by his subordinates in the

Ahmici area on 16 April 1993. Further, the additional evidence admitted on appeal lends support to the Appellant's argument that he had no reason to believe that crimes had been committed in light of the military conflict taking place at that time between the HVO and the ABiH.

The Appeals Chamber considers that the trial evidence assessed together with the additional evidence admitted on appeal shows that the Appellant took the measures that were reasonable within his material ability to denounce the crimes committed, and supports the conclusion that the Appellant requested that an investigation into the crimes committed in Ahmici be carried out, that the investigation was taken over by SIS Mostar, that he was not informed of the results of the investigation, and that the names of the perpetrators were not disclosed to him.

For the foregoing reasons, and having examined the legal requirements for responsibility under Article 7(3) of the Statute, the Appeals Chamber concludes that the Appellant lacked effective control over the military units responsible for the commission of crimes in the Ahmici area on 16 April 1993, in the sense of a material ability to prevent or punish criminal conduct, and therefore the constituent elements of command responsibility have not been satisfied. The Appeals Chamber is therefore not satisfied that the trial evidence, assessed together with the additional evidence admitted on appeal, proves beyond reasonable doubt that the Appellant is responsible under Article 7(3) of the Statute for having failed to prevent the commission of crimes in the Ahmici area on 16 April 1993 or to punish the perpetrators.

6. Alleged errors concerning the Appellant's responsibility for crimes committed in other parts of the Vitez Municipality

The main argument of the Appellant is that the Trial Chamber erred by attributing crimes associated with military action in the Vitez Municipality to the Appellant as a superior officer of the HVO in the area. On the other hand, the Appellant never disputes that he had *de jure* authority to command regular HVO troops in Central Bosnia, generally, or that he ordered certain military actions in the Vitez Municipality in 1993.

A finding that the Appellant is guilty for ordering certain crimes, for failing to prevent the crimes or to punish the perpetrators after the commission of the crimes , cannot stand on the sole ground that he was the *de jure* commander of the perpetrators, as the Trial Chamber found. Second, the Appeals Chamber considers that in the context of this armed conflict which had been in the making for some time, involving both sides, the issue as to which side *initiated* the conflict is irrelevant for the purposes of determining the nature of its actions during the conflict. What concerns the International Tribunal is whether crimes were committed during the conflict and by whom.

a) The Appellant's responsibility under Article 7(1) of the Statute

In respect of the attacks on the town of Vitez on 16 April 1993, the Appeals Chamber accepts that a reasonable trier of fact could have reached the finding of the Trial Chamber that the attack against units of the ABiH army who were present in the town of Vitez was unlawful.

However, in the light of additional evidence, the Appeals Chamber does not consider it to be proved beyond reasonable doubt that the attack was directed at a civilian target, or that the attack targeted the civilian population of the town of Vitez, and it considers that the Trial Chamber's finding regarding civilian casualty figures in connection with the 16 April 1993 attack cannot be relied on in determining the nature of that attack.

Furthermore, no reasonable trier of fact could have found, on the basis of the trial evidence, that the Appellant knew of the risk that crimes might be committed during that attack. *A fortiori*, the trial evidence cannot satisfy beyond reasonable doubt the correct standard pronounced by the Appeals Chamber in this Judgement.

As to the lorry bombingof 18 April 1993, the Appeals Chamber accepts the finding of the Trial Chamber that the bombing of the lorry was a terrorist operation and a crime against humanity. However, no evidence was cited by the Trial Chamber that the Appellant ordered the bombing.

The Appeals Chamber has carefully considered trial and additional evidence and rebuttal material relevant to this argument, and is satisfied beyond reasonable doubt that the explosion was caused by explosives. This part of the finding of the Trial Chamber stands. However, the Appeals Chamber considers that the trial and additional evidence does not satisfy it beyond reasonable doubt that the explosives used could not be secured without the authorization of the Appellant.

As to the 18 July 1993 attack on Stari Vitez, the Appeals Chamber considers that the Appellant has not shown that no reasonable trier of fact could have reached the conclusion of the Trial Chamber that the Appellant ordered the attack on Stari Vitez on 18 July 1993. However, the nature of the attack of 18 July 1993 cannot be categorically defined as that of a criminal act, in that there was still the presence of a considerable number of ABiH soldiers in Stari Vitez at that time.

On the basis of the trial and additional evidence, the Appeals Chamber is not satisfied beyond reasonable doubt either that the attack of 18 July 1993 resulted in heavy casualties among Muslim civilians as a result of the "baby bombs", or that the attack was directed at the Muslim civilian population or civilian property in Stari Vitez.

The Appeals Chamber concludes that the trial and additional evidence does not prove beyond reasonable doubt that the Appellant ordered the attack with the awareness of a substantial likelihood that "baby bombs" would be used against the Muslim civilian population or their property during the attack. The finding that the Appellant ordered the attack as a crime against humanity is therefore reversed.

As to the crimes committed in April and September 1993 in the villages of Donja Veceriska, Gacice, and Grbavica, the Trial Chamber found that the villages attacked could have represented a military interest such as to justify their being the target of an attack, and that the Trial Chamber also found the Appellant guilty of crimes, including destruction, pillage, and forcible transfer of civilians, because he ordered the attacks which "he could only reasonably have anticipated would lead to crimes". The Appeals Chamber has now applied the correct standard in this regard , and considers that trial evidence does not prove beyond reasonable doubt that the Appellant ordered the attacks on the villages with the awareness of a substantial likelihood that crimes would be committed during the attack.

The Appellant's convictions under Article 7(1) of the Statute for the crimes committed in the three villages are all reversed.

b) The Appellant's Responsibility under Article 7(3) of the Statute

The remaining question is whether the Appellant should bear any responsibility under Article 7(3) of the Statute in relation to these attacks.

In relation to the attack of 16 April 1993, and to the lorry bombing of 18 April 1993 the Appeal Chamber considers that there was no finding in the Trial Judgement, and there is no evidence to show, that the Appellant knew or had reason to know before the attack that crimes were about to be committed by the units under his command. The issue of prevention of crimes does not, therefore, arise from these two events.

In respect of the attack on Stari Vitez of 18 July 1993, there was no finding and there is no evidence to show that he knew or had reason to know beforehand that the "baby bombs" would be used in that attack, so the question of preventing the using of those bombs on civilian targets does not arise.

The Appeals Chamber therefore concludes that on the basis of the trial findings and evidence admitted on appeal, the issue of failure to prevent in terms of Article 7(3) of the Statute does not arise in relation to this part of the case.

The Appellant then submits that additional evidence shows that the Vitezovi unit was outside his command and often acted under the direct orders of Kordic and the Ministry of Defence in Mostar.

As to whether the Appellant exercised effective control over the Vitezovi, on the basis of the trial and additional evidence before it, the Appeals Chamber is satisfied beyond reasonable doubt that the Appellant had *de jure* command over that unit. If reporting criminal acts of subordinates to appropriate authorities is evident of the material ability to punish them in the circumstances of a certain case, albeit only to a very limited degree, the Appellant had that limited ability in this case. His command responsibility is, consequently, an issue in this case.

The Trial Chamber did not set out the necessary factual basis for its finding that the Appellant failed to punish, among others, the Vitezovi for their crimes committed in the town of. This lack of analysis of relevant evidence on a critical element of the criminal responsibility of the Appellant alone justifies overturning the relevant convictions of the Appellant under Article 7(3).

However, the Trial Chamber made no assessment of the evidence submitted at trial by the Appellant that he initiated an investigation into the lorry bombing of 18 April 1993 and reported the result of the investigation to his superiors, and that he reported to his superiors the attack of 18 July 1993 by the Vitezovi on Stari Vitez. In relation to the first of these two incidents, no reasonable trier of fact could have reached the conclusion of the Trial Chamber that the Appellant failed to punish in relation to that offence.

As to the report of the attack of 18 July 1993, on the basis of trial and additional evidence, the Appeals Chamber is not satisfied beyond reasonable doubt that the Vitezovi committed an offence by using the "baby bombs". Without the Appellent knowing that his subordinates used "baby bombs" in that attack, the question of his superior responsibility does not arise.

In respect of the attack of 16 April 1993, no reasonable trier of fact could have, in the absence of a proper factual basis, reached the conclusion of the Trial Chamber that the Appellant should be held responsible under Article 7(3) of the Statute for the failure to punish in relation to the crimes that occurred during the attack.

7. Alleged errors concerning the Appellant's responsibility for crimes committed in the Busovaca Municipality

The Trial Chamber found the Appellant responsible for the attacks on the villages of Loncari and Ocehnici in April 1993. The Trial Chamber also found that by giving orders to the Military Police in April 1993, the Appellant intentionally took the risk that very violent crimes would result.

The Appellant submitted that he did not issue any orders for an attack on Loncari or Ocehnici, and that the Trial Chamber erred in attributing crimes committed by the Military Police, including the Jokers, to him.

Having examined the findings of the Trial Chamber outlined above, the Appeals Chamber considers that the Trial Chamber made a finding pursuant to Article 7(1) of the Statute. The Appeals Chamber will apply the correct legal standard to determine whether the Appellant is responsible under Article 7(1) of the Statute for the crimes in Loncari and Ocehnici.

Given the absence of direct evidence that the Appellant ordered the attacks in Loncari and Ocehnici in April 1993, the Appeals Chamber finds that no reasonable trier of fact could conclude beyond reasonable doubt that the Appellant ordered these attacks. The Appeals Chamber notes that the additional evidence admitted on appeal only bolsters this conclusion. As a result, it is not necessary to examine whether the Appellant was aware of a substantial likelihood that crimes would be committed.

In light of the parties' submissions on the issue, and in order to clarify the point, the Appeals Chamber also deems it necessary to discuss the apparent finding of the Trial Chamber that the Appellant was responsible for implementing — not ordering — attacks in January 1993 in Busovaca. The Appeals Chamber considers that the Trial Chamber did not discuss evidence in relation to or assess the Appellant's responsibility for crimes committed in Busovaca in January 1993. As a result, the Appeals Chamber considers that no finding was made pursuant to Article 7(1) of the Statute in relation to the January 1993 attacks in Busovaca.

In relation to the Appellant's command responsibility for the crimes committed in Busovaca, the Appeals Chamber considers that the Trial Chamber failed to examine and to discuss in an adequate manner the evidence before it, in relation to the legal requirements of Article 7(3) of the Statute. As a result, the Appeals Chamber concludes that no finding was made pursuant to Article 7(3) of the Statute concerning the crimes committed in Loncari and Ocehnici in April 1993, and it declines to consider the issue any further.

In relation to Count 14 of the Indictment, concerning the destruction of religious or educational property, the Appellant submitted that the Trial Judgement was vague and failed to identify the evidence of such destruction in Busovaca. In the Disposition, the Trial Chamber found the Appellant guilty on the basis of Count 14 pursuant to Article 7(1) and 7(3), but in the section of the Trial Judgement concerning Busovaca, there is no discussion or analysis pertaining to the charges contained in Count 14, and no specific finding. In light of the foregoing, the Appeals Chamber considers that the conviction under Count 14 of the Indictment in relation to Busovaca must be vacated.

8. Alleged errors concerning the Appellant's responsibility for crimes committed in the Kiseljak Municipality

The Appeals Chamber considers that the Trial Chamber did not find that the Appellant ordered the crimes in Kiseljak in April 1993. Instead, the Trial Chamber found that the Appellant "deliberately ran the risk" of making Muslims and their property the main targets of these offensives, and concluded that he "had to have known" that by ordering such attacks, very violent crimes would result. The Appeals Chamber will apply the correct legal standard to determine whether the Appellant is responsible under Article 7(1) of the Statute for the crimes which occurred in April 1993 in Kiseljak.

The Appeals Chamber notes that the Trial Chamber found that through the offensives and the military assets employed, the Appellant intended to make these populations flee. In the view of the Appeals Chamber, the Trial Chamber seemed to find that the Appellant intended to effect forcible transfers of civilians through these offensives.

In support of its assertion that the Appellant deliberately ran the risk of making Muslim civilians and their property the primary targets of the offensives launched on 18 April 1993, the Trial Chamber had found that the combat preparation order (D299) and combat order (D300) were categorical and hate-engendering, that the Appellant employed terms in these orders which were not strictly military and had emotional connotations which were such as to incite hatred and vengeance against the Muslim populations. The Trial Chamber had further considered that the Appellant used radical words connoting eradication, and cited the term "mop up" contained in D300 as an example.

The Appeals Chamber considers that the trial evidence illustrates that there were military motivations underlying the issuance of the Appellant's orders. The Appeals Chamber finds that on the basis of the evidence relied upon by the Trial Chamber, no reasonable trier of fact could have come to the conclusion beyond reasonable doubt that the Appellant intended to effect forcible transfers of civilians. The Appeals Chamber further finds that this evidence does not prove beyond reasonable doubt that the Appellant was aware of a substantial likelihood that crimes would be committed in the execution of his orders. For the foregoing reasons, the Appeals Chamber finds that no reasonable trier of fact could conclude that the Appellant was responsible under Article 7(1) of the Statute for the crimes committed in April 1993 in Kiseljak.

Additional evidence heard on appeal confirms that the language contained in D300 does not necessarily connote eradication or forcible transfer.

As to the June 1993 attacks, in Kiseljak, the Appeals Chamber observes that in concluding that the Appellant ordered the attacks, the Trial Chamber did not refer to any evidence which would show that he did so. Indeed, there is no evidence on the record showing that the Appellant ordered these attacks. The Appeals Chamber finds that no reasonable trier of fact could have come to the conclusion beyond reasonable doubt that the Appellant ordered the June 1993 attacks in Kiseljak. As a result, it is not necessary to examine whether the Appellant was aware of a substantial likelihood that crimes would be committed. The Appeals Chamber therefore finds that no reasonable trier of fact could conclude that the Appellant was responsible under Article 7(1) of the Statute for the crimes committed in Kiseljak in June 1993.

The Appeals Chamber further observes that in the Trial Judgement, there is no discussion pertaining to Article 7(3) responsibility on the part of the Appellant for crimes committed in April 1993 and June 1993. As a result, the Appeals Chamber concludes that no finding was made pursuant to Article 7(3) in relation to the June 1993 attacks in Kiseljak, and it declines to consider the issue any further.

9. Alleged errors concerning the Appellant's responsibility for detention-related crimes

The Trial Judgement addressed Counts 15 to 20 of the Second Amended Indictment in a section entitled "detention related crimes", as they all entail a deprivation of freedom.

a) Counts 15 and 16: Inhuman and cruel treatment

The Trial Chamber found that the Appellant was guilty pursuant to Article 7(3) of the Statute for the crimes committed in various detention facilities, and pursuant to Article 7(1) of the Statute for crimes associated with trench-digging.

The Appeals Chamber considers that the text of the Trial Judgement is insufficiently clear as to how the Trial Chamber justified its conclusion that the Appellant ordered the detentions, it is a conclusion arrived at by extrapolation. As a result, the Appeals Chamber finds that no reasonable trier of fact could have concluded that the Appellant ordered the detentions, and the finding of the Trial Chamber is overturned.

The Trial Chamber also found the Appellant guilty pursuant to Article 7(1) of the Statute of ordering the detainees to dig trenches, and for the treatment they suffered as a result. The Appeals Chamber finds that the use of persons taking no active part in hostilities to prepare military fortifications for use in operations and against the forces with whom those persons identify or sympathise is a serious attack on human dignity and causes serious mental (and depending on the circumstances physical) suffering or injury and that any order to compel persons taking no active part in the hostilities to dig trenches or to prepare other forms of military installations under such circumstances constitutes cruel treatment.

The Appeals Chamber accordingly finds that a reasonable trier of fact could have come to the conclusion that the Appellant has violated the Laws or Customs of War under Article 3 of the Statute, and is guilty under Count 16 for ordering the use of detainees to dig trenches.

The Trial Chamber further found that the Appellant, by ordering the forced labour, knowingly took the risk that his soldiers might commit violent acts against vulnerable detainees. The Appeals Chamber finds that there is insufficient evidence from which to draw the conclusion beyond reasonable doubt that the Appellant ordered that detainees be used to dig trenches with the awareness of the substantial likelihood that crimes would be committed in the execution of those orders. On the contrary, while there is evidence that the Appellant did order trenches to be dug by detainees in specific instances, the evidence does not prove beyond reasonable doubt that the Appellant ordered that trenches be dug with the awareness of the substantial likelihood that crimes would be committed. The Appellant is therefore not guilty of Counts 15 and 16 under Article 7(1) of the Statute for the crimes associated with trench-digging.

The Appeals Chamber considers that the Trial Chamber found that the Appellant knew of the circumstances and conditions under which the

Muslims were detained in the facilities and in any case did not perform his duties with the necessary reasonable diligence.

The trial evidence considered demonstrates that the Appellant on occasion knew of the mistreatment of non-combatant Bosnian Muslims in detention facilities. Furthermore, the Appeals Chamber has considered evidence from the trial record illustrating that detainees were held in locations in close proximity to the Appellant's headquarters in Vitez, namely: the Vitez Cultural Centre (containing the Cinema Hall) and the Vitez veterinary hospital.

The Appeals Chamber concludes that it was open to a reasonable trier of fact to conclude beyond reasonable doubt that the Appellant knew that detainees had been unlawfully detained in the two locations of the Vitez Cultural Centre (containing the Cinema Hall) and the Vitez veterinary hospital, and that he was aware that the conditions of their detention had been unlawful. This conclusion has not been contradicted by evidence admitted on appeal.

The Appeals Chamber is convinced beyond reasonable doubt that the Appellant, notwithstanding his knowledge that detention-related crimes had been committed in the Vitez Cultural Centre and the Vitez veterinary hospital, failed to punish those subordinates of his who were responsible, and over whom he was able to exercise effective control, and he failed to report the infractions of which he was aware to the competent authorities. The Appellant is, accordingly, guilty under Count 15 of grave breaches of the Geneva Conventions (inhuman treatment) pursuant to Articles 2(b) and 7(3) of the Statute.

b) Counts 17 and 18: Hostage-taking

The Trial Chamber convicted the Appellant of taking hostages, first for use in prisoner exchanges, and second in order to deter ABiH military operations against the HVO.

The Trial Chamber found that the Appellant did not order that hostages be taken or used, but that certain detainees were "threatened with death" in order to prevent the ABiH advance on Vitez, and that the Appellant was responsible by virtue of having ordered the defence of Vitez.

The Appeals Chamber considers, that it does not follow that the Appellant incurred criminal responsibility for someone else's unlawful choice of how to execute his legitimate order. There is no necessary causal nexus between an order to defend a position and the taking of hostages, and the Trial Chamber was wrong so to infer.

The Trial Chamber's finding is not supported by the evidence, and no reasonable trier of fact could have made that finding. The findings of the Trial Chamber with respect to hostage-taking are overturned.

c) Counts 19 and 20: Human Shields

The Trial Chamber found that the Appellant ordered the use of detainees as human shields to protect the headquarters of the Appellant at the Hotel Vitez on 20 April 1993, which inflicted considerable mental suffering upon the persons involved.

The use of prisoners of war or civilian detainees as human shields is prohibited by the provisions of the Geneva Conventions, and it may constitute inhuman or cruel treatment under Articles 2 and 3 of the Statute respectively where the other elements of these crimes are met. Using protected detainees as human shields constitutes a violation of the provisions of the Geneva Conventions regardless of whether those human shields were actually attacked or harmed. Indeed, the prohibition is designed to protect detainees from being exposed to the risk of harm, and not only to the harm itself. To the extent that the Trial Chamber considered the intensity of the shelling of Vitez on 20 April 1993, that consideration was superfluous to an analysis of a breach of the provisions of the Geneva Conventions, but may be relevant to whether the use of the protected detainees as human shields amounts to inhuman treatment for the purposes of Article 2 of the Statute.

The Trial Chamber had no evidence before it permitting it to conclude that the Appellant positively ordered the use of the detainees as human shields. The Appeals Chamber finds that the reasoning of the Trial Chamber in finding the Appellant responsible for positively ordering the use of civilian detainees as human shields is flawed. A factual conclusion that detainees were in fact used as human shields on a particular occasion does not lead to the inference that the Appellant positively ordered that to be done.

A conviction under Article 7(1) is not, however, limited to the positive act of ordering. The Appeals Chamber notes that the Appellant was indicted by the Second Amended Indictment for having – through acts and omissions - planned, instigated, ordered or otherwise aided and abetted in the planning, preparation or execution of the unlawful and inhumane treatment of Bosnian Muslims. The Second Amended Indictment therefore fairly charges the Appellant with other forms of participation under Article 7(1) of the Statute in addition to the positive act of ordering. In particular, criminal responsibility for an omission pursuant to Article 7(1) of the Statute is expressly envisaged by the Second Amended Indictment.

The Appeals Chamber considers that the use of the detainees as human shields caused them serious mental harm and constituted a serious attack on human dignity, and concludes that the Appellant's conviction for the use of human shields under Count 19 was correct in substance. However, in the absence of proof that he positively ordered the use of human shields, the Appellant's criminal responsibility is properly expressed as an omission pursuant to Article 7(1) as charged in the Second Amended Indictment. The Appeals Chamber accordingly finds that the elements constituting the crime of inhuman treatment have been met: and that the Appellant is guilty under Article 7(1) for the inhuman treatment of detainees occasioned by their use as human shields, pursuant to Article 2(b) of the Statute.

10. Appeal Against Sentence

The Trial Chamber sentenced the Appellant to forty-five years' imprisonment, and the Appellant has appealed against this sentence. The Appellant contends that the sentence imposed on him should be vacated.

The Appeals Chamber has emphasised in previous judgements that sentencing is a discretionary decision and that it is inappropriate to set down a definitive list of sentencing guidelines. The sentence must always be decided according to the facts of each particular case and the individual guilt of the perpetrator.

In this case, the Appeals Chamber heard several arguments by the Appellant against the Trial Chamber's sentence. These arguments have been considered in the Judgement of the Appeals Chamber, but will mostly not be discussed in this hearing in the interests of brevity.

However, the Appeals Chamber considers that it was wrong for the Trial Chamber to hold that "it is impossible to identify which acts would relate to which of the various counts - other than those supporting the prosecution for and conviction of persecution under count 1." Where it is impossible to identify which acts would relate to which of the various counts, it is likewise impossible to arrive at distinct convictions. Either an accused person is guilty of different crimes constituted by different elements which may sometimes overlap (but never entirely), or the accused is convicted of that crime with the most specific elements, and the remaining counts in which those elements are duplicated are dismissed as impermissibly cumulative. The Appeals Chamber finds that the reasoning of the Trial Chamber is wrong in law. The Trial Chamber also erred in failing to consider the Appellant's real and sincere remorse as a mitigating factor, and in considering his discriminatory intent as an aggravating factor in light of his conviction for persecutions at trial.

The Appeals Chamber has granted part of the appeal of the Appellant against his sentence. In this case, however, the application of the established test for the revising of a sentence would be inappropriate. The Appeals Chamber in this appeal is being called upon not simply to affirm or revise the sentence imposed by the Trial Chamber, but rather to impose a sentence *de novo*. Instead of revising the sentence of the Trial Chamber, the Appeals Chamber will substitute its own reasoned sentence for that of a Trial Chamber on the basis of its own findings, a function which the Appeals Chamber considers that it may perform in this case without remitting the case to the Trial Chamber.

The Appeals Chamber notes that no evidence has been presented to suggest that the Appellant is of bad character, but that several witnesses were at pains to point out the Appellant's good character, his equitable treatment of Bosnian Muslims both before and during the war and the absence of any bias against Bosnian Muslims, and his professionalism as a soldier. There was also evidence of respect for him by his ABiH opponents, and several witnesses attested to the fact that he is a man of duty. Furthermore, the Appellant is a father to young children.

In its discussion of the factors relevant to sentencing above, the Appeals Chamber has identified the following factors as aggravating circumstances proved beyond reasonable doubt: (i) the position of the accused as a colonel in the HVO, and his position as commander of the regional forces in the CBOZ; and (ii) the fact that many of the victims of the crimes of which the Appellant has been found guilty were civilians.

As mitigating circumstances proved on the balance of probabilities: (i) the Appellant's voluntary surrender to the International Tribunal; (ii) his real and sincere expression of remorse; (iii) his good character with no prior criminal convictions; (iv) his record of good comportment at trial and in detention; (v) his personal and family circumstances, including his poor health; (vi) his having been detained for over 8 years pending a final outcome in his case; and (vii) his particular circumstances at the outbreak of and during the war.

Rule 87(C) provides that a Chamber may decide to exercise its power to impose a single sentence reflecting the totality of the criminal conduct of the accused, and the Appeals Chamber decides to impose a single sentence in this case, as the criminal conduct for which he has been convicted forms part of similar overall behavior, and occurred within a close temporal context.

DISPOSITION

For the foregoing reasons, **THE APPEALS CHAMBER**

PURSUANT to Article 25 of the Statute and Rules 117 and 118 of the Rules;

NOTING the respective written submissions of the parties and the arguments they presented at the hearings of 16 and 17 December 2003;

SITTING in open session;

DISMISSES the Appellant's ground of appeal concerning denial of due process of law;

ALLOWS by majority, Judge Weinberg de Roca dissenting, the Appellant's ground of appeal concerning his responsibility for the crimes committed in Ahmici, Šantici, Pirici, and Nadioci, on 16 April 1993, **REVERSES** the Appellant's convictions pursuant to Article 7(1) of the Statute under Counts 1, 3, 4, 5, 6, 7, 8, 9, 10, 11, 12, 13, and 14 for these crimes, and **REVERSES** the Appellant's convictions pursuant to Article 7(3) of the Statute under Counts 1, 3, 4, 5, 6, 7, 8, 9, 10, 11, 12, 13, and 14 for these crimes;

ALLOWS unanimously, the Appellant's ground of appeal concerning his responsibility for the crimes committed in parts of the Vitez

Municipality other than Ahmici, Santici, Pirici, and Nadioci, in April, July, and September 1993, **REVERSES** his convictions pursuant to Article 7(1) of the Statute under Counts 1, 3, 4, 5, 6, 7, 8, 9, 10, 11, 12, 13, and 14 for these crimes, and **REVERSES**his convictions pursuant to Article 7(3) of the Statute under Counts 1, 3, 4, 5, 6, 7, 8, 9, 10, 11, 12, 13, and 14 for these crimes;

ALLOWS unanimously, the Appellant's ground of appeal concerning his responsibility for crimes committed in Loncari and Ocehnici in the Busovaca Municipality in April 1993, **REVERSES** his convictions under Article 7(1) of the Statute under Counts 1, 3, 4, 5, 6, 7, 8, 9, 10, 11, 12, 13, and 14 for these crimes, and **FINDS** that no finding was made by the Trial Chamber pursuant to Article 7(1) of the Statute in relation to the January 1993 attacks in Busovaca, and that no finding was made by the Trial Chamber pursuant to Article 7(3) of the Statute concerning the crimes committed in Loncari and Ocehnici in April 1993;

ALLOWS unanimously, the Appellant's ground of appeal concerning his responsibility for the crimes committed in April 1993 in Kiseljak, **REVERSES** his conviction under Article 7(1) of the Statute under Counts 1, 3, 4, 5, 6, 7, 8, 9, 10, 11, 12, 13, and 14 for these crimes, and **FINDS** that no finding was made by the Trial Chamber pursuant to Article 7(3) of the Statute in relation to the crimes;

ALLOWS unanimously, the Appellant's ground of appeal concerning his responsibility for detention-related crimes, to the extent that his appeal against the convictions under Counts 17, 18, and 20 pursuant to Article 7(1) of the Statute is granted, and**REVERSES** his convictions under those counts;

AFFIRMS, unanimously, the Appellant's convictions under: 1) Count 15 pursuant to Article 7(3) of the Statute for the detention-related crimes committed in the relevant detention facilities, 2) Count 16 pursuant to Article 7(1) of the Statute for ordering the use of protected persons for the construction of defensive military installations, and 3) Count 19 under Article 7(1) of the Statute for the inhuman treatment of detainees occasioned by their use as human shields, and **FINDS** that no finding was made by the Trial Chamber pursuant to Article 7(3) of the Statute under Counts 15 or 16 in relation to the use of protected persons for the construction of defensive military installations, under Counts 17 or 18 in relation to the taking of hostages, or under Counts 19 and 20 for the inhuman treatment of detainees occasioned by their use as human shields;

DISMISSES the Appellant's appeal against convictions in all other respects;

ALLOWS unanimously, in part, the Appellant's ground of appeal against the sentence, and **IMPOSES** by majority, Judge Weinberg de Roca dissenting, a new sentence;

SENTENCES the Appellant to nine years' imprisonment to run as of this day, subject to credit being given under Rule 101(C) of the Rules for the period the Appellant has already spent in detention, that is from 1 April 1996 to the present day;

ORDERS, in accordance with Rule 103(C) and Rule 107 of the Rules, that the Appellant is to remain in the custody of the International Tribunal pending the finalization of arrangements for his transfer to the State where his sentence will be served.

This Judgement is signed by Judges Mumba, Güney, Schomburg, Weinberg de Roca and myself this twenty-ninth day of July 2004 at The Hague, The Netherlands.

Judge Schomburg appends a separate opinion limited to the sentence.

Judge Weinberg de Roca appends a partial dissenting opinion.

HALILOVIC CASE

JUDGEMENT IN THE CASE THE PROSECUTOR V. SEFER HALILOVIC

16 NOVEMBER 2005

Please find below the summary of the Judgement delivered by **Trial Chamber** I, Section A, composed of Judge Liu (Presiding), Judge El Mahdi, and Judge Mumba, as read out by the Presiding Judge.

Summary in the case Prosecutor v. Sefer Halilovic

Trial Chamber I, Section A is sitting today to render the Judgement in the case of the Prosecutor v. Sefer Halilovic.

For the purposes of this hearing, the Trial Chamber will summarise briefly its findings, emphasising that this is a summary only, and that the only authoritative account of the Trial Chamber's findings, and of its reasons for those findings, is to be found in the written judgement, copies of which will be made available to the parties and to the public at the conclusion of this hearing.

Procedural History

The trial against the Accused, Sefer Halilovic, started on the 31st of January 2005 and closed on the 31st of August 2005. During that time the Trial Chamber heard the evidence of 41 live witnesses and admitted the testimony of another 14 witnesses pursuant to Rule 92*bis*. The Trial Chamber admitted approximately 500 exhibits during trial.

The Alleged Case

The indictment against Sefer Halilovic concerns murders alleged to have been committed by troops belonging to the Army of the Republic of Bosnia and Herzegovina ("ABiH") in the villages of Grabovica and Uzdol in the Jablanica and Prozor areas in Herzegovina in September 1993 during a military operation allegedly called "Operation Neretva". The Prosecution alleges that Sefer Halilovic was the commander of this operation and as such the troops involved in the "Operation Neretva" were under his command and control.

The Prosecution alleges that "the Operation" was commanded and co-ordinated from a Forward Command Post or "IKM" in Jablanica. One axis of attack, which was in the area where Grabovica is situated, was commanded by Zulfikar Ališpago and involved parts of units from the ABiH 1st Corps. These units came from the 9th Motorised Brigade, the 10th Mountain Brigade and the 2nd Independent Battalion. Another axis of attack, which was in the area where Uzdol is situated, involved the Prozor Independent Battalion and was commanded by Enver Buza.

It is alleged that Sefer Halilovic, knowing of the 9th and the 10th Brigades' "notorious reputations for being criminal and uncontrolled in behaviour", ordered the deployment of parts of units of these brigades to Herzegovina. It is further alleged that between the 7th and 8th of September 1993 the unit of the 9th Brigade and a part of the unit of the 10th Brigade as well as the 2nd Independent Battalion were billeted in the village of Grabovica.

The indictment alleges that between the 8th and 9th of September 1993 thirty-three Bosnian Croat civilians were killed in Grabovica. The indictment further alleges that Sefer Halilovic had knowledge of the criminal reputation of the 9th and 10th Brigades and had been present on 8 September when Vehbija Karic, a member of the Inspection Team, told the troops that they should try those Bosnian Croat civilians summarily and throw them into the Neretva River if the villagers did not allow the soldiers to be billeted in their houses. In light of this, the indictment alleges that Sefer Halilovic once notified during the night of the 8th of September about the killing of civilians, was duty bound to act urgently to prevent the commission of any further crimes.

According to the Prosecution, Sefer Halilovic was ordered on the 12th of September by Rasim Delic "to reconsider the scope of the "Neretva-93" Operation, to isolate the perpetrators of the crimes in Grabovica, and to take active measures and to immediately report on the measures he had taken." It is alleged that Sefer Halilovic failed to implement the order of

Rasim Delic resulting in a failure to punish the perpetrators of the crime.

The indictment also alleges that on the 14th of September 1993 in the course of the Operation, the Prozor Independent Battalion attacked the village of Uzdol and killed twenty-nine Bosnian Croat civilians and one HVO prisoner of war.

The Prosecution alleges that Sefer Halilovic, by virtue of his position and authority as Commander of "Operation Neretva", had effective control over the units subordinated to him, including the 9th Brigade, the 10th Brigade, the 2nd Independent Battalion and the Prozor Independent Battalion.

In view of these alleged facts, Sefer Halilovic is charged with murder, punishable under Article 3 of the Statute as recognised by Article 3 (1) (a) of the Geneva Conventions. The indictment alleges that Sefer Halilovic incurs criminal responsibility under Article 7(3) of the Statute since, notwithstanding his duties as a commander, Sefer Halilovic did not take effective measures to prevent the killings of civilians in Grabovica and did not take steps to carry out a proper investigation to identify the perpetrators of the killings in both Grabovica and Uzdol and as commander of the Operation to punish them accordingly.

The Accused

On the 25th of May 1992, Sefer Halilovic was appointed by the Presidency of the Republic of Bosnia and Herzegovina as Commander of the Territorial Defence (TO). After July 1992, he was "Chief of the General Staff" of the ABiH until 18 August 1992 when the RBiH Presidency formed five corps of the ABiH with Sefer Halilovic as "Chief of the Main Staff" of the ABiH. Sefer Halilovic served as the supreme ABiH commander until 8 June 1993 when the President of the Republic of Bosnia and Herzegovina issued a decision restructuring the ABiH supreme command headquarters and creating a new position of "Commander of the Main Staff", which was filled by Rasim Delic, while Sefer Halilovic retained the position of "Chief of the Main Staff" of the ABiH. On 18 July 1993, Alija Izetbegovic issued a further decision making the "Chief of the Main Staff" a Deputy Commander, thus increasing the number of Deputy Commanders to three. According to the decision, the Deputy Commanders would assume the duties of the "Chief of the Main Staff" on rotational basis.

Facts in relation to Grabovica

The Trial Chamber finds that in order to conduct combat operations in Herzegovina to lift the HVO blockade of Mostar at the time relevant to the indictment, units of the 9th Brigade, the 10th Brigade and the 2nd Independent Battalion, all subordinated to the ABiH 1st Corps, were sent from Sarajevo to the Jablanica sector. This was the area where Grabovica was situated and it was at the time the area of responsibility of the 6th Corps. The Trial Chamber finds that those units were deployed to Herzegovina following an order issued by Sefer Halilovic.

Grabovica was a village inhabited by Bosnian Croats. The Trial Chamber notes that Grabovica had been under ABiH control since May 1993 and the relationship between the residents of Grabovica and the ABiH soldiers who were stationed there was good and, as there was no other accommodation available for the arriving troops, they were supposed to be billeted with the inhabitants of the village.

The Trial Chamber has been provided with evidence concerning the nature of the 9th and 10th Brigades, referred to in the indictment as having "notorious reputations for being criminal and uncontrolled". The evidence shows that members of both brigades not only demonstrated a lack of discipline, but also took civilians to dig trenches at the front line and committed thefts or other forms of misappropriation. However, the Trial Chamber finds that this misconduct was not comparable to the crimes committed in Grabovica. The Trial Chamber notes in this respect the testimony of the 1st Corps Commander Vahid Karavelic who, while knowing of breaches of discipline and previous behaviour of members of these brigades, said that it never occurred to him that they might commit atrocities against civilians in Grabovica.

The Trial has also been provided with evidence as to problems encountered by the troops when trying to accommodate themselves with the inhabitants of Grabovica. The Trial Chamber has found the evidence inconsistent as to the circumstances of the alleged statement of Vehbija Karic, in particular when and where it took place and whether Sefer Halilovic was present, and moreover does not find the witnesses reliable in this respect. The Trial Chamber has therefore found that it has not been proven that Vehbija Karic made the alleged comments or that Sefer Halilovic was present at the time.

The Trial Chamber has been presented with evidence that with the arrival of the unit of the 9th Brigade the atmosphere in the village of Grabovica changed and acts of violence started occurring. Throughout the night of the 8th of September shooting was heard in the village. One witness testified that she heard women wailing and crying and that she was "just quiet sitting on the floor and awaiting her fate". The Trial Chamber has established that by the early afternoon of the 9th of September a number of inhabitants had been murdered by members of the ABiH units present in Grabovica at the time. The Trial Chamber takes particular note of the callous way in which a member of the 9th Brigade shot Pero Maric while sitting at a table, facing his victim. The Trial Chamber further notes the brutal way with which Ljubica Zadro and Mladenka Zadro were killed. Ljubica Zadro was carrying her four year old daughter Mladenka, when both were shot at short distance by members of the 9th Brigade.

Facts in relation to Uzdol

In 1993 Uzdol was a Bosnian Croat village, comprised of several hamlets and with a total population of about one hundred inhabitants. In September 1993 the HVO had several positions in and around Uzdol. The Trial Chamber finds that in the early morning hours of the 14th of September, the Prozor Independent Battalion together with some members of the civilian police force of the Ministry of Interior attacked the headquarters of the HVO located in the school building of one of the hamlets of Uzdol. Shortly after the attack began, the HVO started shelling Uzdol. The Trial Chamber has found that during the attack a number of inhabitants were killed by troops under ABiH command.

The Trial Chamber notes that some of the killings committed in Uzdol were particularly cruel in nature. The Trial Chamber notes in this respect the killing of Anica Stojanovic who was half-seated on the ground next to her house when a soldier, who was standing three metres away from her, killed her by a shot to the head. The testimony showed that she cried out the name of her son before she was shot. The Trial Chamber also notes the direct evidence concerning the manner of the killings of Ruza Zelic and her two children, who were 13 and 10 years old at the time of their deaths. The three had tried to flee from the soldiers, but the soldiers caught up with them. Ruza Zelic begged the soldiers not to kill them, but the three of them were shot.

Findings on the crimes charged

As to the crimes committed in Grabovica, the Trial Chambers has found that the fact that the ABiH soldiers were billeted in Grabovica in preparation for combat operations in Herzegovina, played a substantial part in the soldiers' ability to commit the crimes. As for the crimes in Uzdol, the Trial Chamber has found that the crimes were committed during an attack on Uzdol, which was part of military combat operations. The Trial Chamber has therefore found that there was a nexus between the crimes committed in Grabovica and Uzdol and the armed conflict in the area.

With regards to the crimes committed in Grabovica, the Trial Chamber has found that it has been established beyond reasonable doubt that 13 inhabitants, taking no active part in the hostilities, were murdered by members of the 9th Brigade and unidentified members of the ABiH on the 8th or the 9th of September 1993 (Pero Maric, Dragica Maric, Ivan Zadro, Matija Zadro, Mladen Zadro, Ljubica Zadro and Mladenka Zadro, Josip Brekalo, Martin Maric, Živko Dreznjak, Ljuba Dreznjak, Ivan Mandic and Ilka Miletic).

The Trial Chamber has found that the Prosecution failed to prove beyond reasonable doubt that 14 persons listed in the indictment were killed by members of the ABiH in Grabovica at the time relevant to the indictment.

The Trial Chamber notes that during trial, six of the alleged victims listed in the indictment were withdrawn.

With regards to the crimes committed in Uzdol, the Trial Chamber has found that 25 inhabitants were killed by members of units under ABiH command in Uzdol on the 14th of September 1993, and were persons taking no active part in the hostilities (Ruza Zelic, Marija Zelic, Stjepan Zelic, Anica Stojanovic, Ivan Zelenika, Jadranka Zelenika, Ruza Zelenika, Luca Zelenika, Janja Zelenika, Dragica Zelenika, Kata Perkovic, Martin Ratkic, Kata Ratkic, Anto Stojanovic, Franjo Stojanovic, Serafina Stojanovic, Stanko Rajic, Lucija Rajic, Šima Rajic, Mara Rajic, Ivka Rajic (born in 1921), Mijo Rajic, Ivka Rajic (born in 1934), Zorka Glibo, and Mato Ljubic).

The Trial Chamber has found that the Prosecution failed to prove beyond reasonable doubt that two persons listed in the indictment were taking no active part in the hostilities at the time of their deaths on the 14th of September 1993. Moreover, the Trial Chamber has found that the Prosecution failed to prove beyond reasonable doubt that two other persons listed in the indictment were killed by members of units under ABiH command, who attacked Uzdol on the 14th of September 1993.

The Trial Chamber notes that at the end of the trial, one of the alleged victims listed in the indictment was withdrawn.

The Defence has submitted that the cause of death of the victims in Uzdol was either shelling by the HVO or that they were caught in the crossfire between the ABiH and the HVO during the ABiH attack on Uzdol on the 14th of September 1993. The Trial Chamber has found that the HVO shelled the hamlets comprising Uzdol intensively; however, the autopsy report of the victims does not contain any evidence that the victims were killed, or even injured, by shrapnel from falling shells. Therefore, the Trial Chamber has found that the evidence does not support the Defence submission in this respect.

In relation to the Defence submission that the victims were caught in crossfire, the Trial Chamber notes that the evidence shows that there was heavy fighting between the units under ABiH command and the HVO in the Uzdol area during the attack. The evidence also shows that the inhabitants of the area tried to save themselves by leaving their homes and running for their lives. Contrary to the Defence submission, the Trial Chamber has found that the victims were killed intentionally and notes, in particular, that several victims were shot at close range; that two victims were killed in their beds, one of whom was bedridden; that one victim had been mutilated prior to being killed; that one victim was killed by being brutally beaten to death over the head after having been first shot in the chest and leg; that another victim was killed by being beaten over the head with an implement with both sharp and blunt edges, and finally the Trial Chamber notes that even children were killed.

Findings in Relation to the Individual Criminal Responsibility of the Accused

Having found that murders were committed both in Grabovica and Uzdol, the Trial Chamber recalls that the purpose of a trial is not solely to determine whether serious violations of international humanitarian law were committed, but ultimately is to determine whether the Accused bears individual criminal responsibility for those crimes.

The Trial Chamber has assessed the individual criminal responsibility of Sefer Halilovic based on all the evidence presented to it during the trial.

As a preliminary matter, the Trial Chamber notes that it is not convinced that the combat operations carried out in Herzegovina at the time relevant to the indictment were called "Operation Neretva". Except for a map, no other exhibit presented to the Trial Chamber refers to the combat operations as "Operation Neretva". Moreover, the Trial Chamber notes that several of the witnesses involved with the ABiH at the time, including two Corps Commander, did not hear the use of this name during the combat operations. However, for the purposes of this judgement the Trial Chamber used the term "Operation Neretva" to refer to the combat operations which took place in Herzegovina at the time relevant to the indictment.

The Trial Chamber has found that the participants of a meeting held in Zenica on the 21st and 22nd August 1993 and chaired by the Commander of the Main Staff, Rasim Delic, did not discuss "Operation Neretva". It was a briefing by the Corps Commanders on their areas of responsibility at which they expressed their concerns on the direction the conflict had taken and the future direction of the conflict. The Trial Chamber has further found that neither Sefer Halilovic nor anyone else was appointed commander of an "Operation Neretva" or any other operation at this meeting. Furthermore, the Trial Chamber has found that subsequent to the Zenica meeting, Sefer Halilovic among others carried out tasks of reorganisation and re-subordination of units, and that was done pursuant to an order issued by Rasim Delic on the 1st of September.

The Trial Chamber has found that the Prosecution failed to establish that Sefer Halilovic was appointed as commander of "Operation Neretva" by virtue of an order issued by Rasim Delic on 30 August, as alleged in the indictment. Rather, by this order Rasim Delic appointed Sefer Halilovic as Team Leader of an Inspection Team not entrusted with command authority, but with co-ordinating and monitoring functions in the areas of responsibility of the 4th and the 6th Corps, which were the Corps that carried out military operations in the areas mentioned above, where Grabovica and Uzdol were situated. Furthermore, the Trial Chamber has found that the role of Sefer Halilovic, in the implementation of orders issued by Rasim Delic concerning the reorganisation and re-subordination was consistent with his role as Team Leader of an Inspection Team charged with monitoring and co-ordinating functions.

The Trial Chamber has also found that the evidence presented by the Prosecution is insufficient to support a finding that the location where the Inspection Team was accommodated in Jablanica was an IKM from which an "operation" in Herzegovina was commanded, as alleged in the indictment. The Trial Chamber notes that the term IKM was used as "jargon" to denote the location of senior officers.

The Trial Chamber considers the evidence presented to it as to Sefer Halilovic's alleged position as commander of "Operation Neretva" to be inconsistent. The Trial Chamber notes in particular that some of the lower-ranking soldiers who testified before the Trial Chamber considered Sefer Halilovic to be commander of "Operation Neretva". However, the Trial Chamber has found that testimony of some lower-ranking soldiers to that effect is only indicative of the respect which Sefer Halilovic enjoyed as a senior officer and one of the founders of the ABiH. The Trial Chamber cannot find that this evidence *per se* is sufficient to support the Prosecution's allegation that Sefer Halilovic was commander of "Operation Neretva".

The evidence provided by higher-ranking ABiH officers is more consistent in showing that Sefer Halilovic was not a commander of "Operation Neretva", but rather was tasked with co-ordinating combat activities.

The Trial Chamber also notes that at a meeting on the 4th of September in Donja Jablanica, Rasim Delic signed and approved the documents for the "Operation". Rasim Delic's signature can be seen on a map entitled "Operation Neretva". The Prosecution alleges that the signatures on this map, Rasim Delic's on the top-left and Sefer Halilovic's on the bottom-right, indicates that "Halilovic was the commander responsible for the Operation". The Trial Chamber has found, however, that contrary to the Prosecution allegation, the signatures on this map are inconclusive as to who was commander of the "Operation".

Having examined the evidence presented as to the role of Sefer Halilovic in the field in Herzegovina in September 1993, the Trial Chamber has found that Sefer Halilovic carried out tasks consistent with his role as Team Leader of an Inspection Team tasked with reviewing combat readiness and co-ordinating combat operations, as set out in the order issued by Rasim Delic on 30 August 1993. The Trial Chamber notes that the authority of Sefer Halilovic to issue orders was limited in two ways by the 30 August order: first in that for any "drastic proposals" Sefer Halilovic had to consult with Rasim Delic, and secondly, by this order Sefer Halilovic only had the power to issue orders "in keeping with his authority". The Trial Chamber notes, in this regard, that the position of Sefer Halilovic within the structure of the Main Staff was circumscribed as a result of the orders of 8 June and 18 July issued by Alija Izetbegovic. The Trial Chamber also notes that the evidence does not contain a prior order from Sefer Halilovic ordering the start of combat operations on the axes of attack. Furthermore, an analysis of the evidence concerning orders issued by Sefer Halilovic and information sent to him from the field indicates that the orders issued by Sefer Halilovic were issued under the overall authority of Rasim Delic as Commander of the ABiH, and that orders by Sefer Halilovic were, in general, implementing the instructions of Rasim Delic.

The Trial Chamber notes that the evidence only contains one order concerning combat operations issued by Sefer Halilovic after the establishment of the Inspection Team, namely that of 15th of September 1993. The Trial Chamber has found that this evidence is in itself insufficient to support a finding that Sefer Halilovic was in command of combat operations in Herzegovina. Moreover, the Trial Chamber is of the opinion that this order can be seen as part of the Inspection Team's coordination function.

In conclusion, the Trial Chamber has found that the Prosecution failed to prove beyond reasonable doubt that Sefer Halilovic was either *de jure* or *de facto* commander of the alleged operation called "Operation Neretva".

Moreover the Trial Chamber has found the following:

Concerning Grabovica, the Trial Chamber notes that the combat order for the start of combat operations in the axis in that area was issued by Zulfikar Ališpago, as commander of the axis. The Trial Chamber notes in particular that the unit of the 9th Brigade was under the command of Zulfikar Ališpago at the time the crimes were committed. The Trial Chamber has found that the evidence presented is insufficient to establish that Zulfikar Ališpago was subordinated to Sefer Halilovic.

The Trial Chamber has further found that Sefer Halilovic knew of the crimes committed in Grabovica in the evening of the 9th of September, when the last proven crime had already been committed. The Trial Chamber notes that, in relation to the investigation of the crimes in Grabovica, Sefer Halilovic, in the evening of the 9th of September, instructed Namik Dzankovic, a member of the Inspection Team and of the ABiH Main Staff Security Service, to work together with the MUP, as well as with other members of the SVB, in order to investigate the crimes and to keep "Sarajevo", rather than himself, informed. The evidence shows that at this point in time investigations were already under way. The evidence does not show that Sefer Halilovic initiated the investigations or that the investigations were in any way carried forward through his actions. The evidence also shows that the 6th Corps Security Service, the Military Police Battalion of the 6th Corps and the Military Police of the 44th Brigade, which was located in Jablanica, were involved in the investigation into the events in Grabovica. The Chief of Security of the ABiH Main Staff Jusuf Jašarevic was informed of the results of their investigations. The Trial Chamber has found that based on the evidence, it can not be concluded that Sefer Halilovic had the material ability to punish the perpetrators of the crimes committed in Grabovica.

Having examined all the evidence presented to it and in light of its factual findings, the Trial Chamber has found that the Prosecution did not prove beyond reasonable doubt that Sefer Halilovic had effective control over the troops in Grabovica on the 8th and 9th of September 1993, who the Trial Chamber has found committed the crimes.

Concerning Uzdol, the Trial Chamber has found that the crimes were committed by members of units under ABiH command taking part in the attack on HVO positions in and around Uzdol. The Trial Chamber has found that these units were the Prozor Independent Battalion and members of the civilian police forces of the MUP, both under the command of the Prozor Independent Battalion Commander, Enver Buza. The Trial Chamber has found that the evidence presented is insufficient to establish that Enver Buza was subordinated to Sefer Halilovic.

Furthermore, the Trial Chamber considered that the evidence presented to it did not show that Sefer Halilovic had any role in the investigations concerning the crimes committed in Uzdol. These investigations were conducted by the Security Services of the 6th Corps and the Prozor Independent Battalion. Once again, the Chief of Security of the Main Staff Jusuf Jašarevic was informed of the results of the investigations. The Trial Chamber has found that based on the evidence presented, it can not be concluded that that Sefer Halilovic had the material ability to punish the perpetrators of the crimes committed in Uzdol.

Having examined all the evidence presented to it and in light of its factual findings, the Trial Chamber has found that the Prosecution has not proven beyond reasonable doubt that Sefer Halilovic had effective control over the units under ABiH command, which the Trial Chamber has found committed the crimes in Uzdol.

Finally, the Trial Chamber has found that Sefer Halilovic possessed a degree of influence as a high ranking member of the ABiH and as one of its founders. However, the Trial Chamber considers that Sefer Halilovic's influence falls short of the standard required to establish effective control. It is a principle of international criminal law that a commander cannot be held responsible for the crimes of persons who were not under his command at the time the crimes were committed. The Trial Chamber has found that the Prosecution failed to prove beyond reasonable doubt that Sefer Halilovic was either *de jure* or *de facto* commander of an operation called "Operation Neretva", which the Prosecution alleges was carried out in Herzegovina. The Trial Chamber has also found that the Prosecution has failed to establish that Sefer Halilovic had effective control over the troops which committed the crimes in the areas of Grabovica and Uzdo at the time the crimes were committed. The Trial Chamber has therefore found that the Prosecution failed to establish that Sefer Halilovic was responsible under Article 7(3) of the Statute for the murders committed in Grabovica and Uzdol.

Disposition

For the foregoing reasons, the Trial Chamber has decided that:

The Accused **SEFER HALILOVIĆ** is found **NOT GUILTY** and therefore acquitted of Murder, a Violation of the Laws or Customs of War as charged in the indictment.

Pursuant to Rule 99 of the Rules, the Trial Chamber orders that Sefer Halilovic be released immediately from the United Nations Detention Unit after the necessary practical arrangements are made.

HALILOVIC CASE

SUMMARY OF THE APPEALS JUDGEMENT

PROSECUTOR V. SEFER HALILOVIĆ

16 OCTOBER 2007

Please find below the summary of the judgement today read out by Judge Güney:

As the Registrar announced, the case on our agenda today is Prosecutor versus Sefer Halilović. In accordance with the Order Scheduling the Hearing issued on 25 September 2007, the **Appeals Chamber** will deliver its Judgement today.

Following the practice of the International Tribunal, I will not read out the text of the judgement except for the disposition. Instead, I will summarise the issues on appeal and the findings of the Appeals Chamber. This summary is not part of the written judgement, which is the only authoritative account of the Appeals Chamber's rulings and reasons. Copies of the written judgement will be made available to the parties at the conclusion of this hearing.

The events underlying this appeal took place in 1993 in Bosnia and Herzegovina, in the village of Grabovica, about 30 kilometres North of Mostar. The Trial Chamber found that thirteen persons of Croatian descent taking no active part in hostilities were killed in this village between 8 and 9 September 1993 by troops billeted in the village. There is no disagreement among the parties that these crimes occurred.

At the time of these events, Sefer Halilović was Chief of the Main Staff of the Army of the Republic of Bosnia and Herzegovina. According to the Prosecution, Sefer Halilović was the commander of a military operation called Neretva-93.

The Trial Chamber, in its judgement of 16 November 2005, found that the Prosecution had not proven beyond reasonable doubt that Sefer Halilović was either *de jure* or *de facto* commander of Operation Neretva, nor that he had effective control over the troops who committed the crimes in Grabovica. As a result, the Trial Chamber acquitted him of the only charge, murder as violation of the laws or customs of war, punishable under Article 3 and Article 7(3) of the Statute.

The Prosecution appealed the judgement, seeking the reversal of the acquittal for the charge of murder with respect to the killings perpetrated in Grabovica. The parties made oral submissions before the Appeals Chamber in the appeal hearings on 10 and 11 July 2007.

The Prosecution's appeal consists of four grounds. The first ground of appeal, composed of six sub-grounds, hinges upon the issue of whether Sefer Halilović had effective control over the offending troops. The second and third grounds concern the other two requirements of superior responsibility under Article 7(3) of the Statute (the knowledge of the criminal conduct of the subordinates and the failure to prevent or punish). The fourth ground of appeal concerns the admission into evidence of the report and proposed testimony of an expert witness relating to Sefer Halilović's alleged failure to prevent or punish.

Sefer Halilović has submitted that the entire appeal of the Prosecution should be summarily dismissed. The Appeals Chamber has denied this request as unfounded and has therefore examined the Prosecution's appeal on its merits.

I will now briefly summarize the conclusions of the Appeal Chamber with respect to the First Ground of Appeal.

The Prosecution submits that the Trial Chamber erred in law and in fact in concluding that the Prosecution failed to prove that Sefer Halilović was the superior of the troops who committed the murders in Grabovica and in consequently entering an acquittal. The Prosecution requests the Appeals Chamber to apply the correct legal standards, admit evidence erroneously excluded and to proceed by making its own findings of fact regarding the existence of a superior-subordinate relationship between Sefer Halilović and the perpetrators.

The six sub-grounds of appeal advanced under the Prosecution's first ground of appeal are deeply intertwined: they all go to the issue of whether Sefer Halilović was the superior of the troops who committed the crimes in Grabovica. I note that, for reasons explained in the Judgement, the Appeals Chamber has not followed the order proposed by the Prosecution in the presentation of its six sub-grounds.

The Appeals Chamber has first addressed **sub-ground 6**, which seeks the admission into evidence of a statement given by Sefer Halilović to

the Prosecution in 1996. The Prosecution submits that the Trial Chamber erred in law in refusing to admit into evidence the 1996 Statement. The Appeals Chamber unanimously found that the Trial Chamber was correct when it rejected the statement. All judges agree, Judge Meron and Judge Schomburg on different grounds than the majority, that the Trial Chamber enforced the procedural safeguards of the Rules of Procedure and Evidence in order to protect the due process rights of the accused also before the International Tribunal.
The Appeals Chamber has then addressed on the merits **sub-ground 1**, under which the Prosecution claims that the Trial Chamber erred in law in applying the legal standard required to demonstrate effective control.

The Prosecution submits that the Trial Chamber erred in law in treating "command" as a legal requirement of superior responsibility pursuant to Article 7(3) of the Statute. It claims that, as a consequence, the Trial Chamber erroneously focused on Sefer Halilović's role as commander of Operation Neretva and on his control of combat operations to determine his effective control over the offending troops. The Appeals Chamber has considered carefully the way the Prosecution pleaded its case at trial and the fact that a trier of fact is necessarily bound by the theories of the case advanced by the Prosecution. It concluded that the Prosecution clearly pleaded that Sefer Halilović exercised effective control by virtue of his command of Operation Neretva. The Appeals Chamber has therefore dismissed the Prosecution's allegation that the Trial Chamber erred in failing to consider whether Sefer Halilović had effective control over the perpetrators of the crimes charged in the Indictment by reason of his position as Team Leader of the Inspection Team or by virtue of his position as the most senior ranking officer in Herzegovina at the time. As a result, the Appeals Chamber limited its analysis to the Prosecution's submissions regarding Sefer Halilović's effective control as commander of Operation Neretva. In so doing, the Appeals Chamber focused its assessment specifically on the allegation that he was a *de facto* commander, since the Prosecution acknowledged that it failed to prove *de jure* command.

The Appeals Chamber notes that the Trial Chamber correctly set out the elements that must be satisfied to hold a superior responsible under Article 7(3) of the Statute. However, the Appeals Chamber has found that the Trial Chamber erred when it appeared to create a new requirement to the third element of superior responsibility (failure to take the necessary and reasonable measures to prevent the criminal act or punish the perpetrators thereof) by unhelpfully adding an artificial distinction between "general" and "specific" obligations to prevent crimes. In any event, for the reasons I will discuss, this particular error does not have an impact on Sefer Halilović's acquittal.

Under **sub-ground 5**, the Prosecution submits that the Trial Chamber erred in misapplying the standard of proof throughout the Judgement. Under **sub-ground 2 and 3**, the Prosecution raises two specific allegations of errors related to the same alleged mistake.

First, the Appeals Chamber considered that the Prosecution misinterprets the holding by the Trial Chamber that (and I quote) "any ambiguity or doubt" (end of quote) was to be resolved in favour of the Accused. The Trial Chamber in this case simply reworded the beyond reasonable doubt standard in a manner consistent with the jurisprudence.

The Prosecution also alleges that the Trial Chamber erroneously applied the beyond reasonable doubt standard to all exhibits and findings and not only to the ultimate issue of Sefer Halilović's guilt. While not every factual finding must be established beyond reasonable doubt, every fact which is *indispensable for a conviction* must be. Our case-law has made it clear that, apart from the elements of the crime and the requirements for criminal responsibility, there may be other facts indispensable for a conviction depending on the specific circumstances of the case and on the way the case was pleaded.

In any event, since the Prosecution has only identified a handful of findings that were erroneously reached, the Appeals Chamber has limited itself to consider these. The Appeals Chamber has, in this respect, found that the Trial Chamber did not require proof of the name Operation Neretva as a necessary precondition for a finding of effective control. The same can be said of the discussions and decisions taken at a meeting in Zenica to which Halilović is said to have participated.

Similarly, despite having found that the Trial Chamber did err in focusing on whether a formal "forward command post" had been established in the town of Jablanica, the Appeals Chamber has concluded that the Prosecution failed to substantiate its claim that, had the existence of this post been established at trial, the Trial Chamber would have concluded that Sefer Halilović was *de facto* commander of the perpetrators of the crimes.

The Appeals Chamber has further considered **sub-ground 4** of the first ground of appeal, under which the Prosecution submits that the Trial

Chamber erred in concluding that, since Sefer Halilović did not initiate or carry forward investigations, he did not have the material ability to punish the perpetrators of the crimes in Grabovica.

In this regard, the Appeals Chamber first considered that the wording used by the Trial Chamber might be confusing, since the failure to initiate investigations is not, as such, an indication of a lack of power to investigate. However, the Trial Chamber did not base its conclusion that Sefer Halilović lacked the material ability to punish solely on the evidence that Sefer Halilović did not initiate investigations. On the contrary, it carefully analysed the evidence before it, notably the specific rules and the evidence regarding the authority to conduct such criminal investigations, before concluding that Sefer Halilović did not have not the material ability to punish the perpetrators of these crimes. The Appeals Chamber has found that it was not an unreasonable conclusion given the evidence in the record.

In any event, even assuming that Sefer Halilović had the ability to contribute to an investigation or to the punishment of the perpetrators of the crimes committed in Grabovica, these abilities can only amount to effective control relevant for Article 7(3) of the Statute if they are the consequence of a relationship of subordination between Sefer Halilović and these perpetrators. The Prosecution failed to show how Sefer Halilović's alleged position as *de facto* commander of Operation Neretva or his position as Team Leader of the Inspection Team established a chain of command or a hierarchical relationship between him and the perpetrators amounting to such a superior-subordinate relationship.

Therefore, the Prosecution failed to show that no reasonable trier of fact could have reached the conclusion that Sefer Halilović did not have the required degree of "effective control" over the perpetrators, as a commander of Operation Neretva, to establish his superior responsibility under Article 7(3) of the Statute.

As a result, the first ground of appeal is dismissed.

The Appeals Chamber having concluded that the Prosecution has failed to show that the Trial Chamber erred in finding that a superior-subordinate relationship between Sefer Halilović and the offending troops had not been established, the Prosecution's remaining grounds of appeal became moot.

HADŽIHASANOVIĆ CASE

APPEALS JUDGEMENT SUMMARY FOR THE CASE OF HADŽIHASANOVIĆ AND KUBURA.

22 APRIL 2008

BACKGROUND OF THE CASE

This case concerns certain events that unfolded in Central Bosnia in 1993, particularly in the municipalities of Bugojno, Vareš and Zenica. During the period relevant for the Indictment, the Appellant Enver Hadžihasanović was Commander of the 3rd Corps of the Army of Bosnia and Herzegovina. The Appellant Amir Kubura was Commander of the 3rd Corps 7th Muslim Mountain Brigade. On 15 March 2006, the Trial Chamber found Hadžihasanović guilty, pursuant to Articles 3 and 7(3) of the Statute, for having failed in his duty as a superior to prevent or punish the murder by his subordinates of Mladen Havranek at the Slavonija Furniture Salon in the Bugojno Municipality (Count 3); the murder by his subordinates of Dragan Popović at the Orašac Camp (Count 3); and the cruel treatment by his subordinates at the Zenica Music School, at the Orašac Camp and at various detention centres in Bugojno (Count 4). The Trial Chamber acquitted Hadžihasanović on all other counts of the Indictment. Kubura was found guilty, pursuant to Articles 3 and 7(3) of the Statute, for having failed in his duty as a superior to prevent or punish the plunder by his subordinates in the Ovnak area and in Vareš (Count 6). The Trial Chamber acquitted Kubura on all other counts of the Indictment. Hadžihasanović was sentenced to five years of imprisonment; Kubura was sentenced to two years and six months of imprisonment. Hadžihasanović appealed on 18 April 2006, seeking the reversal of the convictions against him. Kubura appealed on 13 April 2006, challenging both his conviction and the sentence imposed on him. The Prosecution appealed the sentence imposed on Hadžihasanović but not the acquittals. The Prosecution appealed Kubura's acquittal under Count 5 of the Indictment, regarding wanton destruction in the town of Vareš in November 1993, and the sentence imposed on him. The Appeals Chamber heard oral submissions of the Parties regarding these appeals on 4 and 5 December 2007.

Following the practice of the International Tribunal, I will not read out the text of the Judgement except for the Disposition. Instead, I will summarise the issues on appeal and the findings of the Appeals Chamber. I emphasise that this summary is not part of the written Judgement, which is the only authoritative account of the Appeals Chamber's rulings and reasons. Copies of the written Judgement will be made available to the Parties at the conclusion of this hearing.

GROUNDS OF APPEAL

I will now address the Parties' grounds of appeal. First, I will address Hadžihasanović's arguments regarding the alleged infringement on his right to a fair trial. Second, I will address the Parties' arguments concerning Hadžihasanović's individual criminal responsibility as a superior. Third, I will address the Parties' arguments concerning Kubura's individual criminal responsibility as a superior. Finally, I will turn to the Parties' arguments regarding the sentences imposed on Hadžihasanović and Kubura.

A. Hadžihasanović's appeal concerning the fairness of the trial and evidentiary issues

In his first, second, and as part of his third and sixth grounds of appeal, Hadžihasanović submits that the Trial Chamber committed numerous errors infringing upon his right to a fair trial under Article 21 of the Statute. For the reasons set out in the Judgement, the Appeals Chamber finds that Hadžihasanović failed to demonstrate that the Trial Chamber erred in law or in fact and that his right to a fair trial was infringed.

B. Appeal concerning Hadžihasanović's individual criminal responsibility as a superior

I now turn to Hadžihasanović's individual criminal responsibility as a superior. Under his third ground of appeal, Hadžihasanović argues that the Trial Chamber erred by finding that he failed to take the adequate measures required to punish those responsible for the murder of Mladen Havranek and the cruel treatment of six prisoners at the Slavonija Furniture Salon on 5 August 1993, as well as to prevent similar crimes in the other detention facilities in Bugojno.

The Appeals Chamber concurs with the Trial Chamber's finding that the evidence before it provided a sufficient basis to conclude that the perpetrators of the 5 August 1993 Slavonija Furniture Salon crimes were held responsible for breaches of military discipline by the military disciplinary organ in Bugojno and that no criminal report was filed with the District Military Prosecutor's Office regarding the matter.

The Appeals Chamber agrees with the Trial Chamber that, given the gravity of the offences for which the perpetrators were being punished – murder and cruel treatment – Hadžihasanović could not consider as acceptable punishment the disciplinary sanction of a period of detention not exceeding 60 days. The Appeals Chamber however finds that no reasonable trier of fact could have found beyond reasonable doubt that the 3rd Corps failed to initiate an investigation or criminal proceedings against the perpetrators of the murder and cruel treatment by filing a report with the Bugojno municipal public prosecutor. The report of 20 August 1993 from the chief of the civilian police in Bugojno regarding alleged war crimes committed against Croats, which establishes that the Bugojno municipal public prosecutor met with European Community observers to discuss alleged war crimes committed against Croats, including the murder of Mladen Havranek, indeed raises a reasonable doubt as to whether the 307th Brigade, subordinated to the 3rd Corps headed by Hadžihasanović, filed a criminal report regarding the 5 August 1993 Slavonija Furniture Salon crimes with the Bugojno municipal public prosecutor.

The Appeals Chamber recalls that a superior need not dispense punishment personally and may discharge his duty by reporting the matter to the competent authority. In the present case, the Appeals Chamber finds that the reporting of the 5 August 1993Slavonija Furniture Salon crimes to the Bugojno municipal public prosecutor, in conjunction with the disciplinary sanctions imposed by the military disciplinary organ, constituted necessary and reasonable measures to punish the perpetrators.

For the reasons set out in the Judgement, the Appeals Chamber reverses Hadžihasanović's convictions for having failed to take the adequate measures required to punish those responsible for the murder of Mladen Havranek and the cruel treatment of six prisoners at the Slavonija Furniture Salon on 5 August 1993.

Under his third ground of appeal, Hadžihasanović also contends that the Trial Chamber erred in finding that he had reason to know of the acts of mistreatment committed in the Bugojno Detention Facilities as of 18 August 1993.

To reach this conclusion, the Trial Chamber mainly relied on its previous finding that Hadžihasanović had failed to take adequate measures to punish the perpetrators of the 5 August 1993 crimes. However, the Appeals Chamber found that this latter finding was in error. Considering that none of the Trial Chamber's remaining findings, whether taken individually or collectively, sufficiently supports the Trial Chamber's conclusion that Hadžihasanović had reason to know of the acts of cruel treatment in the Bugojno Detention Facilities as of 18 August 1993, the Appeals Chamber finds that no reasonable trier of fact could have concluded, given the evidence, that Hadžihasanović possessed the requisite knowledge under Article 7(3) of the Statute, which would trigger his responsibility to prevent or punish such acts.

For the reasons set out in the Judgement, the Appeals Chamber reverses Hadžihasanović's convictions for having failed to take adequate measures to prevent or punish the acts of mistreatment in the Bugojno Detention Facilities as of 18 August 1993. Under his fourth ground of appeal concerning the cruel treatment at the Zenica Music School from May to September 1993, Hadžihasanović argues that the Trial Chambererred by finding that he failed to take the reasonable measures necessary to punish the perpetrators and prevent such acts.

First, Hadžihasanović argues that the Trial Chamber failed to properly consider the evidence provided by Witness Džemal Merdan – his Deputy-Commander – and Witness HF – a senior officer of the 3rd Corps Command – that measures were taken by the 3rd Corps to investigate allegations of mistreatment at the Zenica Music School. The Appeals Chamber notes that the Trial Chamber did not ignore the testimony of these two witnesses but, after reviewing the totality of the evidence before it, decided to accord greater weight to other evidence. The Trial Chamber found, based on the many accounts by former prisoners at the Music School, that the Zenica Music School's basement consistently housed between ten and thirty detainees from 18 April 1993 until 20 August 1993. The Trial Chamber further found that Hadžihasanović received alarming information from other sources, which established the need for further inquiry based on allegations of mistreatment. Thus, the Trial Chamber's finding that an investigation of the allegations of cruel treatment would have enabled Hadžihasanović to identify the persons responsible for the violence does not turn solely on the truthfulness of Witnesses Džemal Merdan and HF.

Second, Hadžihasanović argues that the Trial Chamber failed to properly consider evidence that the arrest, detention and alleged mistreatment of detainees at the Music School was concealed by some members of the 7th Brigade. The Appeals Chamber finds that the Trial Chamber noted that there was an intention on the part of the soldiers present at the School to conceal the mistreatment inflicted on the detainees but concluded that this had no bearing on Hadžihasanović's criminal responsibility. Indeed, the Trial Chamber found that Hadžihasanović had received information that his subordinates were committing mistreatment at the Zenica Music School from sources outside the 7th Brigade, such that any attempted concealment by members of the 7th Brigade was rendered secondary.

Third, Hadžihasanović submits that the measures he took with respect to the Zenica Music School were necessary and reasonable. The Trial Chamber considered Hadžihasanović's arguments that he had taken preventive measures to ensure that civilians and prisoners of war were treated in accordance with international humanitarian law and that he took steps to investigate allegations of mistreatment. The Trial Chamber nevertheless concluded that Hadžihasanović did not make genuine efforts to initiate an appropriate investigation into the allegations of cruel treatment whereas such an investigation would have enabled him to discover the identity of the persons responsible for the violence.

For the reasons set out in the Judgement, the Appeals Chamber finds that Hadžihasanović failed to demonstrate that no reasonable trier of fact could have concluded that, given the evidence, he failed to take necessary and reasonable measures to punish the perpetrators of the cruel treatment at the Zenica Music School and prevent further mistreatment.

I now turn to Hadžihasanović's arguments under his fifth ground of appeal concerning the murder and cruel treatment in Orašac in October 1993.

Hadžihasanović submits that the Trial Chamber erred by finding that he failed to take necessary and reasonable measures to prevent the murder of Dragan Popović and the cruel treatment committed by the El Mujahedin detachment in the Orašac Camp against five civilians abducted on 19 October 1993. He argues that the Trial Chamber erred in finding that he had de jure authority over the members of the El Mujahedin detachment and in finding that he exercised effective control over the El Mujahedin detachment. Since de jure authority is only one factor that helps to establish effective control, and because the question is resolvable on the basis of effective control alone, the Appeals Chamber declines to address whether Hadžihasanović had de jure authority over the El Mujahedin detachment.

The Trial Chamber found that Hadžihasanović exercised effective control over the El Mujahedin detachment on the basis that the evidence before it showed that three types of indicia of effective control were satisfied, namely: the power to give orders to the El Mujahedin detachment and have them executed, the conduct of combat operations involving the El Mujahedin detachment, and the absence of any other authority over the El Mujahedin detachment.

First, the Appeals Chamber recognises that the power to give orders and have them executed can serve as an indicium of effective control. In the present case, the Trial Chamber took certain orders of re-subordination into account, though to varying degrees, as indicia of effective control. However, for the reasons set out in the Judgement, the Appeals Chamber finds that none of the re-subordination orders, either individually or collectively, is sufficient to establish the existence of effective control.

Second, the Appeals Chamber finds that while the findings relied upon by the Trial Chamber confirm that the El Mujahedin detachment took part in several combat operations in September and October 1993 and that this occurred within the framework established by the Operational Group Bosanska Krajina and the 3rd Corps, they do not necessarily provide sufficient support for the conclusion that Hadžihasanović had effective control over the El Mujahedin detachment in the sense of having the material ability to prevent or punish its members should they commit crimes. Notably, several findings of the Trial Chamber demonstrate that the El Mujahedin detachment maintained a significant degree of independence from the units it fought alongside on various issues, which belies the Trial Chamber's conclusion that the El Mujahedin detachment was under the effective control of the 3rd Corps. The Trial Chamber found, for example, that the detachment members were anxious to maintain their independence and reserved the right to decide whether they would take part in combat operations. Thus, while these Trial Chamber's findings indicate that the 3rd Corps cooperated with the El Mujahedin detachment, they are insufficient to establish the existence of a relationship of effective control between the 3rd Corps and the El Mujahedin detachment.

Third, with regard to the absence of any other authority over the El Mujahedin detachment, the Appeals Chamber finds that some of the Trial Chamber's findings suggest that the El Mujahedin detachment was more under the influence of Muslim clerics, than under that of the 3rd Corps. However, the Appeals Chamber disputes the relevance of the criterion identified by the Trial Chamber as an indicator of the existence of effective control. Hadžihasanović's effective control cannot be established by process of elimination. The absence of any other authority over the El Mujahedin detachment in no way implies that Hadžihasanović exercised effective control in this case.

Last, I turn to Hadžihasanović's argument that he could not have effective control over the El Mujahedin detachment if the only way for the 3rd Corps to obtain the release of the civilians abducted on 19 October 1993 was to use force.

The Appeals Chamber finds that the military operation that the Trial Chamber expected the 3rd Corps to undertake to rescue those hostages would be comparable to that necessary to obtain the release of hostages from an enemy force rather than a force under its effective control. Regardless of whether the use of force was materially feasible or advisable to save the lives of the hostages, the facts of the case reveal a situation in which the relationship between the El Mujahedin detachment and the 3rd Corps was not one of subordination. Instead, it was close to overt hostility since the only way to control the El Mujahedin detachment was to attack them as if they were a distinct enemy force. This scenario is at odds with the premise of the Trial Chamber that the El Mujahedin detachment was subordinated to the 3rd Corps. This conclusion further confirms that Hadžihasanović did not have effective control over the El Mujahedin detachment.

For the reasons set out in the Judgement, the Appeals Chamber concludes that no reasonable trier of fact could have concluded that it was established beyond reasonable doubt that Hadžihasanović had effective control over the El Mujahedin detachment between 13 August and 1 November 1993. As a result, the Appeals Chamber reverses Hadžihasanović's conviction for having failed to prevent the crimes of cruel treatment committed between 19 and 31 October 1993 and the murder of Dragan Popović.

C. Kubura's and Prosecution's appeals concerning Kubura's individual criminal responsibility as a superior

I now turn to Kubura's individual criminal responsibility as a superior. Under his first ground of appeal, Kubura submits that the Trial Chamber erred in convicting him of failing to take necessary and reasonable measures to punish the acts of plunder committed in June 1993 in the Ovnak area. He argues that the Trial Chamber erred in finding that the 7th Brigade was involved in the plunder committed in the Ovnak area and/or that he knew of

First, the Appeals Chamber notes that the Trial Chamber examined Kubura's claim that members of the 7th Brigade could not have been responsible for the plunder because they had already left the Ovnak area on 8 June 1993 but, following its review of the evidence, concluded otherwise. While, as Kubura argues, the Trial Chamber indeed found that members of the 7th Brigade did not enter the villages where the plunder was committed and left the sector on 9 June 1993, it also found that, following the end of combat operations, members of the 7th Brigade's military police units entered and systematically plundered the Ovnak area as of 9 June 1993 prior to their departure.

The Appeals Chamber finds that Kubura failed to establish that, given the evidence, no reasonable trier of fact could have concluded that members of the 7th Brigade committed plunder in the Ovnak area in June 1993.

Second, with regard to Kubura's argument that the Trial Chamber only relied on one witness to conclude that he had knowledge of the plunder committed in the Ovnak area on 9 June 1993, the Appeals Chamber finds that he ignores the additional evidence considered by the Trial Chamber and its resulting findings. Moreover, the Trial Chamber noted that Kubura received orders alerting him to plunder in the Ovnak area generally, which Kubura acknowledged and responded to. In addition, the Trial Chamber found that Kubura issued a report on 20 June 1993 to the 3rd Corps Command acknowledging that a standardised procedure for war booty had been implemented by the 7th Brigade.

The Appeals Chamber finds that Kubura failed to demonstrate that, given the evidence, no reasonable trier offact could have concluded that he had knowledge of plunder by his subordinates in the Ovnak area in June 1993.

In light of the foregoing, the Appeals Chamber accordingly upholds Kubura's conviction for failing to take necessary and reasonable measures to punish the plunder committed by his subordinates in June 1993 in the Ovnak area. Under his second ground of appeal, Kubura submits that the Trial Chamber erred in convicting him of failing to take necessary and reasonable measures to prevent or punish the plunder which took place in Vareš in November 1993. He argues that the Trial Chamber erred in finding that the 7th Brigade was involved in the commission of acts of plunder in Vareš in November 1993 and/or that he knew or had reason to know of these acts.

First, with regard to the 7th Brigade's involvement, the Appeals Chamber finds that the documents relied upon by the Trial Chamber in reaching the finding that Kubura's subordinates engaged in plunder in Vareš specifically refer to the 7th Brigade's involvement in these acts. The Appeals Chamber finds that Kubura failed to demonstrate that, given the evidence, no reasonable trier of fact could have concluded that members of the 7th Brigade committed plunder in Vareš in November 1993.

Second, with regard to Kubura's knowledge of the acts of plunder in Vareš triggering his duty to prevent them, the Appeals Chamber notes that the Trial Chamber focused its reasoning on Kubura's failure to punish his subordinates' plunder in the Ovnak area some five months earlier. While portions of the Trial Judgement demonstrate that the Trial Chamber considered factors other than Kubura's past failure to punish his subordinates in determining whether he had reason to know of their acts of plunder in Vareš on 4 November 1993, the Trial Judgement suffers, at the very least, from a lack of clarity as to whether and, if so, how the Trial Chamber took into account the circumstances of the case in determining that Kubura had reason to know sufficient to trigger a duty to prevent his subordinates' plunder in Vareš. The Appeals Chamber deems it of significant import that the Trial Chamber found that, irrespective of the measures taken by Kubura to stop the acts of plunder in Vareš once he had knowledge of them, Kubura remained responsible for failing to prevent these acts in the first place based exclusively on his past failure to punish similar acts in the Ovnak area. Such a conclusion implies that the Trial Chamber considered Kubura's knowledge of and past failure to punish his subordinates' acts of plunder in the Ovnak area as automatically entailing that he had reason to know of their future acts of plunder in Vareš. The Appeals Chamber finds that this constitutes an error of law.

Having applied the correct legal standard to the evidence contained in the trial record, the Appeals Chamber recognises that Kubura's knowledge of and failure to punish his subordinates' past acts of plunder was likely to be understood by his subordinates at least as acceptance, if not encouragement of such conduct, such that it increased the risk that further acts of plunder, such as those in Vareš, would be committed again. The Appeals Chamber notes, however, that the acts of plunder committed by Kubura's subordinates in the Ovnak area on 9 June 1993 and in Vareš on 4 November 1993 were separated by some five months and some 40 kilometres. While the plunder was widespread on each of these two occasions, Kubura's subordinates were not found to have engaged in plunder on a frequent basis while under his command. The Appeals Chamber recalls that the Trial Chamber did not find that Kubura had any other knowledge regarding his subordinates' acts of plunder in Vareš prior to their commission, other than the knowledge it inferred from his past failure to punish.

However, with respect to Kubura's knowledge of his subordinates' acts of plunder whilst they were ongoing, the Appeals Chamber recalls that Kubura received orders on 4 November 1993 alerting him to the ongoing acts of plunder in Vareš and holding him responsible for stopping them. Indeed, the Trial Chamber found that Kubura received orders from the 3rd Corps Command directing him to use military police to prevent property from being plundered in Vareš, as well as instructions from the Operational Group East to cease all unauthorised acts, stop anything from being removed and withdraw his troops from the town. While Kubura's knowledge of his subordinates' past plunder in Ovnak and his failure to punish them did not, in itself, amount to actual knowledge of the acts of plunder in Vareš, the Appeals Chamber concurs with the Trial Chamber that the orders he received on 4 November 1993 constituted, at the very least, sufficiently alarming information justifying further inquiry.

The Appeals Chamber accordingly finds that Kubura possessed knowledge sufficient to trigger a duty to prevent his subordinates from committing further plunder in Vareš as of his receipt of the orders alerting him to the ongoing plunder. For the reasons set out in the Judgement, the Appeals Chamber also finds that Kubura's knowledge of his subordinates' acts of plunder in Vareš was also sufficient to trigger his duty to punish them. With regard to the measures taken by Kubura to prevent his subordinates from committing further acts of plunder in Vareš, the Appeals Chamber recalls that, following the order of 4 November 1993 from the Operational Group Istok Command, Kubura withdrew his troops from Vareš the very same day and then forbade the members of the 7thBrigade from entering or staying in Vareš on 5 November 1993.

For the reasons set out in the Judgement, the Appeals Chamber finds that Kubura took necessary and reasonable measures, given the circumstances of the case, to preventthe plunder by putting a stop to the plunder once it had started so it would not be repeated. The Appeals Chamber however upholds the Trial Chamber's finding that Kubura failed to take necessary and reasonable measures to punish his subordinates' acts of plunder in Vareš on 5 November 1993. Kubura's conviction as a superior under Article 7(3) of the Statute for the plunder in Vareš is accordingly maintained.

I now turn to the Prosecution's second ground of appeal that Kubura should have been convicted under Article 7(3) of the Statute for the wanton destruction committed by his subordinates in Vareš on 4 November 1993.

The Trial Chamber found that Kubura's subordinates committed wanton destruction in Vareš on 4 November 1993 but that it was not proven beyond reasonable doubt that he knew or had reason to know of this crime.

First, as to whether Kubura received information concerning the destruction of property in Vareš, the Trial Chamber found, as correctly remarked by the Prosecution, that the Operational Group Istok issued a combat report to the 3rd Corps Command on 4 November 1993 noting the chaotic situation in Vareš. In this report, the Operational Group Istok requested that the 3rd Corps Command send police military units to the town of Vareš. In response, the 3rd Corps Command issued a combat report stating that it had issued orders that brigades use military police forces to prevent chaos and the destruction of property in Vareš. The

Trial Chamber found that the 7th Brigade neither received the 4 November 1993 Operational Group Istok combat report to the 3rd Corps Command nor the 3rd Corps Command's combat report in response. Yet, from the content of the 3rd Corps Command combat report, it inferred that the 7th Brigade "must have received" orders to use military police forces to prevent chaos and the destruction of property in Vareš given that the 7thBrigade was subordinated to the 3rd Corps Command and present in Vareš. The 3rd Corps Command combat report, however, failed to make explicit the identity of the perpetrators of the acts of wanton destruction in Vareš. The Appeals Chamber notes that other brigades were also present in Vareš on 4 November 1993.
The Trial Chamber also found that the Operational Group Istok issued a separate order on 4 November 1993, specifically directed to the 7th Brigade Commander, which explicitly refers to activities of plunder and the need to prevent them but does not mention acts of destruction. The Appeals Chamber concurs with the Trial Chamber that, given the evidence taken as a whole, the inference that the 7th Brigade must have received orders from the 3rd Corps Command on 4 November 1993 does not establish, by itself, Kubura's knowledge of his subordinates' acts of wanton destruction.

Second, the Appeals Chamber considers that Kubura's knowledge of the acts of wanton destruction cannot automatically be inferred from his awareness of the plunder inVareš on 4 November 1993. Indeed, the Trial Chamber's finding regarding Kubura's knowledge of the plunder in Vareš on 4 November 1993 rests on a much broader evidentiary basis. Furthermore, the Trial Chamber relied on Kubura's knowledge of and failure to punish his subordinates' past acts of plunder. The Trial Chamber made no such findings with respect to any past acts of wanton destruction by Kubura's subordinates. Thus, while there was a sufficient evidentiary basis for the Trial Chamber to conclude that Kubura had knowledge of the acts of plunder in Vareš, it was reasonable for it to conclude that his knowledge as regards the acts of wanton destruction was not established beyond reasonable doubt.

In light of the foregoing, the Appeals Chamber finds that the Prosecution failed to establish that no reasonable trier of fact could have concluded, on the basis of all the admitted evidence, that Kubura's knowledge of wanton destruction in Vareš on 4 November 1993 was not established beyond reasonable doubt. Kubura's acquittal is confirmed. D. Appeals concerning the sentences imposed on Hadžihasanović and Kubura

Finally, I turn to the appeals concerning the sentences rendered. Hadžihasanovićdid not specifically appeal his sentence but alleged that the Trial Chamber erred in that the Disposition of the Trial Judgement does not adequately reflect some of the findings made by the Trial Chamber in the body of the Trial Judgement. Kubura appealed his sentence as manifestly excessive, and the Prosecution appealed both Hadžihasanović and Kubura's sentences as manifestly inadequate.

The Appeals Chamber allows Hadžihasanović's arguments and corrects the Disposition of the Trial Judgement concerning the temporal scope of the cruel treatment at the Zenica Music School to render it consistent with the Trial Chamber's findings. As regards the impact of this shorter period of responsibility on Hadžihasanović's sentence, the Appeals Chamber first recalls that the Trial Chamber, in its sentencing determination, correctly determined that the cruel treatment at the Zenica Music School took place over approximately seven months and not nine months as erroneously indicated in the Disposition of the Trial Judgement. The Appeals Chamber further notes that the Trial Chamber's finding regarding the large number of victims involved in the detention facilities in Zenica, which was considered an aggravating circumstance, remains valid for the relevant period. Thus, these factors remain unaffected by the above correction to the Disposition of the Trial Judgement and there is no impact on the sentence.

For the reasons set out in the Judgement, the Appeals Chamber dismisses the Prosecution's and Kubura's arguments. The Appeals Chamber finds that the Trial Chamber properly considered the gravity of the crimes, the relevant aggravating and mitigating factors, and the sentencing practices in the former Yugoslavia.

I will now read out in full the operative paragraphs of the Appeals Chamber's Judgement, that is, the Disposition. Mr. Hadžihasanović and Mr. Kubura, will you please stand.

DISPOSITION
For the foregoing reasons, THE APPEALS CHAMBER
PURSUANT TO Article 25 of the Statute and Rules 117 and 118 of the Rules;

NOTING the respective written submissions of the Parties and the arguments they presented at the hearings of 4 and 5 December 2007;

SITTING in open session, unanimously:

ALLOWS Hadžihasanović's appeal, in part, with respect to Ground 3;

REVERSES his conviction for failing to take the necessary and reasonable measures to punish those responsible for the murder of Mladen Havranek (Count 3 of the Indictment) and the cruel treatment of six prisoners at the Slavonija Furniture Salon on 5 August 1993 (Count 4 of the Indictment), as well as his conviction for failing to take the necessary and reasonable measures to prevent or punish the cruel treatment at the Gimnazija School Building, the Slavonija Furniture Salon, the Iskra FC Stadium and the Vojin Paleksić Elementary School in Bugojno as of 18 August 1993 (Count 4 of the Indictment);

ALLOWS Hadžihasanovic's appeal, in part, with respect to Ground 4, concerning certain errors in the Disposition of the Trial Judgement with regard to his conviction entered under
Count 4 of the Indictment for his failure to prevent or punish the cruel treatment at the Zenica Music School; SETS ASIDE the related portion of the Disposition of the Trial

Judgement and REPLACES it with the following:
COUNT 4: GUILTY of failure to prevent or punish cruel treatment at the Zenica Music School from 8 May 1993 to 20 August 1993 or 20

September 1993, in addition to failure to punish cruel treatment at the Zenica Music School from 26 January 1993 to 8 May 1993.

ALLOWS Hadžihasanović's appeal, in part, with respect to Ground 5;

REVERSES his conviction for failing to take the necessary and reasonable measures to prevent the murder of Dragan Popović on 21 October 1993 (Count 3 of the Indictment) and his conviction for failing to take the necessary and reasonable measures to prevent cruel treatment at the Orašac camp from 15 October 1993 to 31 October 1993 (Count 4 of the Indictment);

REDUCES the sentence of five years of imprisonment imposed on Hadžihasanović by the Trial Chamber to a sentence of three years and six months of imprisonment, subject to credit being given under Rule 101(C) of the Rules for the period Hadžihasanović has already spent in detention; and

DISMISSES Hadžihasanović's appeal in all other respects;

ALLOWS Kubura's appeal, in part, with respect to Ground 2;

REVERSES his conviction for failing to take the necessary and reasonable measures to prevent, though not to punish, plunder in Vareš on 4 November 1993 (Count 6 of the Indictment);

REDUCES the sentence of thirty months of imprisonment imposed on Kubura by the Trial Chamber to a sentence of two years of imprisonment; and

DISMISSES Kubura's appeal in all other respects;

DISMISSES the Prosecution's appeal in its entirety;

ORDERS that this Judgement shall be enforced immediately pursuant to Rule 118 of the Rules.

AKAYESU CASE

THE PROSECUTORVERSUS JEAN-PAUL AKAYESU

CASE NO. ICTR-96-4-T

2 SEPTEMBER 1998

[...]

6.2. Individual criminal responsibility (Article 6 of the Statute)

The Accused is charged under Article 6(1) of the Statute of the Tribunal with individual criminal responsibility for the crimes alleged in the Indictment. With regard to Counts 13, 14 and 15 on sexual violence, the Accused is charged additionally, or alternatively, under Article 6(3) of the Statute. In the opinion of the Tribunal, Articles 6(1) and 6(3) address distinct principles of criminal liability and should, therefore, be considered separately. Article 6(1) sets forth the basic principles of individual criminal liability, which are undoubtedly common to most national criminal jurisdictions. Article 6(3), by contrast, constitutes something of an exception to the principles articulated in Article 6(1), as it derives from military law, namely the principle of the liability of a commander for the acts of his subordinates or "command responsibility". Article 6(1) provides that:

"A person who planned, instigated, ordered, committed or otherwise aided and abetted in the planning, preparation or execution of a crime referred to in articles 2 to 4 of the present Statute, shall be individually responsible for the crime".

Thus, in addition to responsibility as principal perpetrator, the Accused can be held responsible for the criminal acts of others where he plans with them, instigates them, orders them or aids and abets them to commit those acts.

Thus, Article 6(1) covers various stages of the commission of a crime, ranging from its initial planning to its execution, through its organization. However, the principle of individual criminal responsibility as provided for in Article 6(1) implies that the planning or preparation of the crime actually leads to its commission. Indeed, the principle of individual criminal responsibility for an attempt to commit a crime obtained only in case of genocide See Virginia Morris & Michael P. Scharpf, Ibid., p.235 . Conversely, this would mean that with respect to any other form of criminal participation and, in particular, those referred to in Article 6(1), the perpetrator would incur criminal responsibility only if the offence were completed.

Article 6 (1) thus appears to be in accord with the Judgments of the Nuremberg Tribunal which held that persons other than those who committed the crime, especially those who ordered it, could incur individual criminal responsibility.

The International Law Commission, in Article 2 (3) of the Draft Code of Crimes Against the Peace and Security of Mankind, reaffirmed the principle of individual responsibility for the five forms of participation deemed criminal referred to in Article 6 (1) and consistently included the phrase "which in fact occurs", with the exception of aiding and abetting, which is akin to complicity and therefore implies a principal offence.

The elements of the offences or, more specifically, the forms of participation in the commission of one of the crimes under Articles 2 to 4 of the Statute, as stipulated in Article 6 (1) of the said Statute, their elements are inherent in the forms of participation *per se* which render the perpetrators thereof individually responsible for such crimes. The moral element is reflected in the desire of the Accused that the crime be in fact committed.

In this respect, the International Criminal Tribunal for the former Yugoslavia found in the Tadic case that:"a person may only be criminally responsible for conduct where it is determined that he knowingly participated in the commission of an offence" and that "his participation directly and substantially affected the commission of that offence through supporting the actual commission before, during, or after the incident." Para. 692, page 270, The Prosecutor v. Dusko Tadic, Case No. IT-94-1-T, 7 May 1997, ICTY.

This intent can be inferred from a certain number of facts, as concerns genocide, crimes against humanity and war crimes, for instance, from their massive and/or systematic nature or their atrocity, to be considered *infra* in the judgment, in the Tribunal's findings on the law applicable to each of the three crimes which constitute its *ratione materiae* jurisdiction.

Therefore, as can be seen, the forms of participation referred to in Article 6 (1), cannot render their perpetrator criminally liable where he did not act knowingly, and even where he should have had such knowledge. This greatly differs from Article 6 (3) analyzed here below, which does not necessarily require that the superior acted knowingly to render him criminally liable; it suffices that he had reason to know that his subordinates were about to commit or had committed a crime and failed to take the necessary or reasonable measures to prevent such acts or punish the perpetrators thereof. In a way, this is liability by omission or abstention.

The first form of liability set forth in Article 6 (1) is planning of a crime. Such planning is similar to the notion of *complicity* in Civil law, or *conspiracy* under Common law, as stipulated in Article 2 (3) of the Statute. But the difference is that planning, unlike complicity or plotting, can be an act committed by one person. Planning can thus be defined as implying that one or several persons contemplate designing the commission of a crime at both the preparatory and execution phases.

The second form of liability is 'incitation' (in the french version of the Statute) to commit a crime, reflected in the English version of Article 6 (1) by the word *instigated*. In English, it seems the words incitement and instigation are synonymous See, for example, the "Lexique Anglais-Français (principalement juridique) of the Council of Europe, Strasbourg, January 1997, which translates "incitement" by *incitation, instigation ou provocation* or the "Dictionnaire Français/ Anglais" Larousse, or the "Dictionnaire Francais/ Anglais" Super Senior Robert Collins.. Furthermore, the word "instigated" or "instigation" is used to refer to incitation in several other instruments Article 6 of the Nuremberg Charter, Article 7(1) of the ICTY Statute and Article 2(3)(b) of the Draft Code of Crimes Against the Peace and the Security of Mankind.. However, in certain legal systems and, under Civil law, in particular, the two concepts are very different See, for instance, Article 91 of the Rwandan Penal Code, quoted and analyzed above under Chapter 6.3.2.. Furthermore, and even assuming that the two words were synonymous, the question would be to know whether instigation under Article 6 (1) must include the direct and public elements, required for incitement, particularly, incitement to commit genocide (Article 2 (3)(c) of the Statute) which, in this instance, translates *incitation* into English as "incitement" and no longer "instigation". Some people are of that opinion See Virginia Morris and Michael P. Scharpf, *Ibid.* p.239. Comments on Article 2 (3)(f) of the Draft Code on Crimes Against the Peace and the Security of Mankind by the International Law Commission, which article considers incitement to commit a crime in the same way as Article 6(1) of the Tribunal's Statute.. The Chamber also accepts this interpretation See *infra* the findings of the Chamber on the crime of direct and public incitement to commit genocide..That said, the form of participation through instigation stipulated in Article 6 (1) of the Statute, involves prompting another to commit an offence; but this is different from incitement in that it is punishable only where it leads to the actual commission of an offence desired by the instigator On this issue, also see *infra* the findings of the Chamber on the crime of direct and public incitement to commit genocide.. By ordering the commission of one of the crimes referred to in Articles 2 to 4 of the Statute, a person also incurs individual criminal responsibility. Ordering implies a superior- subordinate relationship between the person giving the order and the one executing it. In other words, the person in a position of authority uses it to convince another to commit an offence. In certain legal systems, including that of Rwanda See Article 91 of the Penal Code, in "Codes et Lois du Rwanda", Université nationale du Rwanda, 31 December 1994 update, Volume I, 2nd edition: 1995, p.395., ordering is a form of complicity through instructions given to the direct perpetrator of an offence. Regarding the position of authority, the Chamber considers that sometimes it can be just a question of fact. Article 6 (1) declares criminally responsible a person who "(...) or otherwise aided and abetted in the planning, preparation or execution of a crime referred to in Articles 2 to 4 (...)". Aiding and abetting, which may appear to be synonymous, are indeed different. Aiding means giving assistance to someone. Abetting, on the other hand, would involve facilitating the commission of an act by being sympathetic thereto. The issue here is to whether the individual criminal responsibility provided for in Article 6(1) is incurred only where there was aiding and abetting at the same time. The Chamber is of the opinion that either aiding or abetting alone is sufficient to render the perpetrator criminally liable. In both instances, it is not necessary for the person aiding or abetting another to commit the offence to be present during the commission of the crime.

The Chamber finds that, in many legal systems, aiding and abetting constitute acts of complicity. However, though akin to the constituent elements of complicity, they themselves constitute one of the crimes referred to in Articles 2 to 4 of the Statute, particularly, genocide. The Chamber is consequently of the opinion that when dealing with a person Accused of having aided and abetted in the planning, preparation and execution of genocide, it must be proven that such a person did have the specific intent to commit genocide, namely that, he or she acted with the intent to destroy in whole or in part, a national, ethnical, racial or religious group, as such; whereas, as stated *supra*, the same requirement is not needed for complicity in genocide See *infra* the findings of the Chamber on the crime of direct and public incitement to commit genocide..Article 6(3) of the Statute deals with the responsibility of the superior, or command responsibility. This principle, which derives from the principle of individual criminal responsibility as applied in the Nuremberg and Tokyo trials, was subsequently codified in Article 86 of the Additional Protocol I to the Geneva Conventions of 8 June 1977. Article 6 (3) stipulates that: "The fact that any of the acts referred to in Articles 2 to 4 of the present Statute was committed by a subordinate does not relieve his or her superior of criminal responsibility if he or she knew or had reason to know that the subordinate was about to commit such acts or had done so and the superior failed to take the necessary and reasonable measures to prevent such acts or to punish the perpetrators thereof".

There are varying views regarding the *Mens rea* required for command responsibility. According to one view it derives from a legal rule of strict liability, that is, the superior is criminally responsible for acts committed by his subordinate, without it being necessary to prove the criminal intent of the superior. Another view holds that negligence which is so serious as to be tantamount to consent or criminal intent, is a lesser requirement. Thus, the "Commentary on the Additional Protocols of 8 June 1977 to the Geneva Conventions of 12 August 1949" stated, in reference to Article 86 of the Additional Protocol I, and the *mens rea* requirement for command responsibility that:"[...] the negligence must be so serious that it is tantamount to malicious intent, apart from any link between the conduct in question and the damage that took place. This element in criminal law is far from being clarified, but it is essential, since it is precisely on the question of intent that the system of penal sanctions in the Conventions is based" Claude Pilloud et al., "Commentary on the Additional Protocols of 8 June 1977 to the Geneva Conventions of 12 August 1949", 1987, p.1036..

The Chamber holds that it is necessary to recall that criminal intent is the moral element required for any crime and that, where the objective is to ascertain the individual criminal responsibility of a person Accused of crimes falling within the jurisdiction of the Chamber, such as genocide, crimes against humanity and violations of Article 3 Common to the Geneva Conventions and of Additional Protocol II thereto, it is certainly proper to ensure that there has been malicious intent, or, at least, ensure that negligence was so serious as to be tantamount to acquiescence or even malicious intent.As to whether the form of individual criminal responsibility referred to Article 6 (3) of the Statute applies to persons in positions of both military and civilian authority, it should be noted that during the Tokyo trials, certain civilian authorities were convicted of war crimes under this principle. Hirota, former Foreign Minister of Japan, was convicted of atrocities - including mass rape - committed in the "rape of Nanking", under a count which charged that he had " recklessly disregarded their legal duty by virtue of their offices to take adequate steps to secure the observance and prevent breaches of the law and customs of war".

The Tokyo Tribunal held that:

"Hirota was derelict in his duty in not insisting before the Cabinet that immediate action be taken to put an end to the atrocities, failing any other action open to him to bring about the same result. He was content to rely on assurances which he knew were not being implemented while hundreds of murders, violations of women, and other atrocities were being committed daily. His inaction amounted to criminal negligence".

It should, however, be noted that Judge Röling strongly dissented from this finding, and held that Hirota should have been acquitted. Concerning the principle of command responsibility as applied to a civilian leader, Judge Röling stated that:

"Generally speaking, a Tribunal should be very careful in holding civil government officials responsible for the behaviour of the army in the field. Moreover, the Tribunal is here to apply the general principles of law as they exist with relation to the responsibility for 'omissions'. Considerations of both law and policy, of both justice and expediency, indicate that this responsibility should only be recognized in a very restricted sense".

The Chamber therefore finds that in the case of civilians, the application of the principle of individual criminal responsibility, enshrined in Article 6 (3), to civilians remains contentious. Against this background, the Chamber holds that it is appropriate to assess on a case by case basis the power of authority actually devolved upon the Accused in order to determine whether or not he had the power to take all necessary and reasonable measures to prevent the commission of the alleged crimes or to punish the perpetrators thereof. [...]

BRIMA ET AL. CASE

PROSECUTOR V ALEX TAMBA BRIMA & ORS - JUDGEMENT - CASE NO. SCSL-04-16-T [2007] SCSL 49

20 JUNE 2007

[...]

3. Individual Criminal Responsibility Pursuant to Article 6(3) of the Statute

779. In addition, or alternatively, the Indictment charges pursuant to Article 6(3) of the Statute that the Accused, while holding positions of superior responsibility and exercising effective control over their subordinates, are each individually criminally responsible for the said crimes in that each Accused is responsible for the criminal acts of his subordinates which he knew or had reason to know that the subordinate was about to commit or had done so and which each Accused failed to take the necessary and reasonable measures to prevent or to punish the perpetrators thereof.[1507]

780. Article 6(3) of the Statute provides:

The fact that any of the acts referred to in Articles 2 to 4 of the present Statute was committed by a subordinate does not relieve his or her superior of criminal responsibility if he or she knew or had reason to know that the subordinate was about to commit such acts or had done so and the superior had failed to take the necessary and reasonable measures to prevent such acts or to punish the perpetrators thereof.

(a) Elements of Superior Responsibility

781. As is evident from its terms, Article 6(3) of the Statute requires a three-pronged test for criminal liability to attach:

1. The existence of a superior-subordinate relationship between the accused as superior and the perpetrator of the crime;
2. The accused knew or had reason to know that the crime was about to be or had been committed; and
3. The Accused failed to take necessary and reasonable measures to prevent the crime or punish the perpetrators thereof.[1508]

782. The principle that an individual may be held responsible as a superior in the course of an armed conflict is enshrined in customary international law.[1509] The scope of Article 6(3) does not only include military commanders, but also political leaders and other civilian superiors in possession of authority.[1510]

783. Under Article 6(3) of the Statute, a superior is held responsible for an omission, *i.e.*, for the failure to perform an act required by international law.[1511] The culpable omission of a superior-consists of his or her failure to prevent or punish crimes under the Statute committed by subordinates. Hence, a superior is responsible not for the principal crimes, but rather for what has been described as a 'dereliction' or 'neglect of duty' to prevent or punish the perpetrators of serious crimes.[1512] Responsibility of a superior is not limited to crimes committed by subordinates in person, but encompasses any modes of criminal liability proscribed in Article 6(1) of the Statute. It follows that a superior can be held responsible for failure to prevent or punish a crime which was planned, ordered, instigated or aided and abetted by subordinates.[1513]

(i) Existence of a Superior-Subordinate Relationship

784. The doctrine of command responsibility is "ultimately predicated upon the power of the superior to control the acts of his subordinates."[1514] It is immaterial whether the power of the superior over the subordinates is based on *de jure* or on *de facto* authority,[1515] as long as the superior possessed the material ability to prevent or punish the commission of the offence.[1516] This requirement has been widely referred to as the exercise of 'effective control'.[1517] It may be presumed that the existence of *de jure* authority *prima facie* results in effective control unless proof to the contrary is produced.[1518] Substantial influence over the conduct of others falls short of effective control.[1519]

785. Indications for effective control include the formality of the procedure used for appointment of a superior,[1520] the power of the superior to issue orders[1521] or take disciplinary action,[1522] the fact that subordinates show greater discipline in the superior's presence,[1523] the level of profile, manifested through public appearances and statements,[1524] or the capacity to transmit reports to competent authorities for the taking of proper measures.[1525]

786. A superior may be held responsible for crimes committed by individuals temporarily subordinated to him, provided he exercises effective control over them.[1526] Further, superior responsibility is not excluded by the concurrent responsibility of other superiors in a chain of command.[1527] If a superior has functioned as a member of a collegiate body with authority shared among various members, the power or authority actually devolved on an accused may be assessed on a case-by-case basis, taking into account the cumulative effect of the accused's various functions.[1528]

787. However, in a conflict characterised by the participation of irregular armies or rebel groups, the traditional indicia of effective control provided in the jurisprudence may not be appropriate or useful. As the Trial Chamber has observed, the formality of an organisation's structure is relevant to, but not determinative of, the question of the effective control of its leaders. The less developed the structure, the more important it becomes to focus on the nature of the superior's authority rather than his or her formal designation.

788. The Trial Chamber considers that indicia which may be useful to assess the ability of superiors in such irregular armies to exercise effective control over their subordinates, include that the superior had first entitlement to the profits of war, such as looted property and natural resources; exercised control over the fate of vulnerable persons such as women and children; the superior had independent access to and/or control of the means to wage war, including arms and ammunition and communications equipment; the superior rewarded himself or herself with positions of power and influence; the superior had the capacity to intimidate subordinates into compliance and was willing to do so; the superior was protected by personal security guards, loyal to him or her, akin to a modern praetorian guard; the superior fuels or represents the ideology of the movement to which the subordinates adhere; and the superior interacts with external bodies or individuals on behalf of the group.

789. Nonetheless, the key traditional indicia of effective control remain central, although they may be more loosely defined. For example, the power of the superior to issue orders is crucial, although these orders may be criminal in nature. Similarly, the superior must be capable of taking disciplinary action, even though the measures taken may be more brutal and arbitrarily utilised.

790. Identification of the principal perpetrator, particularly by name, is not required to establish a superior-subordinate relationship. It is sufficient to identify the subordinates as belonging to a unit or group controlled by the superior.[1529]

(ii) Actual or Imputed Knowledge

791. For a superior to be held responsible pursuant to Article 6(3) of the Statute, it must be established that he knew or had reason to know that the subordinate was about to commit or had committed such crimes.

a. Actual Knowledge

792. Actual knowledge may be defined as the awareness that the relevant crimes were committed or about to be committed.[1530] There is no presumption of such knowledge but, in the absence of direct evidence, it may be established through circumstantial evidence.[1531] Factors indicative of actual knowledge include, first of all, an individual's superior position and the superior's geographical and temporal proximity to the crimes;[1532] also, the type and scope of crimes, the time during which they occurred, the number and type of troops and logistics involved, the widespread occurrence of crimes, the tactical tempo of operations, the*modus operandi* of similar illegal acts and the officers and staff involved.[1533]

793. The evidence required to demonstrate actual knowledge may differ depending on the position of authority held by a superior and the level of responsibility in the chain of command. The membership of the accused in an organised and disciplined structure with reporting and monitoring mechanisms has been found to facilitate proof of actual knowledge. Conversely, the standard of proof of the actual knowledge of a superior exercising a more informal type of authority will be higher.[1534]

b. Imputed Knowledge

794. In determining whether a superior "had reason to know", or imputed knowledge, that his or her subordinates were committing or about to commit a crime, it must be shown that specific information was available which would have put the superior on notice of crimes committed or about to be committed.[1535] The superior may not be held liable for failing to acquire such information in the first

place.[1536] However, it suffices for the superior to be in possession of sufficient information, even general in nature, written or oral, of the likelihood of illegal acts by subordinates.[1537] In other words: failure to conclude, or conduct additional inquiry, in spite of alarming information amounts to imputed knowledge.[1538] It is not necessary that the information would compel the conclusion of the existence of concrete crimes.[1539] Rather, the information must have put the accused on notice of the 'present and real risk' that crimes under the Statute were committed, or about to be committed.[1540] Examples of such information include that a subordinate has a violent or unstable character and that a subordinate has been drinking prior to being sent on a mission.[1541] Furthermore, reports addressed to the superior, the level of training and instruction of subordinate officers are factors to be taken into account when determining imputed knowledge.[1542]

795. The Brima Defence objects to an expansive interpretation of the imputed knowledge standard, especially to hold "a commander [...] liable for the most serious of crimes under a mere negligence standard."[1543]Similarly, the Kamara and Kanu Defences oppose the application of strict liability.[1544] The Kamara Defence says that superiors are not under a duty to know, and are only liable when they had "information which should have enabled them to conclude in the circumstances at the time, that [the perpetrator] was committing or was going to commit such a breach and if they did not take feasible measures within their power to prevent or repress the breach".[1545]

796. It is clear from the case law referred to above that solely negligent ignorance is insufficient to attribute imputed knowledge. What is required is the superior's factual awareness of information which should have prompted him or her to acquire further knowledge.[1546] Responsibility pursuant to Article 6(3) of the Statute will attach when the superior remains wilfully blind to the criminal acts of his or her subordinates.[1547]

(iii) Failure to Prevent or Punish

797. It must be established that the superior failed to take the necessary and reasonable measures to prevent or punish the crimes of his or her subordinates. These are two distinct duties: it is the superior's primary duty to intervene as soon as he or she becomes aware of crimes about to be committed, while taking measures to punish will only suffice if the

superior did not become aware of these crimes until after they were committed.[1548]

798. As regards the duty to prevent the crimes of subordinates, the type of necessary and reasonable measures a superior must take is a matter of evidence rather than one of substantive law.[1549] Generally, it can be said that the measures required of the superior are limited to those within his or her material ability under the circumstances,[1550] including those that may lie beyond his or her formal powers.[1551] The kind and extent of measures to be taken depend on the degree of effective control exercised by the superior at the relevant time, and on the severity and imminence of the crimes that are about to be committed.[1552] A superior must prevent not only the execution and completion of a subordinate's crimes, but also their earlier planning and preparation. The superior must intervene as soon as he becomes aware of the planning or preparation of crimes to be committed by his subordinates and as long as he has the effective ability to prevent them from starting or continuing.[1553]

799. The duty to punish only arises once a crime under the Statute has been committed.[1554] A superior is bound to conduct a meaningful investigation with a view to establish the facts, order or execute appropriate sanctions, or report the perpetrators to the competent authorities in case the superior lacks sanctioning powers.[1555] According to the ICTY Appeals Chamber, there is no support in customary international law for the proposition that a commander can be held responsible for crimes committed by a subordinate prior to the commander's assumption of command over that subordinate.[1556]

4. Relationship Between Article 6(1) and 6(3) of the Statute

800. Article 6(1) and 6(3) of the Statute denote different categories of individual criminal responsibility. Where both Article 6(1) and Article 6(3) responsibility are alleged under the same count, and where the legal requirements pertaining to both of these heads of responsibility are met, it would constitute a legal error invalidating a judgement to enter a concurrent conviction under both provisions.[1557] Where a Trial Chamber enters a conviction on the basis of Article 6(1) only, an accused's superior position may be considered as an aggravating factor in sentencing.[1558]

[...]

[1507] Indictment, para. 36.
[1508] Rule 98 Decision, para. 328, referring to *Čelebići* Trial Judgement, para. 346.
[1509] *Čelebići* Trial Judgement, para. 333, stating "[t]hat military commanders and other persons occupying positions of superior authority may be held criminally responsible for the unlawful conduct of their subordinates is a well-established norm of customary international law." See also *Prosecutor v. Enver Hadžihasanović, Mehmed Alagić and Amir Kubura*, Case No. IT-01-47-AR72, Decision on Interlocutory Appeal Challenging Jurisdiction in Relation to Command Responsibility, 16 July 2003 ("*Hadžihasanović* Appeal Decision on Jurisdiction"), para. 31, holding that "[i]n the opinion of the Appeals Chamber, the Trial Chamber was correct in holding, after a thorough examination of the matter, that command responsibility was at all times material to this case a part of customary international law in its application to war crimes committed in the course of an internal armed conflict."
[1510] *Aleksovski* Appeal Judgement, para. 76; *Stakić* Trial Judgement, para. 459; *Orić* Trial Judgement, para. 308; *Bagilshema* Appeal Judgement, para. 51; *Kajelijeli* Appeal Judgement, para. 85.
[1511] *Halilović* Trial Judgement, para. 54.
[1512] *Halilović* Trial Judgement, paras 42-54; *Prosecutor v. Enver Hadžihasanović and Amir Kubura*, Case No. IT-01-47-T, Judgement, 15 March 2006 ("*Hadžihasanović* Trial Judgement"), para. 75; see Judge Shahabuddeen's partly dissenting opinion in the *Hadžihasanović* Appeal Decision on Jurisdiction, stating that "[t]he position of the appellants seems to be influenced by their belief that Article 7(3) of the Statute has the effect, as they say, of making the commander 'guilty of an offence committed by others even he neither possessed the applicable mens rea nor had any involvement whatsoever in the actus reus.' No doubt, arguments can be made in support of that reading of the provision, but I prefer to interpret the provision as making the commander guilty for failing in his supervisory capacity to take the necessary corrective action after he knows or has reason to know that his subordinate was about to commit the act or had done so"; *Orić* Trial Judgement, para. 293. See also Brima Final Brief, para. 65.

[1513] *Orić* Trial Judgement, paras 301-302; see also *Prosecutor v. Ljube Boškoski and Johan Tarčulovski*, Case No. IT-04-82-PT, Decision on Prosecution's Motion to Amend the Indictment, 26 May 2006, paras 18 et seq.

[1514] *Čelebići* Trial Judgement, para. 377.
[1515] *Orić* Trial Judgement, para. 309, stating that "the broadening of this liability as described above is supported by the fact that the borderline between military and civil authority can be fluid. This is particularly the case with regard to many contemporary conflicts where there may be only de facto self-proclaimed governments and/or de facto armies and paramilitary groups subordinate thereto" (footnotes omitted); see also *Kordić*Trial Judgement, paras 419, 422; Prosecutor v. Juvenal Kajelijeli, Case No. ICTR-98-44A-A, Judgement, 23 May 2005 ("*Kajelijeli* Appeal Judgement"), para. 87; *Prosecutor v. Mladen Naletilić aka "Tuta" and Vinko Martinović aka "Štela"*, Case No. IT-98-34-T, Judgement, 31 March 2003 ("*Naletilić* Trial Judgement"), para. 67.
[1516] *Čelebići* Appeal Judgement, para. 256; see also *Halilović* Trial Judgement, para. 58.
[1517] *Čelebići* Appeal Judgement, para. 256; *Brđanin* Trial Judgement, para. 276; *Orić* Trial Judgement, para. 311; *Limaj* Trial Judgement, para. 522.
[1518] *Čelebići* Appeal Judgement, para. 197; Prosecution Final Brief, para. 437.
[1519] *Čelebići* Appeal Judgement, para. 266; *Blagojević* Trial Judgement, para. 791; *Ntagerura* Trial Judgement, para. 628; Brima Final Brief, para. 100; Kamara Final Brief, para. 61.
[1520] *Halilović* Trial Judgement, para. 58.
[1521] *Aleksovski* Trial Judgement, paras 101, 104; *Blaškić* Trial Judgement, para. 302; *Kordić* Trial Judgement, para. 421; see also *Kajelijeli* Trial Judgement, paras 403-404.
[1522] *Blaškić* Trial Judgement, para. 302; *Hadžihasanović* Trial Judgement, paras 83 et seq.
[1523] *Čelebići* Appeal Judgement, para. 206, endorsing the findings of *Čelebići* Trial Judgement, para. 743.
[1524] *Kordić* Trial Judgement, para. 424; *Stakić* Trial Judgement, para. 454.
[1525] *Aleksovski* Trial Judgement, para. 78; *Blaškić* Trial Judgement, para. 302.
[1526] *Halilović* Trial Judgement, paras 61, 62; *Kunarac* Trial Judgement, para. 399; *Orić* Trial Judgement, para. 313; *Aleksovski* Trial Judgement, para. 106; Prosecution Final Brief, para. 438.
[1527] *Blaškić* Trial Judgement, paras 296, 302, 303; *Krnojelac* Trial Judgement, para. 93; *Naletilić* Trial Judgement, para. 69; *Halilović* Trial Judgement, para. 62; Prosecution Final Brief, paras 439, 440.
[1528] *Brđanin* Trial Judgement, para. 277, referencing *Bagilishema* Appeal Judgement, para. 51; *Musema* Trial

Judgement, para. 135; *Stakić* Trial Judgement, para. 494.
[1529] *Blaškić* Appeal Judgement, para. 217; referring to *Prosecutor v. Milorad Krnojelac*, Case No. IT-97-25-PT, Decision on the Defence Preliminary Motion on the Form of the Indictment, 24 February 1999, para. 46; *Orić* Trial Judgement, para. 311; see also Prosecution Final Brief, para. 444.
[1530] *Kordić* Trial Judgement, para. 427.
[1531] *Kordić* Trial Judgement, para. 427; *Čelebići* Trial Judgement, para. 386; see also *Brđanin* Trial Judgement, para. 278; *Hadžihasanović* Trial Judgement, para. 94.
[1532] *Aleksovski* Trial Judgement, para. 80.
[1533] *Čelebići* Trial Judgement, para. 386; *Galić* Trial Judgement, para. 174; *Limaj* Trial Judgement, para. 524; *Bagilishema* Trial Judgement, para. 968; see also Prosecution Final Brief, para. 446; Brima Final Brief, para. 107.
[1534] *Kordić* Trial Judgement, para. 428; *Galić* Trial Judgement, para. 174; *Orić* Trial Judgement, para. 320; see also Prosecution Final Brief, para. 446.
[1535] *Blaškić* Appeal Judgement, para. 62; *Čelebići* Appeal Judgement, para. 241.

[1536] *Blaškić* Appeals Judgement, paras 62-63, *Čelebići* Appeals Judgement, para 226.
[1537] *Čelebići* Appeal Judgement, para. 238; *Čelebići* Trial Judgement, para. 393; *Kordić* Trial Judgement, para. 437; *Strugar* Trial Judgement, para. 370.
[1538] *Čelebići* Appeal Judgement, para. 232.
[1539] *Čelebići* Trial Judgement, para. 393; *Naletilić* Trial Judgement, para. 74; *Halilović* Trial Judgement, para. 68; *Orić* Trial Judgement, para. 322.
[1540] *Brđanin* Trial Judgement, para. 278, referring to *Čelebići* Appeal Judgement, paras 223, 241; see also *Strugar* Trial Judgement, paras 417-420, wherein it was considered insufficient that the information known to the commander at the time of the offence indicated that illegal acts might occur but rather required that the information indicates that such crimes would occur.
[1541] *Čelebići* Appeal Judgement, para. 238.
[1542] International Committee of the Red Cross ("ICRC"), Commentary to the Additional Protocols, para. 3545.
[1543] Brima Final Brief, para. 65, 69-75.
[1544] Kamara Final Brief, para. 69; Kanu Final Brief, para. 192.
[1545] Kamara Final Brief, para. 69.

[1546] *Orić* Trial Judgement, para. 324.
[1547] *Čelebići* Trial Judgement, para. 387; *Halilović* Trial Judgement, para. 69.
[1548] *Orić* Trial Judgement, para. 326; *Limaj* Trial Judgement, para. 527; *Strugar* Trial Judgement, para. 373.
[1549] *Blaškić* Appeal Judgement, paras 72, 77; *Čelebići* Trial Judgement, para. 394.
[1550] *Limaj* Trial Judgement, para. 528; Prosecution Final Brief, paras 453-454.
[1551] *Čelebići* Trial Judgement, para. 395.
[1552] *Orić* Trial Judgement, para. 329.
[1553] *Orić* Trial Judgement, para. 329; *Halilović* Trial Judgement, para. 79.
[1554] *Blaškić* Appeal Judgement, paras 83, 85.
[1555] *Limaj* Trial Judgement, para. 529; *Orić* Trial Judgement, para. 336; *Strugar* Trial Judgement, para. 376.
[1556] *Hadžihasanović* Appeal Decision on Command Responsibility, paras 45-46, but see Partial Dissenting Opinion of Judge Shahabuddeen, para. 43; Separate and Partially Dissenting Opinion of Judge David Hunt - Command Responsibility Appeal, para. 8; *Orić* Trial Judgement, para. 335.
[1557] *Blaškić* Appeal Judgement, para. 91; *Kordić* Appeal Judgement, para. 34.
[1558] *Blaškić* Appeal Judgement, para. 91; *Aleksovski* Appeal Judgement, para. 183; see also *Orić* Trial Judgement, paras 339-343.

BEMBA CASE

PRE-TRIAL CHAMBER II SITUATION IN THE CENTRAL AFRICAN REPUBLIC IN THE CASE OF THE PROSECUTOR V. JEAN-PIERRE BEMBA GOMBO

DECISION PURSUANT TO ARTICLE 61(7)(A) AND (B) OF THE ROME STATUTE ON THE CHARGES OF THE PROSECUTOR AGAINST JEAN-PIERRE BEMBA GOMBO

15 JUNE 2009

[...]

B. Article 28 of the Statute

402. The Chamber recalls, as stated in paragraph 341, that in the Amended DCC the Prosecutor charged Mr Jean-Pierre Bemba primarily under article 25(3)(a) of the Statute or, in the alternative, as a military commander or person effectively acting as a military commander or superior under article 28(a) or (b) of the Statute. In this regard, the Chamber made it clear that Mr Jean-Pierre Bemba's criminal responsibility under article 28 of the Statute shall not be examined, unless there is a determination that there is not sufficient evidence to establish substantial grounds to believe that the suspect is criminally responsible as a "co-perpetrator" within the meaning of article 25(3)(a) of the Statute for the crimes set out in the Amended DCC.

403.Since the Chamber found, in light of the required standard at the pre-trial stage, that Mr Jean-Pierre Bemba's criminal responsibility cannot be established under article 25(3)(a) of the Statute for the crimes against humanity and war crimes referred to in part V, it will consider his alternative alleged criminal responsibility under article 28 of the Statute.

1. The law and its interpretation

404. Article 28 of the Statute reads:

In addition to other grounds of criminal responsibility under this Statute for crimes wi thin the jurisdiction of the Court:

(a) A military commander or person effectively acting as a military commander shall be criminally responsible for crimes within the jurisdiction of the Court committed by forces under his or her effective command and control, or effective authority and control as the case may be, as a result of his or her failure to exercise control properly over such forces, where:

(i) That military commander or person either knew or, owing to the circumstances at the time, should have known that the forces were committing or about to commit such crimes; and
(ii) That military commander or person failed to take all necessary and reasonable measures within his or her power to prevent or repress their commission or to submit the matter to the competent authorities for investigation and prosecution.
(b) With respect to superior and subordinate relationships not described in paragraph (a), a superior shall be criminally responsible for crimes within the jurisdiction of the Court committed by subordinates under his or her effective authority and control, as a result of his or her failure to exercise control properly over such subordinates, where:
(i) The superior either knew, or consciously disregarded information which clearly indicated, that the subordinates were committing or about to commit such crimes;
(ii) The crimes concerned activities that were within the effective responsibility and control of the superior; and
(iii) The superior failed to take all necessary and reasonable measures within his or her power to prevent or repress their commission or to submit the matter to the competent authorities for investigation and prosecution.

405.The Chamber notes that article 28 of the Statute reflects a different form of criminal responsibility than that found under article 25(3) (a) of the Statute in the sense that a superior may be held responsible for the prohibited conduct of his subordinates for failing to fulfil his duty to prevent or repress their unlawful conduct or submit the matter to the competent authorities. This sort of responsibility can be better understood "when seen against the principle that criminal responsibility for omissions is incurred only where there exists a legal obligation to act".[49]

406.Article 28 of the Statute is drafted in a manner that distinguishes between two main categories of superiors and their relationships - namely, a military or militarylike commander (paragraph (a)) and those who fall short of this category such as civilians occupying de jure and de facto positions of authority (paragraph (b)). For the purpose of this decision, the Chamber is satisfied that the suspect in the case under consideration falls within the ambit of the first category as discussed

[49] Y. Sandoz/Ch. Swinarski/B. Zimmermann (eds.), ICRC Commentary on the Additional Protocols of 8 June 1977 to the Geneva Conventions of 12 Aug 1949 (ICRC, 1987), MN 3537; ICTY, Prosecutor v Delalic et al., Case No. IT-04-83-T,"Judgment", 16 November 1998, para. 334.

later, and, accordingly, it will confine its analysis to article 28(a) of the Statute.

407. **The Chamber considers that, in order to prove criminal responsibility within the meaning of article 28(a) of the Statute for any of the crimes set out in articles 6 to 8 of the Statute,** [50]

(a) The suspect must be either a military commander or a person effectively acting as such;

(b) The suspect must have effective command and control, or effective authority and control over the forces (subordinates) who committed one or more of the crimes set out in articles 6 to 8 of the Statute;

(c) The crimes committed by the forces (subordinates) resulted from the suspect's failure to exercise control properly over them;

(d) The suspect either knew or, owing to the circumstances at the time, should have known that the forces (subordinates) were committing or about to commit one or more of the crimes set out in article 6 to 8 of the Statute; and

(e) The suspect failed to take the necessary and reasonable measures within his or her power to prevent or repress the commission of such crime(s) or failed to submit the matter to the competent authorities for investigation and prosecution.

a) The suspect must be either a military commander or a person effectively acting as such (military-like commander)

408.The Chamber is of the view that the term "military commander" refers to a category of persons who are formally or legally appointed to carry out a military commanding function (i.e., de jure commanders). The concept embodies all persons who have command responsibility within the armed forces, irrespective of their rank or level.

In this respect, a military commander could be a person occupying the highest level in the chain of command or a mere leader with few soldiers under his or her command.

The notion of a military commander under this provision also captures those situations where the superior does not exclusively perform a military function.[51]

---

[50] Although the crime of aggression referred to in article 5 of the Statute falls within the jurisdiction of the Court, the Court cannot exercise jurisdiction over it until a definition is adopted pursuant to articles 121 and 123 of the Statute defining the crime and outlining the conditions on the basis of which the Court shall exercise its competence with respect to this crime.

[51] This is the case in some countries where a head of state is the commander in chief of the armed forces (de jure commander), and although the person does not carry out a military duty in an exclusive manner (also a sort of

409.With respect to a "person effectively acting as a military commander", the Chamber considers that this term is meant to cover a distinct as well as a broader category of commanders. This category refers to those who are not elected by law to carry out a military commander's role, yet they perform it de facto by exercising effective control over a group of persons through a chain of command. This concept was also acknowledged in several cases before the ICTY and the ICTR.[52]

In the Celebici case, the first leading case on the doctrine of command responsibility before the ad hoc tribunals, the ICTY Trial Chamber stated that:

Individuals in positions of authority, (...) within military structures, may incur criminal responsibility under the doctrine of command responsibility on the basis of their de facto as well as de jure positions as superiors. The mere absence of formal legal authority to control the actions of subordinates should therefore not be understood to preclude the imposition of such responsibility (emphasis added).[53]

410.Thus, the Chamber finds that this category of military-like commanders may generally encompass superiors who have authority and control over regular government forces such as armed police units[54] or irregular forces (non-government forces) such as rebel groups, paramilitary units[55] including, inter alia, armed resistance movements

---

quasi de facto commander), that person may be responsible for crimes committed by his forces (i.e., members of the armed forces) This is the case in some countries where a head of state is the commander in chief of the armed forces (de jure commander), and although the person does not carry out a military duty in an

exclusive manner (also a sort of quasi de facto commander), that person may be responsible for crimes committed by his forces (i.e., members of the armed forces)

52 ICTY, Prosecutor v Blaskic, Case No. IT-95-14-T, "Judgment", 3 March 2000, para. 300; ICTY, Prosecutor v Aleksovski, Case No. IT-95-14/1-T, "Judgment", 25 June 1999, para. 76; ICTR, The Prosecutor v. Gacumbitsi, Case No. ICTR-2001-64-A, "Appeals Chamber Judgment", 7 July 2006, para. 143; ICTR, The Prosecutor v. Juvenal Kajelijeli, Case No. ICTR-98-44A-A, "Appeals Chamber Judgment", 23 May 2005, para. 85.

53 ICTY, Prosecutor v Delahc et al, Case No. IT-96-21-T, "Judgment", 16 November 1998, para. 354

54 W. Fenrick, "Article 28", in: O. Triffterer (ed.), Commentary on the Rome Statute of the International Criminal Court, (Nomos Verlag, 1999), pp. 517-518.

55 Working Group on General Principles of Criminal Law, UN Doc. A/CONF. 183/C.1/WGGP/L.7, 22 June 1998, fn 1; W. Fenrick, "Ar t i c le 28", in: O. Tr i

and militias that follow a structure of military hierarchy or a chain of command.

b) The suspect must have effective command and control, or effective authority and control over his forces (subordinates)

411. The second element required for the application of the doctrine of command responsibility is the existence of "effective control" over the forces which committed one or more of the crimes under articles 6 to 8 of the Statute.

412.The Chamber observes that article 28(a) of the Statute refers to the terms "effective command and control" or "effective authority and control" as applicable alternatives in situations of military commanders strictu sensu and military-like commanders. In this regard, the Chamber considers that the additional words "command" and "authority" under the two expressions has no substantial effect on the required level or standard of "control". This is apparent from the express language of the two terms, which uses the words "effective" and "control" as a common denominator under both alternatives. This conclusion is also supported by a review of the travaux préparatoires of the Statute, in which it was acknowledged by some delegations that the addition of the term "effective authority and control" as an alternative to the existing text was "unnecessary and possibly confusing".[56] This suggests that some of the drafters believed that the insertion of this expression did not add or provide a different meaning to the text.

413.In this context, the Chamber underlines that the term "effective command" certainly reveals or reflects "effective authority". Indeed, in the English language the word "command" is defined as "authority, especially over armed forces", and the expression "authority" refers to

---

f f t e r er (ed.), Commentary on the Rome Statute of the International Criminal Court, (Nomos Verlag, 1999), p. 518.

[56] Working Group on General Principles of Criminal Law, UN Doc. A/CONF. 183/C.1/WGGP/L.7, 22 June
1998, fn 2. The term "authority" appeared in square brackets for the first time during the work of the Preparatory Committee in 1997 and remained between square brackets until Rome. See Decisions Taken By the Preparatory Committee At Its Session Held m New York 11 to 21 February 1997, UN Doc. A/AC.249/1997/L.5 (1997), Annex II, Report of the Working Group on General Principles of Criminal Law and Penalties, Article C, p. 23; Report of the Inter-Sessional Meeting From 19 to 30 January 1998 in Zutphen, the Netherlands, UN Doc. A/AC.249/1998/L.13 (1998), Article 19[C], p. 55; Report of the Preparatory Committee on the Establishment of an International Criminal Court, Draft St a tute & Draft Final Act, UN Doc. A/Conf.l83/2/Add.l (1998), Article 25, p. 61.

the "power or right to give orders and enforce obedience".[57] However, the usage of the disjunctive "or" between the expressions "effective command" and "effective authority" calls the Chamber to interpret them as having close, but distinct meanings in order to remedy the appearance of redundancy in the text. Thus, the Chamber is of the view that although the degree of "control" required under both expressions is the same as argued in paragraph 412 above, the term "effective authority" may refer to the modality, manner or nature, according to which, a military or military-like commander exercise "control" over his forces or subordinates.[58]

414.The Chamber wishes to point out that "effective control" is generally a manifestation of a superior-subordinate relationship between the suspect and the forces or subordinates in a de jure or de facto hierarchal relationship (chain of command).[59] As the ICTY Appeals Chamber stated in the Celebici case: "[t]he ability to exercise effective control [...] will almost invariably not be satisfied unless such a relationship of subordination exists".[60]

415.The concept of "effective control" is mainly perceived as "the material ability [or power] to prevent and punish" the commission of offences,[61] and, as such, failure to exercise such abilities of control gives rise to criminal responsibility[62] if other requirements are met. In the

---

[57] C. Soanes/A. Stevenson (eds.), Concise Oxford English Dictionary, (OUP, llth ed., 2004), p. 286

[58] This may refer to superiors who are not in "direct" chain of command with the forces. See on this question, G. Mettraux, The Law of Command Responsibility, (OUP, 2009), p. 29; W. Fenrick, "Article 28", in: O. Triffterer (ed.), Commentary on the Rome Statute of the International Criminal Court, (Nomos Verlag, 1999), p. 518.

[59] see generally, ICTR, The Prosecutor v Bagosora et al, Case No. ICTR-98-41-T, "Judgment and Sentence", 18 December 2008, para. 2012; ICTR, The Prosecutor v. Kajehjeli, Case No. ICTR-98-44A-T,"Judgment and Sentence", 1 December 2003, para. 773; ICTR, The Prosecutor v. Kajehjeli, Case No.ICTR-98-44A-A, "Appeals Chamber Judgment", 23 May 2005, para. 84.

[60] ICTY, Prosecutor v. Delalic et al, Case No. IT-96-21-A, "Judgment", 20 February 2001, para. 303.

[61] ICTY, Prosecutor v. Delalic et al, Case No. IT-96-21-A, "Appeals Chamber Judgment", 20 February 2001, para. 256; ICTR, The Prosecutor v Musema, Case No. ICTR-96-13-A, "Judgment", 27 January 2000, para. 135; ICTR, The Prosecutor v Bagihshema, Case No. ICTR-95-1A-A, "Appeals Chamber Judgment", 3 July 2002, para. 51.

[62] ICTY, Prosecutor v. Krnojelac, Case No. IT-97-25-A, "Appeals Chamber Judgment", 17 September 2003, para. 171 ("It cannot be overemphasised that, where superior responsibility is concerned, an accused is not charged

context of article 28(a) of the Statute, "effective control" also refers to the material ability to prevent or repress the commission of the crimes or submit the matter to the competent authorities. To this end, this notion does not seem to accommodate any lower standard of control such as the simple ability to exercise influence over forces or subordinates,[63] even if such influence turned out to be substantial.[64] As the ICTY Trial Chamber stated in the Hadzihasanovic case:

Since command responsibility is predicated on a superior's power to control the acts of his subordinates, a superior may only be held criminally responsible if he has the necessary powers of control, i.e. if he exercises effective control over his subordinates. The simple exercise of powers of influence over subordinates does not suffice.[65]

416.That said, the Chamber concurs with the view adopted by the ad hoc tribunals that indicia for the existence of effective control are "more a matter of evidence than of substantive law"[66] depending on the circumstances of each case,[67] and that those indicia are confined to showing that the suspect had the power to prevent, repress and/or submit the matter to the competent authorities for investigation.[68]

417. The Chamber takes the view that there are nonetheless several factors which may indicate the existence of a superior's position of authority and effective control. These factors may include: (i) the official

---

with the crimes of his subordinates but with his failure to carry out his duty as a superior to exercise control"); ICTY, Prosecutor v Delalic et al, Case No. IT-96-21-A, "Appeals Chamber Judgment", 20 February 2001, para. 198.

63 iCTY, Prosecutor v. Delic, Case No. IT-04-83-T, "Judgment", 15 September 2008, para. 60; ICTY, Prosecutor v. Kvocka et al, Case No. IT-98-30/1-A, "Appeals Chamber Judgment", 28 February 2005, para. 144.

64 ICTY, Prosecutor v Kordic and Cerkez, Case No. IT-95-14/2-T, "Judgment", 26 February 2001, paras 412-413.

65 ICTY, Prosecutor v Hadzihasanovic, and Kubura, Case No. IT-01-47-T, "Judgment", 15 March 2006, paras 80 and 795.

66 ICTY, Prosecutor v Hahlovic, Case No. IT-01-48-T, "Judgment", 16 November 2005, para. 58; ICTY,Prosecutor v Blaskic, Case No. IT-95-14-A, "Appeals Chamber Judgment", 29 July 2004, para. 69.

67 ICTY, Prosecutor v. Strugar, Case No. IT-01-42-T, "Judgment", 31 January 2005, para. 392.

68 See in the context of the ICTY, Prosecutor v. Blaskic, Case No. IT-95-14-A, "Appeals Chamber Judgment, 29 July 2004, para. 69; ICTY, Prosecutor v Aleksovski, Case No. IT-95-14/1-A, "Appeals Chamber Judgment", 24 March 2000, para. 76 (defining the indicia for effective control as "the power to prevent, punish, or initiate measures leading to proceedings against the alleged perpetrators where appropriate".

position of the suspect;[69](ii) his power to issue or give orders[70];(iii) the capacity to ensure compliance with the orders issued (i.e., ensure that they would be executed)[71];(iv) his position within the military structure and the actual tasks that he carried out[72];(v) the capacity to order forces or units under his command, whether under his immediate command or at a lowerlevels, to engage in hostilities[73];(vi) the capacity to re-subordinate units or make changes to command structure[74];(vii) the power to promote, replace, remove or discipline any member of the forces[75]; and (viii) the authority to send forces where hostilities take place and withdraw them at any given moment.

418.The Chamber also wishes to stress that it is not sufficient to demonstrate that thesuspect had effective control without specifying the time frame required for its existence. In particular, there is a question of temporal coincidence between the "effective control" and the criminal conduct. In this respect, the Chamber takes note of the common position upheld by the ad hoc tribunals, according to which effective control must have existed at the time of the commission of the crime.[76] The Chamber is also aware of the different view embraced by a

---

[69] ICTY, Prosecutor v Kordic and Cerkez, Case No. IT-95-14/2-T, 26 February 2001, para. 438; ICTY, Prosecutor v. Oric, Case No. IT-03-68-A, "Appeals Chamber Judgment", 3 July 2008, paras 91-92; ICTY, Prosecutor v. Hadzihasanovic and Kubura, Case No. IT-01-47-A, "Appeals Chamber Judgment", 22 April 2008, para. 21 (noting that the possession of de jure authority provides some evidence or prima facie indicia of effective control).

[70] iCTY, Prosecutor v. Kordic and Cerkez, Case No. IT-95-14/2-T, "Judgment", 26 February 2001, para.421; ICTY, Prosecutor v. Hadzihasanovic and Kubura, Case No. IT-01-47-A, "Appeals Chamber Judgment", 22 April 2008, para. 199.

[71] ICTY , Prosecutor v Blaskic, Case No. IT-95-14-A, "Appeals Chamber Judgment", 29 July 2004, para. 69

[72] ICTY, Prosecutor v. Hahlovic, Case No. IT-01-48-A, "Appeals Chamber Judgment", 16 October 2007, para. 66.

[73] ICTY, Prosecutor v Strugar, Case No. IT-01-42-T, "Judgment", 31 January 2005, paras 394-396.

[74] ICTY, Prosecutor v Strugar, Case No. IT-01-42-T, "Judgment", 31 January 2005, para. 397.

[75] ICTY, Prosecutor v Délié, Case No. IT-04-83-T, "Judgment", 15 September 2008, para. 62; ICTY, Prosecutor v Strugar, Case No. IT-01-42-T, "Judgment", 31 January 2005, paras 406 and 408; ICTY, Prosecutor v. Delalic et al, Case No. IT-96-21-T, "Judgment", 16 November 1998, para. 767.

[76] See for example, ICTY, Prosecutor v Hahlovic, Case No. IT-01-48-A, "Appeals Chamber Judgment",

16 October 2007, para. 59; ICTR, The Prosecutor v Bagosora et al, Case No. ICTR-98-41-T, "Judgment and Sentence", 18 December 2008, para. 2012.

minority of the ICTY Judges,[77] which was later upheld by Trial Chamber I of the SCSL, according to which the "superior must have had effective control over the perpetrator at the time at which the superior is said to have failed to exercise his powers to prevent or to punish".[78]

419.Having considered the above, the Chamber is of the view that according to article 28(a) of the Statute, the suspect must have had effective control at least when the crimes were about to be committed. This finding is supported by the language of the chapeau of article 28(a) of the Statute, which states in the relevant part that a military commander or a person effectively acting as such shall be criminally responsible for the crimes committed by forces under his effective control "as a result of his or her failure to exercise control properly over such forces [...]". The reference to the phrase "failure to exercise control properly" suggests that the superior was already in control over the forces before the crimes were committed.

c) The crimes committed resulted from the suspect's failure to exercise control properly over the forces (subordinates)

420.The third element to be satisfied for the purpose of article 28(a) of the Statute isto prove that crimes committed by the suspect's forces resulted from his failure to exercise control properly over them.

421.The Chamber recalls the chapeau of article 28(a) of the Statute, which stipulates that:

A military commander or person effectively acting as a mi l i t a ry commander shall be criminally responsible for crimes within the jurisdiction of the Court committed by forces under his or her effective command and control, or effective authority and control as the case may be, as a result of his f a i l u re to exercise control properly over such forces, where: (...)

(ii) That military commander or person failed to take all necessary and reasonable measures within his or her power to prevent or repress their commission or to submit the matter to the competent authorities for investigation.

422.The Chamber now turns to the two expressions, namely "effective control" and "exercise control properly". In this respect, the Chamber considers that it cannot be said that a superior failed to "exercise control properly", without showing that he had "effective control" over his

[77] ICTY, Prosecutor v. Oric, Case No. IT-03-68-A, "Appeals Chamber Judgment", 3 July 2008, (Declaration of Judge Shahabuddeen; Partially Dissenting Opinion and Declaration of Judge Liu), pp. 65-85.

[78] SCSL, The Prosecutor v. Sesay et al, Case No. SCSL-04-15-T, "Judgment", 2 March 2009, para. 299.

forces. Since effective control is actually the "material ability" to prevent, repress or submit the matter to the competent authorities, then a failure to "exercise control properly" is, in fact, a scenario of noncompliance with such duties. This suggests that the reference to the phrase "failure to exercise control properly" must be read and understood in light of article 28(a)(ii) of the Statute.

423.The Chamber also observes that the chapeau of article 28(a) of the Statuteestablishes a link between the commission of the underlying crimes and a superior's "failure to exercise control properly". This is reflected in the words "as a result of", which indicates such relationship.[79] The Chamber therefore considers that thechapeau of article 28(a) of the Statute includes an element of causality between a superior's dereliction of duty and the underlying crimes.[80] This interpretation is consistent with the principle of strict construction mirrored in article 22(2) of the Statute which, as a part of the principle

---

[79] The Chamber acknowledges that the ad hoc tribunals do not recognise causality as an element of superior responsibility. However, unlike article 28(a) of the Statute, the relevant provisions on superior responsibility in the Statues of the ad hoc tribunals do not expressly require such an element. See ICTY, Prosecutor v. Delalic et al, Case No. IT-96-21-T, "Judgment", 16 November 1998, para. 398; ICTY, Prosecutor v. Blaskic, Case No. 1T-95-14-A, "Appealc Chamber Judgment", 29 July 2004, para. 77, ICTY, Prosecutor v Hadzihasanovic et al, Case No. IT-01-47-T, "Appeal Chamber Judgment", 22 April 2008, paras 38-39; ICTY, Prosecutor v Kordic and Cerkez, Case No. IT-95-14/2-A, "Appeals Chamber Judgment", 17 December 2004, paras 830-832; Statute of the International Criminal Tribunal for the Prosecution of Persons Responsible for Serious Violations of International Humanitarian Law Committed in the Territory of the former Yugoslavia since 1991, (1993) 32 ILM p. 1159, as amended by Security Council Resolution 1660 of 28 Feb. 2006, Art. 7(3); Statute of the International Criminal Tribunal for Rwanda, (1994) 33 ILM p. 1602, as amended by Security Council Resolution 1534 of 26 Mar. 2004, Art 6(3); Statute of the Special Court for Sierra Leone, UNTS vol. 2178, p. 138, U.N. Doc. S/2002/246, 16 Jan. 2002, Appendix II, Art. 6(3); Law on the Establishment of the Extraordinary Chambers in the Courts of Cambodia for the Prosecution of Crimes Committed During the Period of Democratic Kampuchea, as amended on 27 Oct. 2004, Doc. No. NS/RKM/1004/006, unofficial translation by the Council of Jurists and the Secretariat of the Task Force, revised on 26 August 2007, Art. 29.

[80] O. Triffterer, 'Causality, A Separate Element of the Doctrine of Superior Responsibility as Expressed in Article 28 Rome Statute?', 15 Leiden J. Int'l L. p. 179, at p. 197 (2002); K. Ambos in A. Cassese/P. Gaeta/J.R.W.J. Jones (eds.), The Rome Statute of the International Criminal Court- A Commentary, vol. 1, (OUP, 2002), p. 860.

nullum crimen sine lege, compels the Chamber to interpret this provision strictly.

424. Although the Chamber finds that causality is a requirement under article 28 of the Statute, its actual scope needs to be further clarified by the Chamber. As stated above, article 28(a)(ii) of the Statute refers to three different duties: the duty to prevent crimes, repress crimes, or submit the matter to the competent authorities for investigation and prosecution. The Chamber considers that a failure to comply with the duties to repress or submit the matter to the competent authorities arise during or after the commission of crimes.[81] Thus, it is illogical to conclude that a failurerelating to those two duties can retroactively cause the crimes to be committed.[82]Accordingly, the Chamber is of the view that the element of causality only relates to the commander's duty to prevent the commission of future crimes. Nonetheless, the Chamber notes that the failure of a superior to fulfil his duties during and after thecrimes can have a causal impact on the commission of further crimes.[83] As punishment is an inherent part of prevention of future crimes, a commander's pastfailure to punish crimes is likely to increase the risk that further crimes will be committed in the future.[84]

425.The Chamber also considers that since article 28(a) of the Statute does not elaborate on the level of causality required, a possible way to determine the level of causality would be to apply a "but for test", in the sense that, but for the superior's failure to fulfil his duty to take reasonable and necessary measures to prevent crimes, those crimes would not have been committed by his forces.[85] However, contrary to the visible and material effect of a positive act, the effect of an omission

---

[81] As explained below under element (e), the duty to repress also may arise during the commission of crimes in the form of a duty to prevent the continuation of the commission of crimes.

[82] This reasoning was used by the ICTY to reject causality altogether, see ICTY, Prosecutor v. Delalic et al, Case No. IT-96-21-T, "Judgment", 16 November 1998, para. 400: "The very existence of the principle of superior responsibility for failure to punish demonstrates the absence of a requirement of causality as a separate element of the doctrine of superior responsibility"; ICTY, Prosecutor v. Blaskic, Case No. IT-95-14-A, "Appeals Chamber Judgment", 29 July 2004, para. 76.

[83] ICTY, Prosecutor v Halilovic, Case No. IT-01-48-T, "Judgment", 16 November 2005, para. 96.

[84] ICTY, Prosecutor v. Hadzihasanovic et al, Case No. IT-01-47-A, "Appeals Chamber Judgment", 22 April 2008, para. 267.

[85] ICTY, Prosecutor v. Delalic et al, Case No. IT-96-21-T, 16 November 1998, para. 399.

cannot be empirically determined with certainty.[86] In other words, it would not bepractical to predict exactly what would have happened if a commander had fulfilled his obligation to prevent crimes. There is no direct causal link that needs to be established between the superior's omission and the crime committed by his subordinates.[87] Therefore, the Chamber considers that it is only necessary to prove that the commander's omission increased the risk of the commission of the crimescharged in order to hold him criminally responsible under article 28(a) of the Statute.[88]

426.Accordingly, to find a military commander or a person acting as a military commander responsible for the crimes committed by his forces, the Prosecutor must demonstrate that his failure to exercise his duty to prevent crimes increased the riskthat the forces would commit these crimes.

d) The suspect either knew or should have known

427. The Chamber, reiterates what it has stated earlier in this decision, that the RomeStatute does not endorse the concept of strict liability. To this end, attribution of criminal responsibility for any of the crimes that fall within the jurisdiction of the Court depends on the existence of the relevant state of mind or degree of fault. This is also the case with respect to criminal responsibility arising under article 28 of the Statute.

428. Thus, in order to hold the suspect criminally responsible under article 28(a) of the Statute for a crime committed by forces (subordinates) under his control, it mustbe proven inter alia that the suspect "either knew or, owing to the circumstances atthe time, should

---

[86] K. Ambos, in: A. Cassese/P. Gaeta/J.R.W.D. Jones (eds.), The Rome Statute of the International Criminal Court A Commentary, vol. 1, (OUP, 2002), p. 860.

[87] K. Ambos, in: A. Cassese/P. Gaeta/J.R.W.D. Jones (eds.), The Rome Statute of the International Criminal Court' A Commentary, vol. 1, (OUP, 2002), p. 860; E. Van Sliedregt, The Criminal Responsibilityof Individuals for Violations of International Humanitarian Law, (T.M.C. Asser Press, 2003), p. 190.

[88] ICTY, Prosecutor v Hadzihasanovic et al, Case No (IT-01-47-A), "Appeals Chamber Judgment", 22 April 2008, para. 31: "a superior's failure to punish a crime of which he has actual knowledge is likely to be understood by his subordinates at least as acceptance, if not encouragement, of such conduct with the effect of increasing the risk of new crimes being committed." (emphasis added); K. Ambos, in:A. Cassese/P. Gaeta/J.R.W.D Jones (eds.), The Rome Statute of the International Criminal Court. A Commentary, vol. 1, (OUP, 2002), p. 860; V. Nerlich, 'Superior Responsibility Under Article 28 ICC Statute - For What Exactly Is the Superior Held Responsible?', 5 *J*. Int'l Crim. Just. p. 655, at p. 673 (2007); see also the AI amicus curiae submission in the Case, ICC-01/05-01/08-406, paras 45-47.

have known that his subordinates were committing or about tocommit" one or more of the crimes embodied in articles 6 to 8 of the Statute. This means that the suspect must have knowledge or should have known that his forces were about to engage or were engaging or had engaged in a conduct constituting the crimes referred to above.[89]

429.In this regard, the Chamber considers that article 28(a) of the Statute encompasses two standards of fault element. The first, which is encapsulated by the term "knew", requires the existence of actual knowledge. The second, which is covered by the term "should have known", is in fact a form of negligence. The Chamber will discuss each of these elements in the following paragraphs.

430.With respect to the suspect's actual knowledge that the forces or subordinates were committing or about to commit a crime, it is the view of the Chamber that such knowledge cannot be "presumed".[90] Rather, the suspect's knowledge must beobtained by way of direct or circumstantial evidence.[91] In this regard, the Chambertakes note of the relevant jurisprudence of the ad hoc tribunals which considered several factors or indicia to reach a finding on a superior's actual knowledge.

431.These factors include the number of illegal acts, their scope, whether their occurrence is widespread, the time during which the prohibited acts took place, thetype and number of forces involved, the means of available communication, the modus operandi of similar acts, the scope and nature of the superior's position and responsibility in the hierarchal structure, the location of the commander at the time and the geographical location of the acts.[92] Actual knowledge may be also

---

[89] ICTY, Prosecutor v Oric, Case No. IT-03-68-A, "Appeals Chamber Judgment", 3 July 2008, paras 57- 60; ICTY, Prosecutor v Milutinovic et al, Case No. IT-05-87-T, "Judgment", 26 February 2009, para. 120; SCSL, The Prosecutor v Sesay et al, Case No. SCSL-04-15-T, "Judgment", 2 March 2009, para. 309.

[90] ICTY, Prosecutor v Délié, Case No. IT-04-83-T, "Judgment", 15 September 2008, para. 64; ICTY, Prosecutor v Erâamn, Case No. IT-99-36-T, "Judgment", 1 September 2004, para. 278 (noting that knowledge "may be presumed if a superior had the means to obtain the relevant information of a crime and deliberately refrained from doing so").

[91] ICTY, Prosecutor v. Kordic and Cerkez, Case No. IT-95-14/2-T, "Judgment", 26 February 2001, para. 427; ICTY, Prosecutor v Hadzihasanovic ct al, Case No. IT-01-47-T, "Judgment", 15 March 2006, para. 94.

[92] See Final Report of the Commission of Experts Established Pursuant of Security Council Resolution 780(1992), UN Doc. S/1994/674, p. 7; see, inter aha, ICTY, Prosecutor v Delalic et al, Case No. IT-96-21-T,"Judgment", 16 November 1998, para. 386; ICTY, Prosecutor v. Blaskic, Case No. IT-95-14-T,"Judgment", 3 March 2000, para. 307; ICTY, Prosecutor v Strugar, Case No. IT-01-42-T, "Judgment", 31January 2005, para. 368; ICTY, Prosecutor v One,

proven if, "a priori, [a military commander] is part of an organised structure with established reporting and monitoring systems".[93] Thus, the Chamber considers that thesefactors are instructive in making a determination on a superior's knowledge within the context of article 28 of the Statute.

432. The "should have known" standard requires the superior to "ha[ve] merely been negligent in failing to acquire knowledge" of his subordinates' illegal conduct.[94] In the Blaskic case, the ICTY Trial Chamber, after having reviewed somepost-Second World War jurisprudence and articles 86(2) and 87 of Additional Protocol I to the Geneva Conventions, supported the inclusion of the "should have known" standard into article 7(3) of the ICTY Statute. In defining this standard, the Chamber stated:

In conclusion, the Trial Chamber finds that if a commander has exercised due diligence in the fulfillment of his duties yet lacks knowledge that crimes are about to be or have been committed, such lack of knowledge cannot be held against him. However, taking into account his particular position of command and the circumstances prevailing at the time, such ignorance cannot be a defence where the absence of knowledge is the result of negligence in the discharge of his duties (...).[95]

433.Thus, it is the Chamber's view that the "should have known" standard requiresmore of an active duty on the part of the superior to take the necessary measures to secure knowledge of the conduct of his troops[96] and to inquire, regardless of the availability of information at

---

Case No. IT-03-68-A, "Appeals Chamber Judgment",3 July 2008, para. 319; ICTR, The Prosecutor v Bagosora et al, Case No. ICTR-98-41-T, "Judgment andSentence", 18 December 2008, para. 2014; SCSL, The Prosecutor v. Sesay et al, Case No. SCSL-04-15-T,"Judgment", 2 March 2009, para. 309.

[93] ICTY, Prosecutor v Hadzihasanovic et al, Case No. IT-01-47-T, "Judgment", 15 March 2006, para. 94.

[94] ICC-01/05-01/08-406, paras 3 and 6

[95] ICTY, Prosecutor v Blaskic, Case No. IT-95-14-T, "Judgment", 3 March 2000, para. 332.

[96] ICTR, The Prosecutor v. Kayishema and Ruzindana, Case No. ICTR-95-1-T, "Judgment and Sentence", 21 May 1999, para. 227 (noting that article 28 (a) of the Statute "imposes a more active duty upon the superior to inform himself of the activities of his subordinates"); Fenrick, W., "Article 28", in: O. Triffterer (ed.), Commentary on the Rome Statute of the International Criminal Court, (Nomos Verlag, 1999), p. 519.

the time on the commission of the crime.[97] The drafting history of this provision reveals that it was the intent of the drafters to take a more stringent approach towards commanders and military-like commanders compared to other superiors that fall within the parameters of article 28(b) of the Statute. This is justified by the nature and type of responsibility assigned to this category of superiors.[98]

434.The Chamber is mindful of the fact that the "had reason to know" criterion embodied in the statutes of the ICTR, ICTY and SCSL[99] sets a different standard to the "should have known" standard under article 28 (a) of the Statute. However, despite such a difference, which the Chamber does not deem necessary to address in the present decision, the criteria or indicia developed by the ad hoc tribunals to meetthe standard of "had reason to know" may also be useful when applying the "should have known" requirement. Moreover, the factors referred to above in relation to the determination of actual knowledge are also relevant in the Chamber's final assessment of whether a superior "should have known" of the commission of the crimes or the risk of their occurrence. In this respect, the suspect may be considered to have known, if inter alia, and depending on the circumstances of each case: (i) he had general information to put him on notice of crimes committed by subordinates or of the possibility of occurrence of the unlawful acts[100];

---

[97] See e.g., E. Van Sliedregt, The Criminal Responsibility of Individuals for Violations of International Humanitarian Law, (T.M.C. Asser Press, 2003), p. 186.

[98] Summary Record of the 7 sf Meeting of the Committee of the Whole, UN Doc. A/CONF.183/C.1/SR.1,] paras 67-82.

[99] Statute of the International Criminal Tribunal for the Prosecution of Persons Responsible for Serious Violations of International Humanitarian Law Committed in the Territory of the former Yugoslavia since 1991, (1993) 32 ILM. 1159, as amended by Security Council Resolution 1660 of 28 Feb. 2006, Art. 7(3); Statute of the International Criminal Tribunal for Rwanda, (1994) 33 ILM 1602, as amended by Security Council Resolution 1534 of 26 Mar. 2004, Art 6(3); Statute of the Special Court for Sierra Leone, UNTS vol. 2178, p. 138, U.N. Doc. S/2002/246,16 Jan. 2002, Appendix II, Art. 6(3).

[100] icTY, Prosecutor v. Délié, Case No. IT-04-83-T, "Judgment", 15 September 2008, paras 65-66; ICTY Prosecutor v Strugar, Case No. IT-01-42-T, "Judgment", 31 January 2005, para. 370; SCSL, The Prosecutor v Fofana et al, Case No. SCSL-04-14-T, para. 244. This information may be obtained from, inter alia, the media or reports prepared by international and non-governmental organisations. ICTY, Prosecutor v. Blaskic, Case No. IT-95-14-A, "Appeals Chamber Judgment", 29 July 2004, para. 618; ICTY, Prosecutor v. Gahc, Case No. IT-98-29-T, "Judgment and Opinion", 5 December 2003, para. 704.

and (ii) such available information was sufficient to justify further inquiry or investigation.[101] The Chamber also believes that failure to punish past crimes committed by the same group of subordinates may be an indication of future risk.[102]

e) The suspect failed to take all the necessary and reasonable measures

435.In order to find the suspect responsible under command responsibility, once the mental element is satisfied, it is necessary to prove that he or she failed at least to fulfil one of the three duties listed under article 28(a)(ii) of the Statute: the duty to prevent crimes, the duty to repress crimes or the duty to submit the matter to the competent authorities for investigation and prosecution.

436. The Chamber first wishes to underline that the three duties under article 28(a)(ii) of the Statute arise at three different stages in the commission of crimes: before, during and after. Thus, a failure to fulfil one of these duties is itself a separate crime under article 28(a) of the Statute.[103] A military commander or a military-like commander can therefore be held criminally responsible for one or more breaches of duty under article 28(a) of the Statute in relation to the same underlying crimes. Consequently, a failure to prevent crimes which the commander knew or should have known about cannot be cured by fulfilling the duty to repress or submit the matter to the competent authorities.[104]

---

101 ICTY, Prosecutor v. Lima] et al, Case No. IT-03-66-T, "Judgment", 30 November 2005, para. 525; ICTY, Prosecutor v. Kordic and Cerkez, Case No. IT-95-14/2-T, "Judgment", 26 February 2001, para. 437.

102 SCSL, The Prosecutor v Sesay et al, Case No. SCSL-04-15-T, "Judgment", 2 March 2009, para. 311. (noting that "while a superior's knowledge of and failure to punish his subordinates' past offences is insufficient on its own to conclude that the superior knew that future offences would be committed, such knowledge may constitute sufficiently alarming information to justify further inquiry").

103 ICTY, Prosecutor v. Dehc, Case No. IT-04-83-T, "Judgment", 15 September 2008, para. 69 (noting that "ft]he failure to punish and failure to prevent involve different crimes committed at different times: the failure to punish concerns past crimes committed by subordinates, whereas the failure to prevent concerns future crimes of subordinates").

104 ICTY Prosecutor v Délié, Case No. IT-04-83-T, "Judgment", 15 September 2008; para 69, ICTY, Prosecutor v Blaskic, Case No. IT-95-14-T, "Judgment", 3 March 2000, para. 336. ICTY, Prosecutor v. Strugar, Case No. IT-01-42-T, "Judgment", 31 January 2005, para. 373; ICTY, Prosecutor v Hadzihasanovic,and Kubura, Case No. IT-01-47-T, "Judgment", 15 March 2006, para. 126.

(i) The duty to prevent

437. The Chamber notes that the duty to prevent arises when the commander or military-like commander knew or should have known that forces under his effective control and command/authority "were committing or about to commit" crimes. Thus, such a duty is triggered at any stage prior to the commission of crimes and before it has actually been committed by the superior's forces.[105]

438.Article 28 of the Statute does not define the specific measures required by the duty to prevent crimes. In this context, the Chamber considers it appropriate to be guided by relevant factors such as measures: (i) to ensure that superior's forces are adequately trained in international humanitarian law[106]; (ii) to secure reports that military actions were carried out in accordance with international law[107]; (iii) to issue orders aiming at bringing the relevant practices into accord with the rules of war[108]; (iv) to take disciplinary measures to prevent the commission of atrocities by the troops under the superior's command.[109]

(ii) The duty to repress

439. The duty to "repress" encompasses two seperate duties arising at two different stages of the commission of crimes.[110] First, the duty to repress includes a duty to stop ongoing crimes from continuing to be committed.[111] It is the obligation to "interrupt a possible chain effect,

105 icTY, Prosecutor v Délie, Case No. IT-04-83-T, "Judgment", 15 September 2008, para. 72.

106 W. Fenrick, "Article 28", in: O. Triffterer (ed.), Commentary on the Rome Statute of the International Criminal Court, (Nomos Verlag, 1999), p. 520.

107 ICTY, Prosecutor v. Strugar, Case No. IT-01-42-T, "Judgment", 31 January 2005, para. 374; ICTY, Prosecutor v Hadzihasanovic, and Kubura, Case No. IT-01-47-T, "Judgment", 15 March 2006, para. 153.

108 ICTY, Prosecutor v. Strugar, Case No. IT-01-42-T, "Judgment", 31 January 2005, para. 374; ICTY, Prosecutor v. Hadzihasanovic, and Kubura, Case No. IT-01-47-T, "Judgment", 15 March 2006, para. 153.

109 icTY, Prosecutor v Strugar, Case No. IT-01-42-T, "Judgment", 31 January 2005, para. 374; ICTY, Prosecutor v. Hadzihasanovic, and Kubura, Case No. IT-01-47-T, "Judgment", 15 March 2006, para. 153.

110 O. Triffterer, "Causality, A Separate Element of the Doctrine of Superior Responsibility as Expressed in Article 28 Rome Statute?," 15 Leiden }. Int'l L., p. 179, at p. 201 (2002).

111 In this respect, the duty to repress is equivalent to the obligation to "suppress" crimes. The latter expression is used in Article 87 of the Additional Protocol I to the Geneva Conventions. See also ICTY, Prosecutor

which may lead to other similar events".[112] Second, the duty to repress encompasses an obligation to punish forces after the commission of crimes.[113]

440.The Chamber wishes to point out that the duty to punish requiring the superior to take the necessary measures to sanction the commission of crimes[114] may be fulfiled in two different ways: either by the superior himself taking the necessary and reasonable measures to punish his forces, or, if he does not have the ability to do so, by referring the matter to the competent authorities. Thus, the duty to punish (as part of the duty to repress) constitutes an alternative to the third duty mentioned under article 28(a)(ii), namely the duty to submit the matter to the competent authorities, when the superior is not himself in a position to take necessary and reasonable measures to punish.[115]

441. Moreover, as explained later, the power of a superior, and thus the punitive measures available to him, will vary according to the circumstances of the case and, in particular, to his position in the chain of command.[116] Accordingly, whether the duty to punish requires

---

v. Hadzihasanovic, and Kubura, Case No. IT-01-47-T, "Judgment", 15 March 2006, para.

127, referring, inter aha, to ICTY, Prosecutor v Strugar, Case No. IT-01-42-T, "Judgment", 31 January 2005, para 446: "The Accused had the legal authority and the material ability to stop the unlawful shelling of the Old Town and to punish the perpetrators" and that he "did not take necessary and reasonable measures to ensure at least that the unlawful shelling of the Old Town be stopped." ICTY, Prosecutor v Kordic and Cerkez, Case No. IT-95-14/2-T, "Judgment", 26 February 2001, para 446.

[112] R. Arnold in: O. Triffterer (ed.), Commentary on the Rome Statute of the International Criminal Court,- Observers' Notes, Article by Article, (Nomos Verlag 2nd ed., 2008), p. 838.

[113] ICTY, Prosecutor v Kordic and Cerkez, Case No. IT-95-14/2-T, "Judgment", 26 February 2001, para 446

[114] w. Fenrick, "Article 28", in O. Triffterer (ed.), Commentary on the Rome Statute of the International Criminal Court, (Baden-Baden: Nomos Verlagsgesllschaft, 1999), p. 520.

[115] ICTY, The Prosecutor v Naser Oric, Case No IT-03-68-A, "Appeals Chamber Judgment", 3 July 2008, para. 336: "The superior need not conduct the investigation or dispense the punishment in person, but he or she must at least ensure that the matter is investigated and transmit a report to the competent authorities for further investigation or sanction." See also ICTY, The Prosecutor v Enver Hadzihasanovic, Amir Kubura, Case No IT-01-47-T, "Judgment", 15 March 2006, para. 154.

[116] Y Fenrick, "Article 28", in O. Triffterer (ed.), Commentary on the Rome Statute of the International Criminal Court, (Baden-Baden: Nomos Verlagsgesllschaft, 1999), p. 520.

exercising his power to take measures himself or to submit the matter to the competent authorities will therefore depend on the facts of the case. (in) The duty to submit the matter to the competent authorities for investigation and prosecution

442. The duty to submit the matter to the competent authorities, like the duty to punish, arises after the commission of the crimes. Such a duty requires that the commander takes active steps in order to ensure that the perpetrators are brought to justice.[117] It remedies a situation where commanders do not have the ability to sanction their forces.[118] This includes circumstances where the superior has the ability to take measures, yet those measures do not seem to be adequate.[119]

(iv) Necessary and Reasonable Measures

443.The Chamber considers that what constitutes "necessary and reasonable measures" must be addressed in concreto.[120] A commander or military-like commander will only be responsible under article 28(a) of the Statute for failing to take measures "within his material possibility".[121] The Chamber's assessment of what may be materially possible will depend on the superior's degree of effective control over his forces at the time his duty arises. This suggests that what constitutes a reasonable and necessary measure will be assessed on the basis of the

---

[117] ICTY, Prosecutor v. Delia, Case No. IT-04-83-T, "Judgment", 15 September 2008; para. 74; see also article 87(3) of Additional Protocol I to the Geneva Conventions which requires a military commander, who is aware that his subordinates have committed a breach of the Geneva Conventions or the Protocol, "where appropriate, to initiate disciplinary or penal action" against them.

[118] ICTY, Prosecutor v. Strugar, Case No. IT-01-42-T, "Judgment", 31 January 2005, para. 376; ICTY, Prosecutor v Kordic and Cerkez, Case No. IT-95-14/2-T, "Judgment", 26 February 2001, para 446.

[119] R. Arnold in: O. Triffterer (ed.), Commentary on the Rome Statute of the International Criminal Court- Observers' Notes, Article by Article (Nomos Verlag, 2nd ed., 2008) p. 838.

[120] ICTY, Prosecutor v. Blaskic, Case No. IT-95-14-A, "Appeals Chamber Judgment", 29 July 2004, para. 417; see also ICTY, Prosecutor v. Hadzihasanovic, and Kubura, Case No. IT-01-47-T, "Judgment", 15 March 2006, para. 155. For the relevant factors to be taken into account see ICTY, Prosecutor v. Dehc, Case No. IT-04-83-T, "Judgment", 15 September 2008, para. 76; ICTY, Prosecutor v Strugar, Case No. IT-01-42-T, "Judgment", 31 January 2005, para. 378.

[121] ICTY, Prosecutor v. Blaskic, Case No. IT-95-14-A, "Appeals Chambers Judgment", 29 July 2004, para. 395.

commander's de jure power as well as his de facto ability to take such measures.[122]

2. Findings of the Chamber

444. Having reviewed the Disclosed Evidence as a whole, the Chamber finds that there is sufficient evidence to establish substantial grounds to believe that Mr JeanPierre Bemba is criminally responsible pursuant to article 28(a) of the Statute for the crimes against humanity of murder (article 7(l)(a) of the Statute) and rape (article 7(l)(g) of the Statute) and the war crimes of murder (article 8(2)(c)(i) of the Statute), rape (article 8(2)(e)(vi) of the Statute) and pillaging (article 8(2)(e)(v) of the Statute) committed by MLC troops in the CAR from on or about 26 October 2002 to 15 March 2003. The Chamber bases this finding on the following considerations.

445.In setting forth its reasoning in relation to the five elements required under article 28(a) of the Statute, the Chamber addresses the first two elements under one sub-heading (a) due to their co-relation. The fourth element concerning the knowledge is dealt with by the Chamber in sub-section (b). The Chamber also covers the third element of causality in the discussion of the f i f th element concerning failure to prevent or to repress under sub-heading (c).

a) Mr lean-Pierre Bemba was effectively acting as a military commander and had effective authority and control over the MLC troops who committed the crimes

446.Having reviewed the Disclosed Evidence as a whole, the Chamber finds that there is sufficient evidence to establish substantial grounds to believe that Mr JeanPierre Bemba, at all times relevant to the charges, effectively acted as a military commander and had effective authority and control over the MLC troops who committed the crimes against

---

122 ICTY, Prosecutor v Kordic and Cerkez, Case No. IT-95-14/2-A, "Appeals Chamber Judgment", 17 December 2004, para. 443: noting that "it is the actual ability, or effective capacity to take measures which is important. The reference to the lack of formal legal competence to take measures should be read in this context. When assessing whether a superior failed to act, the Trial Chamber will look beyond his formal competence to his actual capacity to take measures"; see also ICTY, Prosecutor v. Delahc et al, Case No. IT-96-21, "Judgment", 16 November 1998, para. 395: noting that "for the superior to incur responsibility, he must have had the legal competence to take measures to prevent or repress the crime and the material possibility to take such measures. Thus, a superior would not incur criminal responsibility for failing to perform an act which was impossible to perform in either respect."

humanity of murder and rape and the war crimes of murder, rape and pillaging in the CAR from on or about 26 October 2002 to 15 March 2003.

447.1n reaching the above conclusion, the Chamber was mindful of the Defence's submission which relied on witness statements 9[123], 31[124], 46[125] and 80[126] to allege that in the CAR, the MLC troops were placed under the complete dependence and authority of the members of the Central African government and military hierarchy[127], and were therefore not under the effective authority, control or command of Mr Jean-Pierre Bemba.[128]

448.Upon analysis of the evidence, the Chamber however believes that the MLC – a non governmental force - was a hierarchically organized group over which Mr JeanPierre Bemba had effective authority and control. For the sake of clarity, the following paragraphs will address the different elements taken into consideration by the Chamber.

(i) Mr Jean-Pierre Bemba's official position within the MLC structure

449. In relation to the use of the statement of witness 15, the Chamber would like to underline that this witness was a member of the MLC

---

[123] Statement of witness 9, EVD-P-00148 at 0140, 143, 0154 and 0155. The Defence underlines that at 0140 the witness states that it was not up to Mr Jean-Pierre Bemba to feed the ALC soldiers, since they were in the service of the Central African Republic.

[124] Statement of witness 31, EVD-P-00102 at 0339. The witness states that there was only one commander of the MLC troops in the CAR. The Defence therefore concludes that witness 31 clearly excludes Mr Jean-Pierre Bemba from the chain of command.

[125] Statement of witness 46, EVD-P-02334 at 0299, 0306, 0311 and 0313; EVD-P-02336 at 0365 in which, according to the Defence, it is apparent that Mr Patassé had authority over the MLC troops. EVD-P- 02328 at 0178 in relation to which the Defence states that the witness confirms that, following the rebel
attack of October 2002, President Patassé had asked the CEN-SAD summit to send other troops from the CEN-SAD countries to reinforce the Libyan force which were already present in Bangui since 2001.

[126] Statement of witness 80, EVD-P-02395 at 0189, where, according to the Defence, the witness draws a clear distinction between the commander of the "Banyamulenge" on CAR territory, whom the witness designates as Mr Patassé, and the "Banyamulenge" commander on the other side of the river, on the DRC territory, Mr Jean-Pierre Bemba.

[127] ICC-01/05-01/08-413, paras. 137-148.

[128] ICC-01/05-01/08-413, para. 142.

during all times relevant to the present case, and thus privy to information related to the MLC. However, the Chamber observes that he was later excluded by Mr Jean-Pierre Bemba, and accordingly, the witness describes his relationship with Mr Jean-Pierre Bemba to be "non-existent" and "very poor".[129]

450.The Chamber is of the view that the circumstances surrounding the exclusion of witness 15 from the MLC may raise doubts as to his reliability. Nevertheless, as stated in paragraph 57 of the present decision, the existence of possible political motives does not automatically lead to a rejection of the witness statement. Rather, the Chamber assesses the witness's credibility in relation to each issue to be decided upon and in light of the evidence as a whole. Thus, the Chamber refers to the statement of witness 15 to the extent that the information relied upon is corroborated by other pieces of evidence.

451. According to the Statuts du Mouvement de Libération du Congo signed in Lisala on 30 June 1999 (the "MLC Statute"), a political and military movement was created and called the MLC.[130] According to the statements of witnesses 15 and 36 as well as indirect evidence, the MLC headquarters were established, in or about July 1999 in Gbadolite in the DRC.[131]

452. Pursuant to article 11 of the MLC Statute as well as the statement of witness 36, the MLC is composed of four organs, namely the Presidency, the Conseil PoliticoMilitaire de la Libération (the "Political and Military Council")[132], the Secrétariat Général (the "General Secretariat") and the Armée de Libération du Congo (the "ALC").

453.The Chamber refers to the Statute of the MLC establishing the functions of the President of the MLC as well as of the Political and Military Council assisting the President. Article 12 of the MLC Statute provides that the President of the MLC is the head of the political wing and the Commander-in-Chief of the ALC. The provision further specifies that the President of the MLC who is also the Commander-in-Chief of the ALC inter alia: (i) defines the operations' general policy and determines the military objectives; (ii) approves and signs defence agreements with external partners and (iii) convenes and presides over ALC General Staff

---

[129] Statement of witness 15, EVD-P-02168 at 0511-0518.

[130] Article 1 of the MLC Statute, EVD-P-00024 at 0198

[131] Statement of witness 15, EVD-P-02168 at 0521; statement of witness 36, EVD-P-00142 at 0372; see also Memorandum "Organsiation de l'Armée de Libération du Congo", EVD-D01-00034 at 0637; United States Institute of Peace, Special Report - Elections in the DRC - The Bemba surprise, EVD-P-02153 at 0430.

[132] See also statement of witness 36, EVD-P-00142 at 0360

meetings. The President is assisted by a Political and Military Council, which is composed of nine members appointed by him.[133] The President may appoint and dismiss members of the MLC after hearing the opinion of the Political and Military Council.[134]

454. According to article 16 of the MLC Statute and the statement of witness 36,[135] the ALC, which is the military wing of the MLC, is placed under the control of the President. Each member of the General Staff of the ALC is appointed and dismissed by the Commander in Chief of the ALC (i.e., the President of the MLC) after a positive opinion of the Political and Military Council.[136]The Chief of Staff, who is subordinated to the Commander-in-Chief (President of the MLC) coordinates the activities of the General Staff and troops, and executes the decisions of the Commander-in-Chief of the ALC. In this respect, he prepares the decisions of the Commander-in-Chief, coordinates the General Staff's activities and reports to the Commander-in-Chief on the implementations of the orders transmitted.[137]

455. The Disclosed Evidence shows that MLC members as well as the ALC soldiers chose Mr Jean-Pierre Bemba as the President of the MLC and Commander-in-Chief of its military wing (the ALC).[138]

The Chamber notes, based on the evidence that, at all times relevant to the charges, Mr Jean-Pierre Bemba retained such positions: this is clearly manifested by the fact that Mr Jean-Pierre Bemba specifically signed documents as the President of the MLC and Commander-in-Chief of the ALC.[139]

456.The Chamber also notes that the ALC, which consisted of approximately 20,000soldiers,[140] was structured like a conventional army. As stated in article 16 of the MLC Statute and corroborated by witness 36, it had an état-major which comprised(i) a commander of the army, the Chief of Staff; (ii) a Gl in charge of administration; (iii) a G2 in charge of intelligence; (iv) a G3 in charge of operations; (v) a G4 in charge of logistics; and (vi) a G5 in charge of political and civilian

[133] Article 13 of the MLC Statute, EVD-P-00024 at 0200.

[134] Article 12 of the MLC Statute, EVD-P-00024 at 0199-0200.

[135] Statement of witness 36, EVD-P-00142 at 0359.

[136] Article 16 of the MLC Statute, EVD-P-00024 at 0200

[137] Article 16 of the MLC Statute, EVD-P-00024 at 0200-0201.

[138] Article 30 of the MLC Statute, EVD-P-00024 at 0202; see also statement of witness 36, EVD-P-00142 at 0361-0362.

[139] See for instance, Decree No. 035/PRES/MLC of 16 November 2002 on the establishment of military jurisdiction within the ALC, EVD-P-00087 at 0018

[140] Statement of witness 36 at EVD-P-00142 at 0367; statement of witness 15 at EVD-P-02168 at 0520.

affairs.[141] The ALC[142] wasdivided into 7 brigades. Each brigade consisted of 2,500 to 3,000 men and was headed by a brigade commander.[143] A brigade was divided into battalions, each headed by a battalion commander and comprising General Staff.[144] Finally, each battalion was sub-divided into companies and platoons.[145] The companies and platoons were also divided into sections.[146] The evidence, particularly the statements of witnesses 36 and 40,[147] shows that the brigade and battalion commanders were all appointed by Mr Jean-Pierre Bemba.

457. In sum, based on the aforementioned evidence, the Chamber considers that from the creation of the politico-military movement (MLC/ALC) in 1999[148] and at all times relevant to the present case Mr Jean-Pierre Bemba served as the de jure Commander-in-Chief of the ALC. He also had the de facto ultimate control over MLC commanders.

(ii) Mr Jean-Pierre Bemba had the power to issue orders that were complied with

458. The Chamber further considers that Mr Jean-Pierre Bemba had the power to issue or give orders. According to witnesses 15[149] and 45[150], Mr Jean-Pierre Bemba retained control over the military apparatus.[151] He signed important decisions as the MLC President and the ALC Commander-in-Chief such as those involving the nomination of commanders of operations.[152]

459.The Chamber also notes that the Disclosed Evidence, in particular the statements of witnesses 36, 45 and the summary statement of witness 33, shows that a reporting system, which was facilitated by the

---

141 Article 16 of the MLC Statute, EVD-P-00024 at 0200; statement of witness 36 at EVD-P-00142 at 0359.

142 Hereinafter also referred to as "MLC."

143 Statement of witness 36, EVD-P-00142 at 0362-0363.

144 Statement of witness 40, EVD-P-02293 at 0164 (line 462), and EVD-P-02294 at 0183 (lines 406-409

145 Statement of witness 36, EVD-P-00143 at 0441; statement of witness 40, EVD-P-02293 at 0155 (lines 460-472).

146 Statement of witness 36, EVD-P-00143 at 0441; statement of witness 40, EVD-P-02293 at 0155 (lines 460-472).

147 Statement of witness 40, EVD-P-02293 at 0155 and 0164, and EVD-P-02294 at 0183; statement of witness 36, EVD-P-00143 at 0441.

148 MLC Statute, EVD-P-00024.

149 Statement of witness 15, EVD-P-02168.

150 Statement of witness 45, EVD-P-02392

151 Statement of witness 15, EVD-P-02168 at 0508.

152 Statement of witness 45, EVD-P-02392 at 0442-0443

means of communication available, was in place within the MLC. This reporting system allowed Mr Jean-Pierre Bemba to receive daily information in the form of oral or written reports, as stated by witnesses 15, 33 and 45. According to witnesses 15 and 65, the reporting system in place also enabled Mr Jean-Pierre Bemba to monitor the military operations conducted by the MLC and to transmit his orders. In this regard, although article 16 of the MLC Statute stated that the Chief of Staff is entrusted with the implementation of the Commander-in-Chief's orders, witnesses 33, 36, 44, 45 and 65 state that Mr Jean-Pierre Bemba bypassed him and directly contacted commanders in the field and issued orders. Evidence shows that these orders were complied with by the troops and cases of disobedience were punished.

(iii) Mr Jean-Pierre Bemba had the power to appoint, promote, demote, dismiss as well as arrest, detain and release MLC commanders

460. It follows from the statements of witnesses 15, 32, 36, 45 and the summary statement of witness 33 that Mr Jean-Pierre Bemba not only had the power to appoint, promote, demote and dismiss MLC commanders, but also the ability to unilaterally arrest as well as to detain and release those who were arrested.

(iv) Mr Jean-Pierre Bemba had the power to prevent and repress the commission of crimes

461.The Disclosed Evidence further demonstrates that Mr Jean-Pierre Bemba had the power to prevent and to repress the commission of crimes. The Chamber refers to the existence, within the MLC structure, of a military judicial system to which Mr Jean-Pierre Bema was able to submit matters for investigation and prosecution.

462.In this regard, the Chamber first notes that the MLC troops were required to comply with a Code of Conduct which organised the military discipline within the MLC. The code of conduct states that the Martial Court is the third organ under the code and that its members are appointed by the High Command. In addition to the Martial Court, there is also a Disciplinary Board in each unit of the army. This Board has jurisdiction to judge any junior officer for all offences with the exception of inter alia murder, theft and rape. In the latter complex cases, the Disciplinary Board is required to refer such matters to the Martial Court. The Chamber further observes that, according to the code of conduct, the Commander of the army (i.e., Mr JeanPierre Bemba) can also suspend any unit commander.

463. Evidence also shows that Mr Jean-Pierre Bemba had the ability to issue decrees which impacted on the organization of the MLC military

judicial system. For instance, Mr Jean-Pierre Bemba issued Decree No 002/PRES/MLC/2002 of 25 March 2002 on the establishment of a Court Martial within the ALC. He also issued Decree No 035/PRES/MLC of 16 November 2002 on the establishment of a military jurisdiction within the ALC, which established a Conseil de Guerre Supérieur and a Conseil de Guerre de Garnison.

464.The Chamber notes that, according to witnesses 15 and 45, Mr Jean-Pierre Bemba imposed disciplinary measures and took some other measures in relation to the alleged crimes committed by MLC troops during the 2001 intervnetion in the CAR and the 2002 Mambasa attack.

(v) Mr Jean-Pierre Bemba retained his effective authority and control over the MLC troops throughout the 2002-2003 intervnetion in the CAR

465. The Chamber would first like to observe that the Disclosed Evidence shows that:

(1) the Central African government provided the MLC troops with governmental bases including the naval base and Régiment de Soutien/Camp Béai, and provided them with transportation, uniforms and fuel;

(2) a coordination cell, from which operations were planned with the FACA, was created on Mr Patassé's instructions;

(3) The transport of MLC troops was coordinated by Mr Patassé's subalterns who also relayed the MLC to an area designated for them based on Mr Patassé's instructions;

(4) These activities were reported to Mr Patassé on a daily basis; and

(5) The FACA and USP were deployed to support the MLC troops when they were unfamiliar with the territory.

466.Notwithstanding the above, the Chamber still considers that, throughout the 2002-2003 intervention in the CAR, Mr Jean-Pierre Bemba retained his effective authority and control over the MLC troops deployed in the CAR during the fivemonth period of intervention. He had the material ability to prevent and repress thecrimes committed throughout the entire period. The Chamber reached this conclusion based on Disclosed Evidence relating to the elements developed hereafter which show that Mr Jean-Pierre Bemba notably resorted to his de jure and de facto control over the MLC.

467. According to witness 36, it was Mr Jean-Pierre Bemba who took the decision to send MLC troops to the CAR and he informed his Chief of Staff of this decision. This information finds support in the statements of witnesses 45 and 32 and the summary of the statement of witness 3S.

468.Witness 36 stated that Mr Jean-Pierre Bemba also took the decision on the selection of the battalions to be deployed into the CAR. Thus, following his orders, three battalions were deployed and were headed by an MLC Commander of Operations.

469.The Chamber notes that during the 2002-2003 intervention in the CAR, Mr JeanPierre Bemba resorted to his powers to initiate investigation and to punish. As the Chamber previously underlined, according to a letter addressed to the President of the FIDH, Mr Jean-Pierre Bemba took steps to establish a commission of enquiry to verify facts relating to the commission of alleged crimes in the CAR, identify the soldiers responsible, and remit them to the military justice system. To that end, a team of five ALC soldiers travelled to Bangui on 30 October 2002.

470. Moreover, RFI reported that during a telephone conversation they had had with Mr Jean-Pierre Bemba, he told them that if his men had committed "atrocities, they would [have been] arrested and undergo[ne] trial under their Movement's military laws". Based on the conclusions of the report submitted by the commission of enquiry on 28 November 2002, seven soldiers were charged with pillaging before the Military Court in Gbadolite previously established on 25 March 2002.

471. The Chamber also recalls that several witness statements, coupled with two summary statements, revealed that Mr Jean-Pierre Bemba, along with senior MLC commanders, travelled to Bangui in November 2002 to address his troops. In particular, witness 31 stated that Mr Jean-Pierre Bemba learned about the crimes committed by the MLC soldiers, and accordingly suspended two commanders who were suspected of pillaging. Furthermore, according to witness 40, during his visit, Mr Jean-Pierre Bemba cautioned members of his army against any misconduct and stated that "the one who [...] make mistakes, [...] will respond [...] to his mistakes".

472.The Chamber further notes that according to a report sent by the MLC Commander of Operations in the CAR to Mr Jean-Pierre Bemba, the MLC and the FACA were each responsible for trying their own soldiers. In this respect, the MLC Commander of Operations in the CAR reported some cases of pillaging, which occurred on 7 and 8 November 2002, to Gbadolite. This was followed by the commencement of an investigation and the suspected persons were transferred to Gbadolite to be tried.

473. Based on the Disclosed Evidence, particularly the statements of witnesses 31 and 44, the Chamber considers that throughout the 2002-2003 intervention in the CAR, Mr Jean-Pierre Bemba had the material ability to contact his Commander of Operations in the CAR. In this respect, the Chamber notes that both the Prosecutor and the Defence

rely on the statement of witness 40 and draw different conclusions. Both the Prosecutor and the Defence disagree about whether Mr Jean-Pierre Bemba was in direct contact with the MLC Commander of Operations in the CAR. They also disagree about the subject-matter of such contact, if any. In particular, the Defence underlines that, according to witness 40, the reports the MLC Commander of Operations in the CAR was required to make to his hierarchy were addressed to the Chief of Staff and not to Mr Jean-Pierre Bemba. Such reports were limited to three points: (1) the troops' state of discipline with no reference to any of the crimes with which Mr Jean-Pierre Bemba is charged with; (2) the names of dead soldiers and wounded soldiers who required treatment; and (3) the manpower reinforcement needed by him in December 2002.

474. After a careful review of the statement of witness 40 and in light of the Disclosed Evidence as a whole, the Chamber finds that, albeit the number of contacts Mr Jean-Pierre Bemba might have had with the MLC Commander of Operations in the CAR, the latter was still in contact with his hierarchy in Gbadolite during the 2002-2003 intervention in the CAR. The Chamber underlines that the MLC Commander of Operations was contacted at least once by Mr Jean-Pierre Bemba in February 2003 when he was given the order to withdraw the MLC troops from the CAR. This was an order which he immediately started to implement.

475.Wirness 40 further states that in compliance with the hierarchical military structure of the MLC, the MLC Commander of Operations in the CAR contacted the Chief of Staff of the MLC. The MLC Commander of Operations in the CAR also submitted reports on issues relating to the Congolese soldiers to the MLC Chief of Staff, who in turn was under a duty pursuant to article 16 of the MLC Statute, to report to the Commander-in-Chief of the MLC (i.e., Mr Jean-Pierre Bemba).

476.The Chamber is not persuaded by the Defence submission that since the three points addressed in the reports did not involve military operations, Mr Jean-Pierre Bemba lacked authority and control over the MLC in the CAR. On the contrary, the Chamber is of the opinion that the three points referred to by the Defence demonstrate that the MLC troops remained under the control of MLC headquarters in Gbadolite. This is apparent from the fact that the MLC Commander of Operations in the CAR referred to his hierarchy in Gbadolite for disciplinary matters, logistical purposes, and for manpower reinforcements. For instance, as mentioned in paragraph 472 above, the MLC Commander of Operations in the CAR referred some cases of pillaging to his hierarchy in Gbadolite, which led to the opening of an investigation. Moreover, when the MLC Commander of Operation requested a reinforcement battalion, the 5th Battalion was sent to the CAR in the course of the intervention.

477. Finally, Disclosed Evidence demonstrates that Mr Jean-Pierre Bemba took the decision to withdraw his troops from the CAR and signed a joint "communiqué" with Mr Ange-Félix Patassé in January 2003 announcing the gradual withdrawal of the MLC troops from the CAR. Consequently, Mr Jean-Pierre Bemba contacted his Commander of Operations in the CAR in February 2003 ordering him to start withdrawing his troops.

b) Mr Jean-Pierre Bemba knew that MLC troops were committing or were about to commit crimes

478.Having reviewed the Disclosed Evidence as a whole, the Chamber finds sufficient evidence to establish substantial grounds to believe that Mr Jean-Pierre Bemba knew that the MLC troops were committing or were about to commit the crimes against humanity of murder and rape and the war crimes of murder, rape and pillaging in the CAR from on or about 26 October 2002 to 15 March 2003.

479. The Chamber is of the view that there is a distinction between the knowledge required under article 30(3) and article 28(a) of the Statute. This is justified on the ground that the cognitive element under article 30 of the Statute is only applicable to the forms of participation as provided in article 25 of the Statute. Under article 30 of the Stählte the person is aware of the occurrence of a result of his own act, whether as a principal or an accessory, while this is not the case with article 28, where the person does not participate in the commission of the crime (i.e., the crime is not a direct result of his own act).

480. The Chamber further wishes to clarify that, bearing in mind its findings with respect to Mr Jean-Pierre Bemba's criminal responsibility under article 25(3)(a) of the Statute, in particular paragraphs 394, 396 and 397, some of the arguments presented by the Prosecutor in support of its demonstration on Mr Jean-Pierre Bemba's mens rea under article 28 of the Statute can no longer be entertained. The Chamber refers in particular to the arguments put forward by the Prosecutor in paragraphs 113 and 115 of the Amended DCC.

481.The Chamber recalls the written submission of the Defence in which it was asserted that Mr Jean-Pierre Bemba was geographically distant from the theatre of operations since he was mainly in the DRC and simultaneously involved in the conclusion of peace agreements, and was therefore not aware of the crimes committed by MLC troops during the 2002-2003 intervention in the CAR. The Defence further contends that there is no evidence that Mr Jean-Pierre Bemba received concrete information from the Operational Commander of the CAR General Staff or from the MLC Commander of Operations in the CAR. To this end, the

Defence refers to witnesses 9, 44, 45 and 46, who stated that Mr Jean-Pierre Bembadid not receive direct information concerning the commission of the crimes. In this context, the Defence submitted a log book containing messages from Bangui to the MLC headquarters alleging that no reference was made to the commission of the crimes and that they were not addressed to Mr Jean-Pierre Bemba.

482.The Chamber recalls its earlier finding that knowledge may be obtained by way of direct or circumstantial evidence.

483.The Chamber will first address the last point of the Defence's arguments pertaining to the information found in the log book. The Chamber observes that only four pages of the entire log book were disclosed to the Prosecutor by the Defence and that, taken out of its context, the Chamber is unable to assess the information contained therein. Therefore, the Chamber accords little weight to this piece of evidence.

484.With respect to the Defence's second contention, the Chamber concurs with the jurisprudence of the ICTY which made clear that:

(...) The more physically distant the superior was f rom the commission of the crimes, the more additional indicia are necessary to prove that he knew them. On the other hand, if the crimes were committed next to the superior's duty-station this suf f i c es as an important indicium that the superior had knowledge of the crimes, and even more so if the crimes were repeatedly committed.[153]

485.The Chamber acknowledges the fact that at all times relevant to the period of the intervention in the CAR, Mr Jean-Pierre Bemba was mainly stationed in the DRC. But, this does not deny the fact that he traveled to the CAR at least once during this period, and that there are several indications of Mr Jean-Pierre Bemba's knowledge of the crimes throughout the period of intervention. In particular, the Chamber refers to the statements of witnesses 6, 31 and 40 and the summary of the statement of witness 38, according to which, Mr Jean-Pierre Bemba travelled to Bangui in November 2002 to address his troops. Witness 31 stated that Mr JeanPierre Bemba learned about the crimes committed by the MLC soldiers, and accordingly, suspended two commanders who were suspected of pillaging. Additionally, according to witness 40, Mr Jean-Pierre Bemba during this visit cautioned his army members against any misconduct and stated that "the one who [...] make mistakes, [...] will respond [...] to his mistakes". This statement was followed by a speech given by the MLC Commander of Operations in the CAR who excused for the troops' misconduct and promised to ensure their discipline.The

[153] ICTY, Prosecutor v. Stakic, Case No. IT-97-24-T, "Judgment", 31 July 2003, para. 460.

speech provided by the MLC Commander of Operations in the CAR was then reported in a Central African news paper.

486. Moreover, the Chamber recalls its previous finding that crimes against humanity of murder and rape and war crimes of murder, rape and pillaging were committed in the CAR from on or about 26 October 2002 to 15 March 2003. The attack directed against the CAR civilian population was widespread targeting various locations such as Bangui (districts of Boy-Rabé and Fouh), PK 12 and Mongoumba as well as Bossangoa, Damara, Bossembélé, Sibut, Bozoum, Bossemptélé and PK 22. The attack on those locations also lasted for a period of approximately five months. Disclosed direct evidence further corroborated by media sources establish that throughout the approximately five-month period of the MLC intervention in the CAR, the acts of murder, rape and pillaging were regularly broadcasted by international media such as RFI, BBC, Africa Numero l and the Voice of America. According to the statement of witness 44, these media can be listened to throughout the Congo and Africa. Witness 44 further states that Mr Jean-Pierre Bemba regularly read the press or listened to the radio.

487. In addition, witnesses 15, 37 and 45 confirmed that Mr Jean-Pierre Bemba was directly told by his political circle and intelligence advisors about the acts of murder, rape and pillaging committed by MLC troops in the CAR. According to witness 45, he denied the accuracy of the information claiming that "it was a plot against him". In addition, witness 37 stated that on a daily basis, Mr Jean-Pierre Bemba discussed the events that occurred in the CAR with him as they were broadcast, yet he did not believe. In the witness's opinion, Mr Jean-Pierre Bemba did not trust the media "very much", because he claimed that it was "bought". Still, on 4 January 2003 Mr Jean-Pierre Bemba sent a letter to the Special Representative of the UN Secretary-General in the CAR refuting the allegations that his troops had committed serious human rights violations as they were bound by the military code. The letter also stated that he believed that public opinion had been manipulated and misinformed.

488.The Chamber is not persuaded by Mr Jean-Pierre Bemba's statement denying the accuracy of the information provided to him and which stated that his troops had committed these crimes. In the Chamber's opinion, there are several facts that lead the Chamber to reach such a conclusion. These facts include inter alia the availability of effective means of communications and an established reporting system within the MLC. These were not the only means of communication since Mr Jean-Pierre Bemba possessed a phonie at his house. As stated earlier in this section, Mr Jean-Pierre Bemba had the material ability, throughout the 2002-2003 intervention in the CAR, to contact his Commander of Operations in the CAR. Direct evidence, particularly the statements of witnesses 32 and 36 coupled with the summaries of the statements of witnesses 33 and 65, demonstrate that he used such means of communication in order to contact the commanders in the field directly.

489. In sum and based on a thorough analysis of the evidence, the Chamber considers that Mr Jean-Pierre Bemba actually knew about the occurrence of the crimes committed during the five-month period of intervention. In reaching this conclusion, the Chamber has given particular weight to: the widespread nature of the illegal acts committed by the MLC troops; the length of the period over which these acts were committed; Mr Jean-Pierre Bemba's visit to his forces in Bangui in early November 2002 after the commission of crimes in late October 2002; his suspension of two commanders after his visit; his statement cautioning his forces about future misconduct; the existence of an effective reporting system at Mr JeanPierre Bemba's disposal; his ability to use the existing means of communication to contact the commanders in the field during the entire period of intervention; the fact that he was informed by his political circle and intelligence adviser of the commission of murder, rape and pillaging by his MLC forces at least 3 months before the complete withdrawal of his troops; and the existence of media broadcasts throughout the entire period of intervention which reported about the commission of murder, rapes and pillaging by MLC forces. These facts established by the evidence clearly indicate that Mr Jean-Pierre Bemba was aware of the occurrence of these crimes as of the beginning of the operations and throughout the entire period of intervention.

c) Mr Tean-Pierre Bemba failed to take all necessary and reasonable measures within his power to prevent or repress the commission of the crimes by MLC troops

490.The Chamber finds sufficient evidence to establish substantial grounds to believe that Mr Jean Pierre Bemba - who was at all times relevant to the charges, a military-like commander with effective authority and control over the MLC troops - failed to take all necessary and reasonable measures within his power to prevent or repress the commission by the MLC troops of the crimes against humanity of murder and rape and the war crimes of murder, rape and pillaging in the CAR from on or about 26 October 2002 to 15 March 2003. The Chamber bases this finding on the following considerations.

491. The Chamber acknowledges that MLC soldiers received military training which encompassed training on the use of arms, deployment and intelligence as well as training on discipline. The MLC also placed at its command many officers who had been trained in military academies. Furthermore, the MLC soldiers had been informed about the importance of respect for international humanitarian law and the code of conduct, which regulated the military discipline, the established Disciplinary Board, and the court martial. Moreover, the Chamber observes that, according to the code of conduct, the Commander of the Army, i.e. Mr Jean-Pierre Bemba, can also suspend any unit commander.

492. In this regard, the Chamber observes that according to witness 36, the code of conduct was not distributed to all soldiers. Instead, political commissioners were there to popularize the code amongst soldiers. The Chamber also notes that the code of conduct was written in French and was interpreted into Lingala to the MLC soldiers by the political commissioners.

493.The Chamber recalls the existence of a military judicial system as referred to above enabling Mr Jean-Pierre Bemba to initiate investigation and prosecution within the MLC structure. In addition, Mr Jean-Pierre Bemba had the ability to issue decrees impacting on the organization of the said military judicial system as was the case with the Decree on the establishment of military jurisdiction within the ALC, which created a Conseil de Guerre Supérieur and a Conseil de Guerre. He also had the power to unilaterally arrest, detain and release soldiers.

494. The Chamber notes that Mr Jean-Pierre Bemba specifically established a commission of enquiry to verify facts relating to alleged crimes committed by MLC soldiers. Consequently, a team of five ALC soldiers travelled to Bangui on 30 October 2002 in order to investigate the alleged crimes. Eventually, seven MLC soldiers were charged with attempted extortion or theft with the use of force. Moreover, during his visit in November 2002, Mr Jean-Pierre Bemba suspended two commanders, who had been suspected of pillaging, and cautioned his army members against any future misconduct.

495.The Chamber considers that, regardless of Mr Jean-Pierre Bemba's warning to his troops that any soldier who was involved in misconduct would be arrested and tried under the Movement's military law, only two commanders were preventively suspended and seven soldiers were charged of pillaging before the military court in Gbadolite. In this regard, the Chamber recalls the conclusion reached by the ICTY Appeals Chamber in the Ku b u ra and the Halilovic cases in which it was stated that the measures taken by a superior does not depend on whether they "were of a disciplinary or criminal nature" so far as they were necessary and reasonable in the circumstances of the case.[154] Thus, it is the Chamber's view that its assessment in the present case is not dependent on the fact that Mr Jean-Pierre Bemba merely took a disciplinary measure against the two commanders or any other measure of a specific nature, if at all. Rather, the Chamber believes that the assessment of any measures taken by Mr Jean-Pierre Bemba should be first and foremost based on his material ability.[155] Moreover, the reasonable and necessary measures were those "suitable to contain the situation" at the time in term of preventing and/or repressing the crimes[156] and thus were within his powers and abilities.[157] The Chamber considers that this was not the case and that Mr Jean-Pierre Bemba disregarded the scale and gravity of the crimes committed and opted for measures that were not reasonably proportionate to those crimes during his visit in November 2002. This was followed by a passive attitude in relation to the prevention of future crimes that were committed thereafter or repression thereof. According to the evidence before the Chamber, such disproportionate measures taken by Mr JeanPierre Bemba with respect to the acts of pillaging were the only measure resorted to by him throughout the five-month period of intervention, and accordingly, crimes continued to be carried out thereafter.[158]

496.Moreover, the Chamber recognises that the statement made by Mr Jean-Pierre Bemba to caution his troops against any future misconduct only addressed around 200 soldiers out of the two battalions deployed at the time. In the Chamber's view, this was not sufficient to ensure that the warning would reach the remaining majority of the soldiers who

---

154 ICTY, Prosecutor v Hadzihasanoinc and Kubura, Case No. IT-01-47-A, "Appeals Chamber Judgment",22 April 2008, para.142; ICTY, Prosecutor v Halilovic, Case No. IT-01-48-A, "Appeals Chamber Judgment", paras. 63-64.

155 Article 86 of the Additional Protocol I; J. Pictet, (ed.), ICRC Commentary on IV Geneva Convention Relative to the Protection of Civilian Persons in Time of War, (ICRC, 1958), pp. 35-36; Y. Sandoz/Ch. Swmarski/B. Zimmermann (eds.), ICRC Commentary on the Additional Protocols of 8 June 1977 to the Geneva Conventions of U August 1949, (TCRC, 1987), MN 3548.

156 ICTY, Prosecutor v Dehc, Case No. 1T-04-83-T, "Judgment", 15 September 2008, para. 76; ICTY, Prosecutor v. Aleksovskl, Case No. IT-95-14/1-A, "Appeals Chamber Judgment", 24 March 2000, paras. 73-74.

157 ICTY, Prosecutor v. Mdutmovic et al, Case No. IT-05-87-T, "Judgment", 26 February 2009, para. 122.

158 See for example, Hostages Case, 11 TWC 759, p. 1311 ("ft]his defendant, with full knowledge of what was going on, did absolutely nothing about it [...] As commander [...] it was his duty to act and when he failed to do so and permitted these inhumane and unlawiful killings to continue, he is criminally responsible").

were not present, especially since this was the only occasion on which he directly addressed his forces during the five-month period of intervention.[159] As the International Military Tribunal for the Far East stated: "[t]he duty of Army commander in such circumstances is not discharged by the mere issue of routine orders [...] His duty is to take such steps and issue such orders as will prevent thereafter the commission of war crimes and to satisfy himself that such orders are being carried out".[160] In this regard, the Chamber reiterates that Mr JeanPierre Bemba neither addressed his troops any further, nor followed up on his statement to the troops or took the reasonable and necessary preventive measures to avoid the occurrence of future crimes or any repressive measures to punish those responsible from his troops after crimes were committed during the relevant time referred to in the Amended DCC.

497. In its written submission, the Defence contends that Mr Jean-Pierre Bemba called upon the United Nation Secretary General Special Representative to open an international investigation into any crimes that were committed in the CAR during the 2002-2003 intervention.

498.With respect to the Defence submission, the Chamber observes that the letter was only sent on 4 January 2003 -i.e., more than two months after the beginning of the 2002-2003 intervention in the CAR. In the Chamber's opinion, Mr Jean-Pierre Bemba had the material ability to trigger internal investigations into the allegations at the time, as he had previously done during the first week of the 2002-2003 intervention in the CAR (although the measure was not proportionate). Yet, he failed to do so since the beginning of November 2002 throughout the remaining period of intervention. Thus, sending a letter to the United Nations to request an international investigation, let alone two months after the beginning of the intervention, is in the Chamber's opinion neither a necessary nor a reasonable a measure.

499.The Chamber also notes that, by the 13 January 2003, Mr Jean-Pierre Bemba was advised by the MLC Secretary General to withdraw his troops from the CAR. Mr Jean-Pierre Bemba then signed a joint communiqué with Mr Ange-Félix Patassé, on mid-January 2003,

---

[159] As the International Military Tribunal for the Far East stated: "The duty of Army commander in such circumstances is not discharged by the mere issue of routine orders [...] His duty is to take such steps and issue such orders as will prevent thereafter the commission of war crimes and to satisfy himself that such orders are being carried out", see the Tokyo Judgment, The International Military Tribunal for the Far East, vol. I, p. 452.

[160] See the Tokyo Judgment, The International Military Tribunal for the Far East, vol. I, p. 452.

announcing the gradual withdrawal of the MLC troops from the CAR starting in mid-February 2003. Consequently, Mr Jean-Pierre Bemba issued an order to this effect to his Commander of Operations in the CAR in mid-February 2003. The order was complied with immediately and the troops took approximately one month to complete the withdrawal on 15 March 2003.

500.In this regard, the Chamber has concerns about the time taken by Mr Jean-Pierre Bemba to decide to withdraw his troops from the CAR, knowing that crimes had been committed as early as the first weeks of the operations, which even led to the crimes continuing to be committed. It is apparent that the MLC troops could have been withdrawn at any stage during the intervention. However, despite the need felt by Mr Jean-Pierre Bemba in January 2003 to withdraw, essentially as a result of international pressure, he delayed giving the order for withdrawal for at least a month, thus inevitably failing to prevent the crimes that took place between mid January and mid February 2003.

501. In light of the foregoing and having thoroughly assessed the evidence, the Chamber reiterates its finding that Mr Jean Pierre-Bemba neither took the necessary nor the reasonable measures within his material ability to prevent or to repress the crimes committed by his MLC subordinates throughout the five-month period of the intervention in the CAR. The evidence shows that a genuine will to take the necessary and reasonable measures to protect the civilian population by preventing crimes or even repressing their commission was lacking. Mr Jena-Pierre Bemba's failure to fulfil his duties to prevent crimes increased the risk of their commission by the MLC troops in the CAR at all times relevant to the Case. In reaching this finding the Chamber has given particular weight to Mr Jean-Pierre Bemba's material ability to prevent and repress crimes; the availability of a functional military judicial system within the MLC through which he could have punished crimes committed and prevented their future repetition during the period of intervention; the absence of any measures with respect to the crimes committed by MLC troops between November 2002 and January 2003 which increased the risk of their future occurrence; and the length of time taken to announce the troop withdrawal and to issue an order to this effect, which led to the continuing commission of the crimes at least between mid January to mid February 2003. [...]